JOSEPH E. ILLICK is professor of history at San Francisco State University and author of a biography of William Penn. He was born and raised in Pennsylvania, where his German ancestors came in the early eighteenth century and where his family still lives.

COLONIAL
PENNSYLVANIA

A HISTORY

A HISTORY OF THE AMERICAN COLONIES
IN THIRTEEN VOLUMES

GENERAL EDITORS:
MILTON M. KLEIN & JACOB E. COOKE

JOSEPH E. ILLICK

COLONIAL PENNSYLVANIA

A HISTORY

CHARLES SCRIBNER'S SONS, NEW YORK

Copyright © 1976 Charles Scribner's Sons

Library of Congress Cataloging in Publication Data

Illick, Joseph E
  Colonial Pennsylvania: a history.

  (A History of the American colonies)
  Bibliography: p. 322
  Includes index.
    1. Pennsylvania—History—Colonial period, ca.
1600–1775. 2. Pennsylvania—History—Revolution,
1775–1783. I. Title. II. Series.
F152.I44   974.8'02   75-37551
ISBN 0-684-14565-0

1 3 5 7 9 11 13 15 17 19 C/C 20 18 16 14 12 10 8 6 4 2

Printed in the United States of America

for
Margaret Flexer Illick
and
Joseph E. Illick, Jr.

CONTENTS

ILLUSTRATIONS

EDITORS' INTRODUCTION

The American colonies have not lacked their Boswells. Almost from the time of their founding, the English settlements in the New World became the subjects of historical narratives by promoters, politicians, and clergymen. Some, like John Smith's *General History of Virginia*, sought to stir interest in New World colonization. Others, such as Cotton Mather's *Magnalia Christi Americana*, used New England's past as an object lesson to guide its next generation. And others still, like William Smith's *History of the Province of New-York*, aimed at enhancing the colony's reputation in England by explaining its failures and emphasizing its accomplishments. All of these early chroniclers had their shortcomings but no more so than every generation of historians which essayed the same task thereafter. For it is both the strength and the challenge of the historical guild that in each age its practitioners should readdress themselves to the same subjects of inquiry as their predecessors. If the past is prologue, it must be constantly reenacted. The human drama is unchanging, but the audience is always new: its expectations of the past are different, its mood uniquely its own.

The tercentenary of John Smith's history is almost coterminous with the bicentenary of the end of the American colonial era. It is more than appropriate that the two occasions should be observed by a fresh retelling of the story of the colonization of English America not, as in the case of the earliest histories, in self-justification, national exaltation, or moral purgation but as a plain effort to reexamine the past through the lenses of the present.

Apart from the national observance of the bicentennial of American independence, there is ample justification in the era of the 1970s for a modern history of each of the original thirteen colonies. For many of them, there exists no single-volume narrative published in the present century and, for some, none written since those undertaken by contemporaries in the eighteenth century. The standard multivolume histories of the colonial period—those of Herbert L. Osgood, Charles M. Andrews, and Lawrence H. Gipson—are too comprehensive to provide adequate treatment of individual colonies, too political and institutional in emphasis to deal adequately with social, economic, and cultural developments, and too intercolonial and Anglo-American in focus to permit intensive examination of a single colony's distinctive evolution. The most recent of these comprehensive accounts, that of Gipson, was begun as far back as 1936; since then a considerable body of new scholarship has been produced.

The present series, *A History of the American Colonies*, of which *Colonial Pennsylvania* is a part, seeks to synthesize the new research, to treat social, economic, and cultural as well as political developments, and to delineate the broad outlines of each colony's history during the years before independence. No uniformity of organization has been imposed on the authors, although each volume attempts to give some attention to every aspect of the colony's historical development. Each author is a specialist in his own field and has shaped his material to the configuration of the colony about which he writes. While the Revolutionary Era is the terminal point of each volume, the authors have not read the history of the colony backward, as mere preludes to the inevitable movement toward independence and statehood.

Despite their local orientation, the individual volumes, taken together, will provide a collective account that should help us understand the broad foundation on which the future history of the colonies in the new nation was to rest and, at the same time, help clarify that still not completely explained melodrama of 1776 which saw, in John Adams's words, thirteen clocks somewhat amazingly strike as one. In larger perspective, *A History of* *the American Colonies* seeks to remind today's generation of Americans of its earliest heritage as a contribution to an understanding of its contemporary purpose. The link between past and present is as certain as it is at times indiscernible, for as Michael Kammen has so aptly observed, "the historian is the memory of civilization. A civilization without memory ceases to be civilized. A civilization without history ceases to have identity. Without identity there is no purpose; without purpose civilization will wither." *

Colonial Pennsylvania has attracted many able scholars and has been the subject of shelf upon shelf of books. Yet Professor Illick is the first historian of recent times to provide a general survey of the richly textured history of a province that prefigured in significant ways the diverse characteristics of the new nation of which Pennsylvania would be a prominent member.

That historians previously have shied away from such an undertaking is understandable. To compress the complexities and contradictions of colonial Pennsylvania into a single short volume is a challenging assignment. Although William Penn conceived of Pennsylvania as a "holy experiment," the colony soon displayed a conspicuously secular society. Although its founder envisaged a haven for Quakers, the province was an early version of the famous American "melting pot." Although the property of a "true and absolute" proprietor, Pennsylvania successfully pitted provincial autonomy against proprietary privilege. It became, too, the cultural center of British North America. Colonial Pennsylvania was, in fine, a pluralistic society, characterized by religious and ethnic variety, economic diversity, comparative political maturity, and cultural accomplishment.

The transformation of a proprietary colony into a New World commonwealth is engagingly recounted by Professor Illick with succinctness, clarity, and interpretative originality. Eschewing the topical approach by which colonial historians characteristically attempt to render their complex subjects manageable, Illick casts his narrative in a chronological mold. More novel yet, he

---

* Michael Kammen, *People of Paradox* (New York, 1972), 13.

personifies much of Pennsylvania's colonial history in two men: William Penn and Benjamin Franklin. Penn, the seventeenth-century English Quaker, not only founded the province and inspired its political, economic, and social institutions, but also largely dominated the first half-century or so of its development. Franklin, the archetypal Pennsylvanian (and, indeed, American) of his day, symbol and spokesman of the bourgeois values that pervaded provincial society, epitomized the major trends of the second half of the colony's history.

Although by the mid-eighteenth century Pennsylvania bore only a faint resemblance to the province its creator had envisioned, Penn's influence had not been erased. "The principles of his 'holy experiment,' " in Illick's words, "became tenets of the American faith, if not always of national practice." So, too, did Pennsylvania—and indirectly the nation-to-be—bear the imprint of Penn's fellow Quakers, a sufficient reason for the leading role that the Friends play in this volume. Just as their insistence on following an Inner Light, their submission to persecution, their belief in "a Faith that overcomes the World," posed a challenge to seventeenth-century English society, so their political, social, and religious principles were institutionalized in Pennsylvania. Particularly notable were their emphasis on liberty of conscience and their strictures on the evil and barbarousness of slavery (a subject that Illick discusses with rare knowledge and insight).

But as large numbers of German, Scotch-Irish, and other immigrants joined the original English and Welsh settlers, what had started as a Quaker colony became a heterogeneous province that included Anglicans, Presbyterians, Lutherans, Mennonites, Dunkards, Schwenkfelders, and Moravians who, combined, greatly outnumbered the Friends. Political factionalism, often grudging and petty, mirrored the colony's ethnic and religious diversity; yet from the political wrangling there emerged a large degree of home rule, and despite its religious, regional, ethnic, and economic divisions, the province joined in resisting the imperial measures by which the British government sought to tighten its control of the American colonies. Although many Pennsylvanians were reluctant to endorse independence or to take up arms to establish it, a majority of them did both, and they then proceeded to establish a new frame of government, which was the most democratic in America. Pennsylvania's colonial history, viewed in conjunction with the histories of the other twelve colonies, clarifies the meaning of a revolution whose inception, however fortuitous, produced consequences so momentous that they live with us still.

MILTON M. KLEIN
JACOB E. COOKE

PREFACE

Pennsylvania is a large state; and from the policy of its founder and the government since, and especially from the celebrity of Philadelphia, has become the general receptacle of foreigners from all countries and of all descriptions, many of whom soon take an active part in the politics of the state; and coming over full of prejudice against their government—some against all governments—you will be enabled without any comment of mine to draw your own inference of their conduct.

GEORGE WASHINGTON

An observing traveler, without the aid of the quadrant may always know his latitude by the character of the people among whom he finds himself. It is in Pennsylvania that the two characters seem to meet and blend and to form a people free from the extremes both of vice and virtue.

THOMAS JEFFERSON

Perhaps these seemingly contradictory statements by two venerated Americans are better indices to their characters than to the personality of Pennsylvania. But, after struggling with the writing of this book, I would prefer to think that the combined wisdom of the Founding Fathers bears unmistakable testimony to the complexity of their subject and mine. Certainly my own personal experience admits of two Pennsylvanias, for the small German Protestant community where I grew up never acknowledged the existence of a polyglot steel town only ten miles away. Nevertheless, I have tried in this volume to treat all the people of Penn's province, and if I have seemed to pay excessive attention to one religious or economic group, I can only plead that their colonial contemporaries had the same bias.

I did, however, feel the subject was complex enough to require an approach which would render it manageable for both reader and writer, a perspective which—when I recognized it—was surprisingly and gratifyingly logical. The first fifty years of Pennsylvania's history were dominated by the personality and the plans of William Penn, a seventeenth-century English Quaker who had definite ideas for New World development. The second half century of provincial life reflected the influence of Benjamin Franklin, an eighteenth-century Yankee whose behavior was pragmatic rather than dogmatic, whose expressions were aphoristic rather than philosophical or theological. He was an indigenous American, rejecting the authority of tradition. I hope my use of these characterizations has not been heavy-handed as I have moved through the century of Pennsylvania's colonial history.

I began this work at the urging of Jacob E. Cooke, who has steadfastly supported me while I took far too long to do it. He, Elsie Kearns, and Milton M. Klein have read the full manuscript and given me helpful suggestions, not all of which were followed, and I have profited also from comments by Jack D. Marietta and Thomas Wendel. My cousin, John F. Walzer, who was raised with me in the Pennsylvania countryside and drew on that experience to write about the inland trade of the province, has been an unfailing source of sustenance. He and a number of other historians will recognize, not too clearly, I hope, their work here; I have tried to acknowledge those debts in my bibliography. David Lundberg regularly brought me books from the University of California library, along with wry remarks about their contents, helping me keep a sense of humor if not historical perspective. Sally Cohen met every typing deadline with a smile and words of encouragement; Diane Litchfield was also unfailingly and good-naturedly willing to aid in the typing; Carol W. Williams gave last-minute aid on the illustrations; and Kati Boland saved me from stylistic errors with her copyediting.

At one point my work was interrupted, or so I then thought, by my service as president of AFL-CIO # 1352. Only later did I realize that the experience, not because it was a labor union or a gathering of faculty members but because it was political, taught me lessons I had never learned from reading: the need for mediocrity as well as intelligence, the inevitability of petty intrigue as well as wise maneuver, the functions of tedium in assembly and gossip in the hallways, the overwhelming force of inertia. In addition to my many opponents, I want to thank several friends for clarifying these messages: David Novogrodsky, Joyce Weinstein, and, in the course of many years of political discussions, Stanley Boxer.

To Toni, Joe, and Katie, who bore with me, or without me, during the final months I worked on this book, I am grateful for forbearance. To my parents, who gave me the confidence necessary for accomplishment and the ability to laugh or make a few puns along the way, I have dedicated this book with great love.

JOSEPH E. ILLICK

COLONIAL PENNSYLVANIA

A HISTORY

1

PLANNING: WILLIAM PENN, THE QUAKERS, AND THE "HOLY EXPERIMENT"

On March 4, 1681, thirty-six-year-old William Penn was granted a charter by Charles II appointing him and his heirs "true and absolute Proprietaries" of a sparsely populated tract of land lying north of Maryland (whose charter was already a half-century old), south of New York (a recent English acquisition from the Dutch), and extending five longitudinal degrees westward from the Delaware River (on the east bank of which were the Jersies, a haven for persecuted Quakers). Stated another way, the conjunction of English politics, Quaker persecution, and prior seventeenth-century colonization with the aims of a middle-aged religious leader and social activist explain the founding of Pennsylvania.

When Charles II ascended to the throne in 1660, Englishmen were looking back on two decades of tumult. Armies had clashed in the field of civil war, Parliament had been purged, and a king, Charles II's father, had been executed. There followed Oliver Cromwell's flawed experiment in republican government, which was insufficiently radical for vociferous political and religious sectarians. Judging by the prophecies and preachments of men wandering through the English countryside, and considering the vigor of Cromwell's partisans, the monarchy and the church were obsolete.

Yet in 1660 both were restored. The Stuart family reigned once more, while an Act of Uniformity again made Anglicanism

William Penn, an early portrait. *Historical Society of Pennsylvania.*

the only officially recognized religion. The regicides were executed and fanatics were seized and jailed. Chaos was turned into
order, as Charles II moved slowly but steadily toward the
reconsolidation of power in the monarchy. English society froze
into place. Men recalled with a shudder what had happened in
the middle years of the century, and this recollection was a key to
their conservatism and support of the king. Yet while turmoil
had been quieted, the anxieties it produced remained active. Any
signs of unorthodoxy which could upset the status quo were dealt
with accordingly.

No group was more disturbing than the Quakers, whose
challenge to English society was undisguised. The movement was
born of the vision of George Fox, an intense, semiliterate young
man whose quest for meaning within the Church of England
drew only ridicule from its curates. Forced back on his own
resources, Fox discovered God: "I found that there were two
thirsts in me, the one after creatures, to have gotten help and
strength there, and the other after the Lord the creator. . . . The
Lord did stay my desires on himself."

In the late 1640s and early 1650s he wandered through the
countryside preaching of an Inner Light, whereby the holy spirit
was revealed to and acted through man. Gathering to himself
followers who shared the zeal born of cosmic discovery, Fox at
first imposed no discipline on them. After all, if the Inner Light
transformed men into vessels of God's will, then rules, ministers,
and even the church as an institution might be done away with.

But the Quakers did not stop at the rejection of church
tradititon. The Puritans had gone that far, and there can be little
doubt that Quakers inherited such Puritan attitudes as the
attachment of primary importance to personal experience,
especially the conversion to a godly life; the concept of man as a
pilgrim, a stranger to the world, yet a voyager determined to
remake the world for the Lord; and, consequently, a seemingly
limitless capacity for moral protest against the world's wicked
ways. Thus, Puritans outraged Anglicans by denying man-made
church tradition, citing the Bible as their only guide. And
Quakers infuriated Puritans by claiming that the Scriptures
alone were not guidance enough. Robert Barclay, the first man

to attempt a systemization of Quaker thought, declared that the Bible was "a declaration of the *fountain*, but not the *fountain* itself." The written word was not to be a restraint on the Inner Light. Where Puritans were literal, Quakers were mystic.

The contrast was more than theological. George Fox was the son of a weaver whose neighbors contemptuously referred to him as a "Righteous Christer." His mother, too, was deeply religious. Fox's preaching attracted men and women like himself, spiritually thirsty and, if not always of humble origins, at least disdainful of the polite conventions which acknowledged a social status then generally accepted as inevitable. Puritans could count among their number members of the gentry, and they supported both the principle and the practice of social stratification. Indeed, their belief in predestination and election, the restriction of salvation to a chosen few, reflected an elitist attitude. Conversely, Quakers believed that any man could discover the Inner Light. And if any man could achieve this spiritual condition, then every man could. Quaker zeal was fired with a belief in the possibility of achieving earthly perfection.

A zealous perfectionism demanded the elimination of man-made obstacles on the road to attainment. No time, no place, no conditions were inappropriate for the preaching of the Word, even if church services must be disrupted or bizarre behavior were necessary to attract attention. Fox wrote of one William Simpson: "He went three years naked and in sackcloth in the days of Oliver and his Parliament, as a sign to them and to the priests showing how God would strip them of their power, and that they would be as naked as he was, and should be stripped of their benefices. All which came to pass after King Charles the Second came in. And moreover he was made oftentimes to colour his face black, and so black they should be and appear so to people for all their great profession."

Perfectionism also dictated a disregard for meaningless social distinctions as were symbolized in dress, custom, and manner of speaking. William Penn, one of the most aristocratic of the early converts, stated flatly, "We are not to respect persons," for which act of social deviance he cited the authority of the apostle James. John Evelyn, of Penn's social class but not his persuasion, recorded in his diary: "At *Ipswitch* I had the curiosity to visit some *Quakers* there in prison, a new phanatic sect of dangerous principles, they show no respect to any man, magistrate or other." Yet it was these very excesses of the first Quakers which led increasing numbers of them to call for self-restraint.

This discipline did not come fast enough to suit most Englishmen. To the government which came to power in 1660, bent on establishing calm and conformity throughout the land, the behavior and aims of the Quakers still seemed excessively radical. "Tho the Restoration of King *Charles* the second was usher'd in with a specious Declaration for Liberty of Conscience," wrote Joseph Besse, the chronicler of Quaker suffering, "yet 'twas not long before the poor *Quakers* . . . were grevously persecuted, as well as by the Execution of Old Laws made in former reigns against *Popish Recusants,* as the enactment of New Ones against themselves, extending even to banishment on pain of death." In 1661, as a result of an uprising of Fifth Monarchy Men and consequent prohibition of sectarian meetings, over four thousand Quakers were jailed. After that time their number in prison was almost always above a thousand. It was in this period of persecution that William Penn joined them. His motives for enlisting with the Quakers, the indignities he suffered for doing so, and his changing outlook on the tactics of religious dissent demonstrate in miniature the situation and consequent change in Quakerism during the Restoration.

The elder William Penn, father of the future proprietor, was successfully forging a career in the navy at the time of his son's birth in 1644. Despite his reputation for a spotless personal life, even a deep strain of piety, he could serve only as a distant model for his son during the lad's first dozen years, since he was almost always at sea. His wife, Margaret (née Jasper) Van der Schuren Penn, a widow when he married her in 1644, is virtually unknown through historical record. William was her only child until his sister, Margaret, was born in 1652; a brother, Richard, arrived four years later. The Penns lived in London until, shortly after William's serious bout with smallpox at the age of three, they moved into the Essex countryside near the village of Chigwell, the seat of a renowned grammar school. From his sixth to his twelfth year young Penn pored over Greek and Latin eight to ten hours a day, laying the firm foundations of his classical education. A strong sense of the past no doubt confirmed the feeling of security in his youth.

This stable world was shaken by Admiral Penn's naval defeat in the West Indies and brief imprisonment in the autumn of 1655, which caused the family to move back to London and, due to continuing political uncertainty, to Ireland the following year. William Penn later recalled that "the Lord first appeared unto me . . . about the 12th Year of my Age, Anno 1656," a divine encounter fostered by the Puritan influence of Chigwell and by his being uprooted in early adolescence. In Ireland he heard Thomas Loe, a Quaker itinerant, preach to his family at the Admiral's invitation, an experience which apparently intensified his religious feelings.

Four years were spent in Ireland, with tutors tending to Penn's education. He was now in closer association than ever before with his land-bound father. At the Restoration of the Stuarts in 1660, the Admiral was knighted and named a commissioner of the navy. William, academically well prepared, entered Oxford the same year, where he demonstrated his piety by rejecting the Anglican formalism of the university. He was first fined for refusing to attend chapel and then dismissed in his second year. Admiral Penn was outraged; he determined to thwart his son's religiosity by sending him on a worldly tour of the Continent, where the eighteen-year-old would also complete his studies in the Protestant college at Saumur in France. The Admiral's purpose was to prepare the young man for high public office, but William devoted most of two years to the study of theology at Saumur. Summoned back to England, he entered Lincoln's Inn and spent a year reading law before his studies were cut short in early 1666 by the London plague.

His limited legal knowledge, however, could be put to use in managing the family estate in Ireland. Barely twenty-one, he accepted his father's decision to follow this worldly pursuit, only to cross paths again with Thomas Loe. At a meeting in Cork, Penn heard Loe preach on the text: "There is a Faith that overcomes the World, and there is a Faith that is overcome by the World." He committed himself from that moment to the Quakers.

Penn joined the sect in the spirit of its first members who, bent on converting a reluctant world to righteousness, would stop at nothing to preach the Truth. He was imprisoned four times for publicly stating his beliefs in word and print. He published forty-two books and pamphlets in the seven years immediately following his conversion, including the famous *No Cross, No Crown* in 1669, a defense of his beliefs written in the Tower of London. Penn's willingness to withstand the harshness of these confinements, when he might have used his father's position to obtain release, as well as his missionary efforts on the Continent, convinced other Quakers of his commitment and paved the way to his position of leadership at a time when Quakerism was in process of change.

What was occurring was the accommodation of "a Faith that overcomes the World" to the necessities of social survival. The cause was clear enough. Penn's own experience was testimony that Quakers were imprisoned almost at the caprice of public officials, such were the variety of laws and nature of justice applying to nonconformists. There were occasional respites from persecution, but the fear of subversion was far too pervasive not to demand scapegoats. The Quakers suffered most. At least fifteen thousand of them were imprisoned in England and Wales during the Restoration, and four hundred and fifty or more died during their suffering. Persecution did not deter the Quakers. They met openly in defiance of threats and sure arrest. Yet their numbers, estimated at thirty to forty thousand in 1660, doubled during the next two decades. They seemed to thrive on persecution, but not on that alone. Martyrdom may have been necessary to prove the ultimate fidelity of the believer, but it did not ensure the perpetuation of the group. The alternative was to combat persecution through organization. It was during the Restoration that the individualistic Quakers coalesced into the Society of Friends.

This conscious transformation did not occur without a struggle over strategy. Some of the most vital men in the movement were the persons most resistant to corporate discipline. Thus, the very effort to counter persecution from without led to schism within. Complicating matters even more was the problem of leadership. The death or confinement of the most prominent First Publishers of Truth in the 1660s, coupled with the fact that future leaders such as Penn were only now joining the ranks, made discipline more imperative but also more difficult to achieve. Again it was the boundless energy of George Fox which turned the tide.

Emerging from a long imprisonment in 1666, Fox began a four-year canvass of England and Ireland in the cause of group discipline. He set up Men's Monthly Meetings, separate from the weekly worship meetings held on First Day (Sunday), to handle such business as defining membership, preserving good conduct (by means of Quakers keeping watch on one another), and giving mutual aid through funds collected in the name of charity. Monthly Meetings sent delegates to Quarterly Meetings, regional rather than local but handling the same sort of business and keeping in touch with London, where a Yearly Meeting was established during the 1670s. A parallel system of Women's Meetings was also instituted, in addition to a Meeting for Sufferings, initiated to collect and publish accounts of persecution and later utilized to defend Friends against these official acts, and a First-Day Morning Meeting (originally composed of traveling ministers in London who would declare what meeting for worship each would attend) which controlled Quaker printed matter.

This imposition of church government was the object of a protest which rocked the Society during the mid-1670s, until it was quelled by Fox and his allies. But it was only natural that a major controversy should arise from a transformation in the movement. Spontaneity and self-expression were becoming less characteristic than regularity and group discipline. Conformity of behavior had roots in the Quaker concept of conversion—faith must be proved by action—as well as in the emerging institutional controls. Submission to persecution and martyrdom were being replaced by legal challenge and political lobbying. The expectation of converting the world to righteousness declined, superseded by the hope of obtaining toleration of religious dissent by society.

The same move from zeal to moderation was evident in

William Penn's life. His early enthusiasm had outraged his father and, given the circumstances of his adolescent religious awakening, it is not merely speculative to surmise that his Quakerism was in part a matter of youthful rebellion. Indeed, it was characteristic of young Friends that their most irritating behavior was not in society but in the family, where they did not accord their parents the expected courtesies. It might, then, have been expected that the death of Admiral Penn in 1670 would moderate his son's activities, a mellowing accentuated by the death of William's brother Richard in 1673, and of several of his children in infancy after his marriage to Gulielma Springett in 1672.

But Penn had never changed in his devotion to liberty of conscience, the basic principle of his political thought and action, and he always favored practical steps to alleviate persecution. The alteration came in his tactics. While in Newgate Prison he had written *The Great Case of Liberty of Conscience, Once More Briefly Debated and Defended by the Authority of Reason, Scripture and Antiquity* (1670), in which he stated the immorality and irrationality of persecution. Less than a decade later, in his tract *England's Great Interest in the Choice of This New Parliament* (1679), he made clear his determination to engage in politics to eliminate persecution. In the interim, the English political picture had changed as party platforms were enunciated on the two great issues of the seventeenth century, the constitutional conflict between king and Parliament and the religious struggle between the Church of England and dissenters.

The tories, advocates of the throne and the national church, were not without attraction for Penn, since he numbered among his friends Charles II, the king's brother James, Duke of York, and several influential courtiers, all of whom he had approached on the Quakers' behalf. But with political principles deriving from his study of classical republicanism and a vital interest in dissent, Penn naturally gravitated to the opposition group, the whigs. He had already encouraged fellow Quakers to compile a record of persecutions, institutionalized in the Meeting for Sufferings which he took the lead in organizing in 1675, and to lay petitions before Parliament. *England's Great Interest* was issued as one of the first clear statements of whig policy.

Within the Society of Friends, however, there was resentment to the worldly militance Penn represented; older Quakers stymied his strategy. Nor did Penn's foray into politics serve him well, since the whigs faded before a tory resurgence. Frustrated in England, Penn turned toward America as a means of institutionalizing his political and religious principles.

For a quarter of a century Friends had been traveling to the New World, not seeking escape but sowing the Word. "In 1655 many went beyond the sea," wrote Fox, "where truth also sprang up; and in 1656 it broke forth in America." But it was a Quaker truth, considered a falsehood in Massachusetts, where the early arrivals were jailed, deported, whipped, and finally executed. Quakers fared better in New York, Virginia, and Maryland, and best in Carolina and Rhode Island, where they held positions in government. Fox visited them in the latter colony, though the usually tolerant Roger Williams cared neither for him nor for his followers. As early as 1660 the Quaker Josiah Coale, a friend of Penn's, spoke to the Susquehanna Indians about purchasing land. By 1674 two Quakers were in possession of West New Jersey, formerly the proprietary of John, Lord Berkeley, and it was here that Penn became directly involved in American affairs.

John Fenwick bought West New Jersey in trust for Edward Byllynge; both erroneously thought they had acquired the rights of government as well as title to the soil. Fenwick held the deeds and refused to convey them to Byllynge unless he was in return granted a tenth of the holding. Penn and two other Quakers were called upon to arbitrate between Fenwick and Byllynge lest the matter go to court, a circumstance Quakers tried to avoid, but Fenwick proved obstinate until Byllynge conceded. Penn wrote to Fenwick in disgust: "Thy Great Gran Children may be in the other world before w't Land thou has allotted will be employed." Fenwick went right ahead with his plans to plant a colony, issuing propaganda, selling land, and announcing a plan of government.

Penn and his two colleagues became trustees of Byllynge's estate, attempting to straighten out his finances and obtain official recognition of West New Jersey. A boundary agreement was reached with Sir George Carteret, proprietor of East New

Jersey, and a joint stock company was set up to sell shares in the colonial venture. Penn was a trustee of but not a shareholder in West New Jersey, and his business and legal experience drew him more and more into the tangled affairs of the colony. He also wrote some promotional literature and had a hand in drafting the libertarian "Concessions and Agreements of the Proprietors, Freeholders and Inhabitants of the Province of West New-Jersey, in America" (March 3, 1676/77), which was drawn up before the Duke of York had even confirmed the right of government to the colony in August 1680. The nature of the Duke's grant led to even further confusion.

The complications of organizing a colony so encumbered by personal and legal conflicts as West New Jersey showed Penn, not the most patient of Quakers, the virtues of clear and single proprietorship as a prerequisite to planting a settlement. Although the new Quaker emphasis was on group action, Penn saw the pragmatic advantage to be gained by individual effort, not only in controlling the settlement but even in getting a royal charter through his connections at court. But his conception of Pennsylvania as a "holy experiment," a whiggish combination of republicanism and religious toleration, could hardly appeal to royalists; even some Quakers were unfriendly to his goals. To proceed alone allowed him to be secretive. Finally, he took personal satisfaction from his role as sole proprietary lord, despite his proclaimed republicanism and Quaker egalitarianism.

Penn's solitary venture, motivated in part by conservative opposition within the Society of Friends, should not disguise the fact that colonization was a vital part of the Quaker movement. Just as the Massachusetts Bay settlement was preceded by the more tentative but no less permanent Puritan plantation at Plymouth, so the gradual Quaker movement into the New World was capped by the founding of Pennsylvania. It strengthened the Friends' position in America, yet it was tied to England in spirit and by direct correspondence. It was of more than symbolic significance that in 1681 the London Yearly Meeting issued its first letter abroad, and that William Penn was a member of the Epistle Committee. Quakers in Pennsylvania would never be unaware of their counterparts across the sea, unlike the Massachusetts men who cut themselves off from English Puritanism.

If colonization was expressive of the spirit of Quakerism, a charter granting the privilege of a private plantation in America ran counter to the aim of the English government. When Charles II came to power in 1660, England had no colonial policy, certainly no colonial office, though the commercial value of colonies was dimly recognized. But the establishment in 1675 of the Lords of Trade, an executive body charged with the enforcement of the Navigation Acts, signalized a determination to bring the New World settlements under closer control. This policy was confirmed by the transformation of New Hampshire into a royal colony, the nullification of the Bermuda and Massachusetts charters, and the creation of the Dominion of New England.

Yet in the midst of this activity, Penn was able to get a royal patent naming him and his heirs proprietors of Pennsylvania with "free, full and absolute power . . . to ordeyne, make, Enact and under his and their Seales to publish any Lawes whatsoever . . . by and with the advice, assent and approbation of the freemen of the said Countrey," as well as "such power and authoritie to appoint and establish any Judges, and Justices, Magistrates and Officers whatsoever." The charter was not without its restrictions: no earlier patent had explicitly called for obedience to the Navigation Acts, an order reinforced by clauses stipulating the admission of royal officials to the province for enforcement purposes and the presence of a colonial agent in London, answerable for violations. Furthermore, provincial laws had to pass the Privy Council's scrutiny, while the king could hear all appeals from colonial courts and reverse judgments.

But these restrictions were not crippling. The charter for Pennsylvania was an exception to the policy of increasing colonial control. The king and the Duke of York, who apparently had jurisdiction over the territory west of the Delaware through the proprietorship of New York, were willing that Penn should receive the grant for personal reasons; their respect for his father outweighed the repugnance of his political principles. Both men had shown sympathy for religious dissent, though neither would mind if whig adherents left the country. Furthermore, even though Pennsylvania was to be Quaker, it would have the strategic virtue of filling the sparsely populated gap between New York and Maryland. Nor could the commercial potential of the colony be overlooked. In 1680 Penn published *The Benefit of Plantations, or Colonies*, giving the orthodox mercantilist explanation for overseas ventures: they strengthened the mother country.

Though often careless about personal financial matters, Penn knew how to look after his political fortunes. He drew upon his friendships with influential courtiers and he consulted knowledgeable advisers to guide his charter safely through official channels. The result was a broad grant of proprietary power which would allow him to implement his vision of an ideal state. Shortly after he received his patent, he wrote: "For my country, I eyed the Lord in the obtaining of it, and more was I drawn inward to look to him and to owe it to his hand and power, than to any other way. I have so obtained it, and desire that I may not be unworthy of his love, but do that which may answer his kind providence, and serve his truth and people; that an example may be set up to the nations; there may be room there, though not here, for such an holy experiment." Thus did the proprietor merge his concept of Pennsylvania with divine guidance.

Penn was not the first Englishman to view America as the place to build a new and better world. His most famous predecessor, John Winthrop, planned with Puritan associates to erect a "city upon a hill," an exercise in godly living for the uncleansed to witness and emulate. But while Penn and Winthrop were in agreement on the efficacy of example and the necessity of beginning anew in the wilderness, they did not share a view concerning the means of achieving these goals. Aboard ship to Massachusetts, Winthrop reminded his followers that a safe landing would symbolize God's confirmation of His side of the covenant with His people; the Puritans must reciprocate by constant service to the Truth. To Winthrop this meant an undeviating adherence to orthodox Calvinism as interpreted by ministers and practiced by magistrates. In Massachusetts there would be "liberty to do that only which is good, just, and honest." Dissent would be tolerated no more than it had been in England. A political system controlled by the religious elite would ensure loyalty.

Penn was no democrat. But he was devoted to the contract theory of government, the political consequences of which were strikingly different from those which proceeded from Winthrop's covenant theology. Penn believed that the contract between citizen and government guaranteed the former personal freedom and the protection of his property, as well as participation in government and trial by jury. Justice was to be mutual, fair, and proportionate to the crime. Of these axioms, the one which stood in clearest contrast to the principles on which Massachusetts operated was individual liberty. From this sprang Penn's defense of dissent which, far from being a civil crime, was an integral part of personal freedom, a civil right. Persecution was the crime.

Penn's original contract with the citizens of Pennsylvania was a Frame of Government drawn up in England in 1682, presumably expressive of the proprietor's political philosophy and an immutable agreement with his prospective settlers. To it were attached Forty Laws agreed upon in England, to be ratified in the province itself. The latter document explicitly guaranteed freedom of worship to all who believed in God; strict observation of the Sabbath was also promised "that they may better dispose themselves to worship God according to their understandings." Toleration did not vitiate sobriety. In addition to their underwriting individual liberty, the Forty Laws made ample provision for the protection of property, not only through such safeguards as requiring that taxes be levied solely by law but also by fostering attitudes congenial to economic success: children must be taught trades, prisons would be workhouses, debts had to be paid on penalty of forfeiting goods.

Participation in government was acknowledged in the Forty Laws through the definition of the freeman, or voter, as any Christian male over twenty-one who held requisite property (100 acres by purchase or 50 acres by release from servitude) or paid a personal tax; the same qualifications applied to officeholding. (Probably half the adult males in early Pennsylvania were enfranchised, as compared to one quarter or less in early Massachusetts.) The elected bodies would be "the sole judges of the regularity or irregularity of the elections of their own respective members." Trial by jury, "twelve men, and as near as may be peers, or equals, and of the neighborhood," was guaranteed, court fees were to be moderate, and prisons, with which Penn had had such unpleasant experience, were to be free. Only treason and murder were capital crimes, as compared to Massachusetts, where Quakers suffered the death penalty for their beliefs, or early Virginia, where blasphemy was sufficient cause for execution; this penalty was attached to both acts by the royal charter.

Although it would take the consent of the governor and six-sevenths of the legislature to alter any of these Forty Laws, which were also subject to repeal by the Privy Council, they were not so fundamental to the operation of the political system as the principles that were embodied in the contract itself—the Frame of 1682. Here it was stated: "The government of this province shall, according to the powers of the patent, consist of the Governor and freemen of the said province, in form of a Provincial Council and General Assembly, by whom all laws shall be made, officers chosen, and publick affairs transacted." The proprietor would serve as governor or appoint a deputy to the post. The Provincial Council was to consist of seventy-two men, one-third of whom would be chosen anew annually by the freemen for a three-year term. It would be presided over by the governor and, with him, responsible for initiating all legislation and executing all laws. To gain "the more full concurence of the freemen," there was a two-hundred-member Assembly with the powers of proposing amendments to and approving or disapproving of the emergent bills. But the governor and Council would manage the treasury, erect the courts, and choose the judges. Local officials, such as sheriffs, would be chosen by the governor from a freemen's list of candidates.

In *The Common-wealth of Oceana*, published a quarter century before Penn devised his Frame and probably known to him, James Harrington had written: "An equal Common-wealth . . . is a Government established upon an equall Agrarian, arising into the superstructure or three orders, the Senate debating and proposing, the people resolving, and the Magistracy executing by an equal Rotation through the suffrage of the people given by the Ballot." Three of these four principles appeared in Penn's

Frame of 1682: the separation of debate, resolution, and execution through the divisions of Council, Assembly, and governor, respectively; rotation in office, with a limited term for members of the Council; and the exercise of franchise through the secret ballot.

Absent from Penn's plan of government was the so-called "equall Agrarian," and the omission was significant. Harrington's idea was to limit landed estates to a certain value in order to eliminate by statute a landed aristocracy, in the belief that popular government could exist only where the ownership of land was broadly diffused. Indeed, as he stated, this principle was the foundation of Oceana. But Penn could not afford all the luxuries of political theory in 1682. Obtaining a royal charter had been a costly process, and getting Pennsylvania off to a sound start would require capital beyond Penn's resources. Land, 47 million acres by his grant, was his untapped reservoir of wealth. Allowed by his charter to dispose of his New World territory as he saw fit, even to erect manors, Penn did not rule out the sale of large blocks of land to interested individuals. Of the approximately 500,000 acres sold to the so-called "first purchasers" by the middle of 1682, nearly half of it was parceled out in chunks of 5,000 and 10,000 acres to forty-one men, less than one-tenth the total number of buyers. Selling at £100 per 5,000 acres, Penn realized £10,000 on paper, which compared favorably to the £12,000 he claimed to have spent in launching the colony in the first two years.

Still, Penn was more interested in encouraging settlement than land speculation, specifying that large purchasers were "not to have above one thousand acres together, unless in three years they plant a family upon every thousand acres." Purchasers of 5,000 acres or more were allowed to form townships, where the immediate allotment of land, hence settlement, was encouraged. Penn's aim of rapidly establishing people on the land appears to have been motivated less by a forward-looking belief in the relationship between property and political power than by his distress with conditions in England: "Of old time the Nobility and Gentry spent their Estates in the Country, and that kept people in it; . . . Now the Great men (too much loving the Town and resorting to London) draw people thither to attend. . . . The Country being thus neglected, [there is] no due Balance kept between Trade and Husbandry, City and Country."

Clearly, there was an ambiguity in Penn's mind about the past and the present. As proprietor of Pennsylvania, he was a feudal lord; theoretically, the lands he granted were subject to quitrent, forfeiture, and escheat. His charter allowed him to grant manors, a privilege from which members of his family and other favored persons benefited. In addition he withheld from sale one-tenth of all land as a proprietary reserve. He enjoyed his anachronistic role as proprietor, just as he longed for an England past. Yet simultaneously he placed Pennsylvania in the vanguard of seventeenth-century political and economic life, pointing up the liberal nature of government and the commercial possibilities of his province. This unresolved tension between past and present pervaded Penn's New World planning.

It was evident again in his mercantile design. As much as Penn might have wanted to be the sole support of his proprietary, he had enough experience with colonizing to know that his personal investment would have to be supplemented with wider financial support. Revenue from the sale of land was one source of capital, but probably not sufficient for a growing colony, even assuming that after 1684 he would be collecting quitrents. Penn could force the dynamic potential of commerce, however. Its growth and the prosperity of the province might be virtually synonymous. Quakerism had, by 1680, attracted its share of merchants. Penn's task was to tie them to Pennsylvania, and he moved to do so through his proprietary powers.

His most notable effort in this regard was the encouragement he gave to the Free Society of Traders in Pennsylvania, a joint stock company organized primarily by Quaker merchants in London. The leaders invested in Pennsylvania real estate, with individual holdings ranging up to 10,000 acres, and Penn correspondingly bought stock in the company. Furthermore, out of the Society's purchase of 20,000 acres, he erected the Manor of Frank, a privilege which included not only the customary civil jurisdiction within the holding but also abolition of quitrents, a choice spot on the Philadelphia waterfront, and three seats on the Provincial Council. The president of the society, Nicholas More, became chief justice of the Provincial Court, provincial secretary, and clerk of the Provincial Council. James Claypoole, another company officer, became a commissioner of propriety. The mercantile interest was thus attached to the proprietary grant by traditional means: commercial monopoly and real estate rewards.

Other purchasers of large tracts of land, outside the Free Society, were also rewarded with provincial officers. Most of these men were Quakers; Nicholas More and William Markham, a distant cousin of Penn's who went as his deputy to Pennsylvania in 1681, were the sole Anglicans. It appeared in England that the government along the Delaware would be in the hands of well-to-do Friends. Indeed, a second and harder look at the Frame of Government, and especially its evolution, showed that Penn had made concessions in principle to ensure financial backing for the colony.

In the first of seventeen drafts of a political system, Penn had proposed that the governor be assisted by a two-house parliament: the "lords" and the "renters." The latter, delegates of the small landholders, would initiate legislation. The "lords," composed of the first fifty purchasers of five thousand acres or more, were given the veto power on all laws, in addition to other important duties. By stipulating that the "lords" would pass their seats to their heirs, the proprietor again showed his penchant for the past, as well as his gratitude for present support.

The hereditary feature of the upper house was soon dropped, not to diminish the power of that body but probably in response to the warning of one of Penn's advisers that it would "reflect on us a people who affect Grandure beyond our pretensions." Nor was there good reason to segregate wealth in the upper house, bereft of the right to initiate legislation. Experience showed that English voters chose their economic superiors to sit in an elective assembly. A draft of government now emerged, "The Fundamentall Constitutions," in which the powers both of proposing and passing laws were vested in the lower house, whose members stood annually for election. The upper house became a body merely consultative to the governor.

This scheme, though it had the blessing of Benjamin Furley,

prominent Quaker merchant in Rotterdam, and was probably approved by Algernon Sidney, political theorist and erstwhile whig politician, had the disadvantage of appearing too liberal to the bulk of Penn's backers. Dependent on their financial support and himself torn between feudal and modern ideas about government, Penn finally settled on a Frame of Government in which the Assembly was stripped of every power but that of passing on bills initiated jointly by the governor and the Provincial Council. Lest the voters missed the point, they were instructed in the frame to choose "persons of most note for their wisdom, virtue and ability" to the Council, while no criterion was set for the Assembly.

If the frame met Harrington's requirements for the separation of debate and resolution, it was not satisfactory to other political theorists. Sidney supposedly referred to this final instrument of government as "the basest laws in the world," his exaggeration no doubt stemming from a feeling of betrayal, and several Quakers, including Furley, deplored the weakness of the Assembly. Penn, because he was honestly sympathetic to republican ideas, rationalized in the preface to the Frame: "Any government is free to the people under it (whatever be the frame) where the laws rule, and the people are a party to those laws. . . . there is hardly one frame of government in the world so ill designed by its first founders, that in good hands would not do well enough." Ironically enough, political experience in Pennsylvania would be the proving ground of that statement.

Yet Penn could not be expected to anticipate in England the practical political problems which might arise in America. In creating an instrument of government he had been pragmatically responsive to his financial backers, yet he had not impaired his essential ideal, liberty of conscience. As the policy of Charles II became more authoritarian, Penn maintained the integrity of his beliefs, though not openly. Immediately after receiving his charter and before the Frame had reached its final stage, he wrote from Westminster: "For matters of liberty and privilege, I propose that which is extraordinary, and to leave myself and successors no power of doing mischief, that the will of one may not hinder the good of an whole country. But to publish these things now, and here, as matters stand, would not be wise; and I am advised to reserve that till I come there."

If men in high places and of elevated station considered him too liberal, Penn had reason to believe that humble Quakers were not vitally concerned with the governmental features of Pennsylvania so long as the system was representative and, more important, freedom of worship was guaranteed. In 1659 a prominent Friend had written: "For what is a King, and what is Parliament, what is a Protector, and what is a Council, while the presence of the Lord is not with them? And we are not for names, nor men, nor titles of Government, but we are for justice, and mercy and truth and peace." Penn's devotion to these principles was never doubted.

Furthermore, he made an outright appeal for colonists through the medium of promotional literature. In *Some Account of the Province of Pennsylvania* (1681), Penn repeated his mercantilistic arguments concerning the benefit of colonies, glad news to prospective traders, and then soared into a description of the place, "600 miles nearer the Sun than England," abundant with timber, "Fowl, Fish, and Wild-Deer." He pointed to the popular nature of the government and laid down the liberal conditions of land disposal, not only for purchasers but also renters, "one peny per Acre," and servants, "Fifty Acres shall be allowed to the Master for every Head, and Fifty Acres to every Servant when their time is expired." Penn's observation that planting in the New World best suited the industrious, the ingenious, the genteel but disinherited, and "Men of universal spirits" was reminiscent of the propagandistic tactics of Captain John Smith; what self-respecting man could consider himself exempt? He could take his wife, two children, and servant to Pennsylvania, with 500 acres awaiting him, for £20, not including cost of clothes and goods transported. A good third of English households earned this much or more annually, enabling Penn to attract yeomen and artisans as well as wealthy merchants and tradesmen.

Those purchasing land, who clearly must have been persons of some means, were more often of urban than rural background; the ratio may have been as high as four to one. More than eighty occupations were represented among them, most of which were of the artisan-shopkeeping variety, surely a clue to the commercial success of Philadelphia. Old World experience, stimulated by New World opportunity, would turn the "holy experiment" into a thriving enterprise.

It was Penn who set it in motion. With the help of Benjamin Furley he translated and published his promotional tracts in Dutch and German. He appointed three men in London to handle inquiries and promote the overseas venture, and he maintained agents in Dublin, Edinburgh, Hamilton, and Aberdeen as well. Penn himself traveled to Bristol on several occasions to stimulate interest in the colony. Some eight thousand people, almost entirely English, Welsh, and Irish Quakers, migrated to Pennsylvania by 1685.

It could truly be said that Penn was responsible not only for the planning of his colony but also for getting the initial settlers there. For Quakers, whose lot was that of a persecuted minority, these details were less important than the fact that a haven from suffering had been established. The colony might have been regarded as an escape from the real work of conversion had it been founded at an earlier time. But as the zeal and religious individualism characteristic of the first Quakers was being subjected to group discipline, emphasis changed from reform of society to toleration by it. Pennsylvania, offering the alternative of a fresh start, appeared not as a violation of Quaker ideals but as the very way to put them into practice. Thus, where Friends had once gone to America as missionaries into alien communities, braving threats and almost expecting martyrdom, they now were going in a body to establish a separate place for themselves.

Though the political, economic, and social institutions of the colony were the creation of one man, his ideas were tempered by the restraint of his wealthy backers. Nevertheless, Penn had been generous, a fact which he was perhaps too conscious of and his Quaker followers too little acquainted with. Paternalistic at heart, the proprietor had asked the prospective settlers to contribute nothing but themselves to the "holy experiment." In Pennsylvania, the wilderness laboratory, they would have the opportunity to work out the experiment with fuller control over their own destinies.

2

PLANTING: EARLIER INHABITANTS AND NEW SETTLERS

The idea for Pennsylvania was English, born in the mind of William Penn. The colonists whom he encouraged brought with them Old World notions, which would have a determinative effect on how they settled into place. But they were not the first arrivals. Penn's wilderness laboratory was already populated, though sparsely, by aborigines and transplanted Europeans, who had to be acknowledged and dealt with.

For twelve to eighteen thousand years Pennsylvania had been inhabited by Indians. In the seventeenth century there were Lenni Lenape, or Delawares, living on or near the river of that name; Susquehannocks farther west in the Susquehanna River basin; tribes on the upper Ohio and its tributaries; and Eries on the shores of the easternmost Great Lake. Their culture was that of the late stages of the Stone Age. The Indians had a mature agricultural economy, based primarily on the cultivation of corn. Tribes traded with one another, sometimes over long distances. Although hunting was on the decline, animals were still brought in for food and clothing. There was no livestock, since there were no domesticable animals. Gathered together as farmers in villages, the Indians developed a political life. Social relations among them were characterized by restraint, and religious ritual showed a sophisticated imagination. Nevertheless, though the population was increasing, villages were not cities; sporadic trade was not an established commerce; and that hallmark of advanced civilization, a written language, had not yet been invented. In this regard, pictography was the limit of aboriginal endeavor, symbols being drawn on bark, etched on rock, or woven into wampum belts.

The Indians were also less developed industrially than the Europeans. Although they potted, worked leather, and wove, they were acquainted with only the primitive uses of metals. Europeans tools, implements, and utensils were understood by the Indians and recognized as superior to their own metalware. Hence, the material disparity between the two cultures worked to the disadvantage of the aborigines, who changed their methods of hunting, farming, cooking, dressing, and even behaving, once liquor was discovered. The formerly autonomous Indians became dependent on the intruders.

Before Pennsylvania was founded a pattern had been set. Indians, watching the initial European attempts at survival in a land from which the natives easily obtained a living, condescended to save settlers from starvation. Europeans, likewise certain of the superiority of their own way of life, responded to Indian aid by increasing the size and strength of their colonies, changing the face of the landscape, and depleting its natural resources, always moving westward. Often land was purchased from the Indians, but the European concept of private property and the Indian assumption of the inalienability of the earth from the families who lived on it led to conflict over the permanence of sale. When warfare came, the Indians won some of the preliminary skirmishes but, inferior in numbers, organization, and technology, they lost the major battles.

William Penn was not fully aware of the dynamics of cultural conflict in America, but he believed that a bellicose resolution of it should be avoided. He was no student of the Indian way of life or the religious precepts which underlay it. But he was essentially kind and paternalistic, and he wanted to deal with the native Americans in that spirit. In *Certain Conditions and Concessions* (1681), he dictated a careful regulation of trade for the Indians' protection as well as a policy of equal rights and privileges before the law, though it would, of course, be English law. In a letter addressed specially to the Indians, Penn emphasized his and their mutual dependence on "one Great God" who "hath been

Benjamin West's famous rendition of Penn's treaty with the Indians in 1682 (opposite) later appeared in the background of Edward Hicks' *A Peaceable Kingdom* (above). Both men were Quakers, West serving as president of the Royal Academy in London and being buried in St. Paul's Cathedral, Hicks preaching mysticism and depicting Pennsylvania as heaven on earth. (opposite) *Philadelphia Museum of Art.* (above) *From the collection of the Mercer Museum of the Bucks County Historical Society.*

pleased to make me concerned in your part of the world." But, he continued: "I desire to enjoy it with your love and consent. . . . I am very sensible of the unkindness and injustice that hath been too much exercised toward you by the people of these parts of the world. . . . But I am not such a man . . . and I desire to win and gain your love and friendship by a kind, just and peaceable life, and the people I send are of the same mind, and shall in all things behave themselves accordingly. . . . I have sent my commissioners to you to treat with you about land, and a firm league of peace."

Penn's caution to his commissioners, "buy land of them, where any justly pretend, for they will sell one another's, if you are not careful," was no more than a conventional prejudice based on a misunderstanding of aboriginal views of real estate. Once he arrived in Pennsylvania, witnessed native ceremonies, and learned the language, Penn wrote about the Indians with rare understanding. Perhaps the simplicity of the aborigines appealed to his Quaker spirit, although there were many other educated Europeans who were not Friends, who had never encountered Indians, and who were quite susceptible to the naive charms, real or supposed, of the native Americans.

Penn's reporting on the Indians was straightforward, but occasionally he was willing to overlook important differences between his and their outlooks. He observed that although the Indians were "under a dark Night" regarding religious tradition, "yet they believe a God and Immortality, without the help of Metaphysicks." Indeed, Penn thought the aborigines were descended from the Old Testament Jews, which probably strengthened his mistaken notion that their religious beliefs closely resembled Christianity. While the prevailing attitude in Massachusetts was that Indians were savage or, even worse, agents of the devil, Penn erred in the opposite direction by failing to give due weight to the real differences between the natives and the intruders. European society was dynamic, aggressive, and organized to act concertedly; otherwise it would not have invaded the western hemisphere. Indian society was static, passive, and internally divided. Despite an initial numerical advantage and continuing skills in trade and warfare, the Indians could not resist the Europeans, even in Pennsylvania.

The wellsprings of Penn's actions toward the Indians—love, a desire for equity and justice—were, nevertheless, unusual. Yet the policies he adopted to implement his ideals were not without precedents. Earlier settlers along the Delaware and the governor of New York, respectively, had purchased land from the natives and forged a league of peace. Pennsylvania, far from being a virgin wilderness when Penn first encountered it, was inhabited not only by Algonquian-speaking Indians in its southeastern corner and several Iroquois-related tribes farther west in the Susquehanna River valley, but also housed Swedes, Dutch, and English along the banks of the Delaware; and its interior was jealously regarded by the fur interests of Maryland and New York.

Only two years after the settlement of Jamestown, Henry Hudson sailed into Delaware Bay, and soon other Dutch mariners were exploring the South (Delaware) River. The Dutch West India Company, though far more interested in exploiting the Hudson River Valley, attempted several commercial ventures along the Delaware. Settled in this region were the Lenni Lenape or Delawares, Indians of the Algonquian linguistic stock which included all tribes along the Atlantic coast from Florida to Canada except those of the Iroquois tongue, who existed as an island in and around New York. The Dutch, unlike Penn, were interested in the Indians solely because of the fur trade, and thus they had no need for extensive real estate in the region that became Pennsylvania. Still, as early as 1633 an employee of the Dutch West India Company bought a parcel of land beside the Schuylkill River on which to build a trading post.

Five years later Peter Minuit, former director general of New Netherland, the Dutch settlement on the Hudson, headed an expedition up the Delaware for the New Sweden Company. Minuit also purchased land from the Indians. This plot on the west bank of the Delaware below the Schuylkill was divided into farms by the Swedish settlers, who never prospered in the fur trade but expended much energy simply in defense against the

Dutch until 1655, when the Swedes surrendered. Meanwhile, colonists from New England had begun forays into the Delaware territory. But the capture of New Netherland in 1664 and the transfer of ownership to the Duke of York led to no more than a trickle of English migration into the upper Delaware. Only with the revived interest in West New Jersey under Quaker control did settlers begin to stream in, and then mainly to the east bank of the river. But farther south, in the area adjacent to Maryland, tobacco planters were moving in on the basis of land patents acquired from the Duke of York in the 1670s.

Although the Swedes, Dutch, and English living in the Delaware region would force an alteration in Penn's plans for locating and laying out Philadelphia, they contributed to the colonization effort by preparing resident Indians for the Quaker migration. They anticipated Penn's intention of buying land from the natives, and their presence was accepted. Indians were quite sincerely applying the term "brother" to whites. Eventually the Lenni Lenape would surrender their identity to the interests of harmony by taking on the English name Delaware. Those colonial officials steeped in the diplomacy of the Continent regarded Indian protestations of friendship with skepticism, but egalitarian Quakers were prepared to accept them at face value. In fact, Penn encountered no native resistance to colonizing the southeastern portion of his province. Land was immediately bought in that area; by 1685 Penn had generously expended £1,200 in purchases and presents.

But Penn was constantly in need of capital to underwrite settlement, and one way to earn a return on his investment was the fur trade. Pelts in the Delaware Valley had been largely depleted by the time of his arrival; the Susquehanna Valley, farther west, had to be the source of this precious commodity. This region had been populated by the Susquehannocks, Iroquois-speaking tribes who, unlike their erstwhile tributaries the Lenni Lenape, were militaristic and politically well organized. The Susquehannocks had traded with the Dutch and Swedes in the Delaware Valley, as well as with the English in Maryland and Virginia; and their hunting grounds were well stocked. But only a few years before the founding of Pennsylvania, the situation of the Susquehannocks and, consequently, the valley in which they trapped and from which they traded changed radically.

Since the middle of the seventeenth century the Susquehannocks had been at war with the Iroquois of New York who, having stripped their own forests bare of furs, sought to control the territory south of them. In 1675 the Susquehannocks were defeated and dispersed, so that when Penn entered upon the scene the Susquehanna Valley was almost uninhabited. The few Susquehannocks who returned were part of a "covenant chain" of Indian nations, forged by the governor of New York and dominated by the Iroquois. The purpose of alliance was to control the fur trade of the Middle Colonies. Thus, when Penn sent commissioners to Albany to negotiate for the sale of land claims in the Susquehanna region, the Albany merchants, with the full support of their government, persuaded the Iroquois not to cooperate with the Quaker proprietor. By this devious method, Pennsylvania traders were temporarily barred from the Susquehanna Valley.

In the initial years of settlement, then, the activity of Pennsylvanians was confined to the Delaware Valley. But even here there was a conflict over land ownership, not with the natives but with the colony of Maryland. Control of the lower Delaware River, in Penn's mind, was crucial to uninhibited access to the sea from a port city farther north. The east bank clearly belonged to Quaker New Jersey, but the west bank was in the somewhat shaky clutches of Maryland. Although Lord Baltimore apparently had been deeded this area in his charter of 1632, the Dutch settlements along the west bank had been under the aegis of New Netherland and, later, New York. It was on this precedent, the presence of colonists unattached to Maryland, that Penn based his hopes. As soon as he received his royal charter in 1681, Penn began pressing the Duke of York for legal title to the region but was told that it was "improper for him [the Duke] to give a graunt of what he has not a patent for himself." It took the persuasive proprietor little more than a year to obtain from Charles II, the Duke's brother, the necessary deeds to the so-called Three Lower Counties, and he wasted no time in assuming political control once he had arrived in Pennsylvania, though his title was dubious. Penn's conscience was less tender when dealing with his fellow countrymen than with the Indians.

If the earlier settlement of Europeans was an aid to Penn in establishing control over the future state of Delaware, still their presence was not entirely beneficial. When Penn's deputy governor, William Markham, started seeking a site for a port city in 1681, he was discouraged to find that all habitable waterfront property was occupied by Hollanders, Swedes, or Englishmen. The spot which Penn had thought would be the best port location, Upland (now Chester), had been settled for over thirty years; real estate there was too dear to fulfill the proprietor's scheme, which had been sketched without full recognition of American conditions.

Penn's plan for a port city was conceived in terms of England, where the drawing power of Quakers was greatest in urban areas. However much he may have wanted to return to a rural past, and he clearly believed the decay of country life in England to be a calamity, he was restrained by the knowledge that his settlers would probably have city skills. Penn also recognized the requirement for commercial prosperity when he declared that "a certain quantity of land or ground plat shall be laid out for a large town or city, in the most convenient place upon the river for health and navigation. . . ." Location of land in this "first great town" was to be determined by lottery.

Yet Penn realized that the cramped and squalid conditions of London nurtured the plague and fanned the fire which destroyed part of the metropolis. In the next stage of city planning he instructed the commissioners going to Pennsylvania not only to locate a place that was "navigable, high, dry, and healthy" but also: "Let every house be placed . . . in the middle of its plat, as to the breadth way of it, that so there may be ground on each side for gardens or orchards, or fields, that it may be a green country town, which will never be burnt, and always be wholesome." Penn wanted 10,000 acres in one place, for he had promised the purchasers of the first 500,000 rural acres sold in Pennsylvania a 2 percent bonus in urban property. (City plots would, under this plan, have ranged from ten to 200 acres!) No urban land would be sold outright, allowing property holders to benefit from the inevitable rise in real estate values.

Still, Penn sensed the practical obstacle to total realization of his plan, and he wisely instructed his commissioners: "If you cannot find enough land by the water side to allow an hundred acres to five thousand acres, get what you can, and proportionately divide it, though it were but fifty acres a share." Having rejected Upland as a site, Penn's agents concluded that the best location for a port city lay on a sparsely settled peninsula, formed by the confluence of the Schuylkill and Delaware rivers and varying from two to five miles in width. The land here was largely undeveloped, and at the narrowest point it was high, wooded, well watered, and served by a good harbor on the Delaware side. Titles to it had been granted only recently by the Duke of York, while further inland a large part of the land was unpatented. As Penn's appointed land commissioners arrived, they concurred with Deputy Governor Markham's decision and, although not all the titles could be purchased immediately, a large tract was bought from some Swedes in early 1682. Time could not be squandered bargaining or looking farther, as the first purchasers were growing impatient to occupy their town lots.

Among the early migrants was an Irish Quaker, Thomas Holme, whom Penn had commissioned surveyor general of the province. Armed with lists of the purchasers and Penn's several specifications, Holme faced the task of laying out a city in the wilderness. It was immediately clear that the proprietor's vision of a "green country town" did not square with the possibilities of the place. His promise, "each share [5,000-acre purchase] to have 50 poles upon the front to the river," could not be realized, for it would have meant that the hundred shareholders would occupy fifteen miles of waterfront, when less than a mile had been bought. Given this situation, how were 10,000 acres to be proportionately divided into city lots, all of which would have fairly easy access to the harbor?

If Penn anticipated the problem of land scarcity, his instructions left open to interpretation whether he intended Philadelphia to be made up of large plots, directly proportional to rural holdings, or whether he envisioned a small commercial center built around the harbor and surrounded by "liberty lands," that is, contiguous suburbs. In the latter case, the purchasers would hold small lots in the town and the remainder of their due land in the surrounding liberties. Not only would this plan be more equitable, placing all settlers close to the source of commerce, but it was less a deviation from past experience. And to the colonists who had already arrived, living close together in Philadelphia seemed more immediately appealing than pushing on into the inhospitable forest.

Holme began the work of town planning in the tract on the Delaware by laying out four streets and holding a lottery to determine the positions of purchasers on each. Lots were accorded equal frontage along the street, therefore being considerably deeper than wide, and subdivisions were permissible in accord with the proportions of rural holdings. Before these properties were surveyed, however, word came that Penn was on his way. Despite the clamoring of settlers to occupy their lots, Holme and Markham stopped work in anticipation of the proprietor's coming.

When Penn arrived he was satisfied with the site chosen for Philadelphia, but he insisted on altering its use. His modifications were to some extent due to changes that had taken place in the ranks of first purchasers: several had backed out while others had bought in, and the proprietor wanted to apply the up-to-date list to the allotment of city property. More important, however, was Penn's determination to construct some semblance of his "green country town" rather than allow crowding about the Delaware harbor.

He moved first to acquire frontage on the Schuylkill, less as an attempt to establish two ports than to develop an expanded city tract between the two rivers. The town would now have about one mile of waterfront real estate on either side and two miles from shore to shore, or 1,200 acres, surrounded by approximately 8,000 acres of liberty lands. In the former would be town houses, in the latter "gentlemen's seats or modest estates large enough to preserve rural delights" close to the city. Lots would be measured out regularly and carefully, but not all of Philadelphia would be

immediately surveyed or occupied. Some land would be reserved
to attract inhabitants in the future.

The actual layout of the city was dictated by the physical
features of the site, as well as by concepts of town planning
known to Penn and Holme. The product was a fortuitous but
fortunate blend of function and form. Philadelphia was a
rectangle, the long side of which ran east and west. The
watershed on the peninsula, from which streams traversed the
plane to either river, cut through the center of the city in a
north-south direction. It was a nearly perfect spot on which to
impose a gridiron pattern, with the principal axes virtually
determined. The adoption of this plan by Penn and Holme was
not a startling innovation. It was frequently employed in the
Spanish and French colonies. As early as 1638, New Haven had
been laid out in nine regular squares, the central one given to
public use. Burlington, in nearby Jersey, was divided into
quadrants by two wide thoroughfares, Broad and High streets,
and subdivided by smaller avenues. The name of its designer,
Richard Noble, appeared on early Pennsylvania land surveys.

Penn and Holme probably were acquainted with grid-plan
towns in northern Ireland. Neither man could have avoided
notice of building along these lines in London, and especially the
numerous plans drawn up after the great fire of 1666. One of
these, utilizing the popular open public square, was Richard
Newcourt's blueprint for an area one by one and a half miles,
strikingly similar to the subsequent Penn-Holme plan for Philadelphia.

When Holme's carefully drawn "Portraiture of the City of
Philadelphia" was published in 1683 with a descriptive text, not
only was the new town plan presented but also an innovation
regarding the placement of first purchasers.

The City, (as the Model shows) consists of a large Front-street to each
River, and a High-street (near the middle) from Front (or River) to
Front, of one hundred Foot broad, and a Broad-street in the middle of
the City, from side to side, of the like breadth. In the Center of the City
is a Square of ten Acres; at each Angle are to be Houses for publick
Affairs, as a Meeting-House, Assembly or State-House, Market-House,
School-House, and several other Buildings for Publick Concerns. There

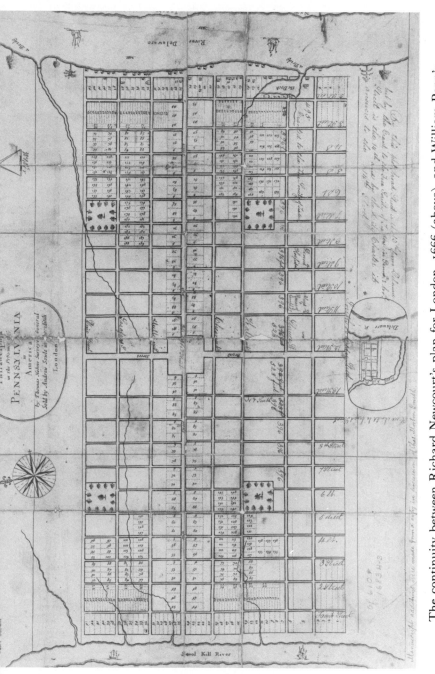

The continuity between Richard Newcourt's plan for London, 1666 (above), and William Penn's plan for Philadelphia, 1682 (below), demonstrates a direct relationship of Old World thought to New. (above) *Courtesy of Town Planning Review and John Reps.* (below) *Historical Society of Pennsylvania.*

are also in each Quarter of the City a Square of eight Acres, to be for the like Uses, as the Moore-fields in London; and eight Streets, (besides the High-street) that run from Front to Front, and twenty Streets, (besides the Broad street) that run cross the City, from side to side; all these Streets are of fifty Foot breadth.

In each Number in the Draught, in the Fronts and High-street, are placed the Purchasers of One Thousand Acres, and upwards, to make up five Thousand Acres Lot . . .

The lesser Purchasers begin at Number 1, in the second Streets, . . . the biggest of them being first placed, nearest to the Fronts.

More specifically, the purchasers of 1,000 to 10,000 acres received 20 to 204 feet of water frontage and one to four lots (varying in size) on High Street, a choice position. Purchasers of 250 and 500 acres would have to be satisfied with small back lots.

In other words, Penn jettisoned the agreement to choose town sites by lottery. It was, to be sure, another instance of preferential treatment for those who were crucial to the economic success of the colony, underscored by the special concession given the Free Society of Traders, which had purchased 20,000 acres in Pennsylvania. The Society was given almost 100 acres in the city, fronting on Dock Creek, the best harbor on the Delaware. Many grants to individual members of the society, whose land purchases amounted to over 61,000 acres, were also made in the Dock Creek area. Yet Penn could argue that such placement was rational as well as preferential. Merchants needed locations on the waterfront, whereas shopkeepers, artisans, and the like could as easily work and trade inland. The pragmatic principle behind Penn's assignments was apparent when he placed large purchasers who did not migrate on the Schuylkill; it was already clear to settlers that this river would not become a center of commerce. Furthermore, resident merchants on the Delaware would give the town a settled appearance.

Penn's concern for the financial prosperity of his province was complemented by the attention that he paid to his own fortunes. He retained control of the narrow strip of land between the Front Street lots and the water, potentially the most valuable property in Pennsylvania. He held back city real estate for rent and future sale rather than parceling it all out to first purchasers. Yet these material concerns notwithstanding, Philadelphia reflected Quaker ideals. The gridiron plan itself represented simplicity and order; it was significant that Penn did not draw on Baroque models of planning. If large purchasers got favorable locations, still it was decreed that the city would be residential and without grandiose public buildings. Far from mirroring Paris, Rome, or London, Philadelphia would not even resemble a New England town, dominated by an unpretentious Puritan meetinghouse. Instead, settlement was scattered, suggesting the Quakers' lack of dependence on institutions. The streets of the city, though initially several had been named after men, including Holme, were simply numbered or given the plainest designations: High (later Market), Broad, Front, Walnut, Race.

The actual work of surveying and clearing lots was carried on with vigor, if not exactly according to the representation on Holme's "Portraiture." In late 1683, Penn exulted that "our Wildernesse flourishes as a Garden," Philadelphia having "about 600 people in it & 100 houses built," not to mention "many hundred Farms settled and settling about her." But the economic picture in Pennsylvania was less rosy than this would suggest. Lack of currency was ever a problem in colonial America, and Philadelphians suffered the pinch. Penn, financially hard pressed as he was, only exacerbated matters by attempting to collect quitrents a year before they were due. But this was unfortunately symptomatic of a proprietary land policy which, more than anything else at the time, caused conflict in the colony.

Some settlers were irritated, others angered, by the locations assigned them in the city. Then, in early 1684 when lot holders in large numbers sought to legalize their surveys through patents, it was discovered that Penn intended to charge quitrents on city as well as country land, an unexpected exaction. Nor was it clear that he would assign full powers and privileges to property owners. The proprietor, it appeared, was always willing to benefit at the settlers' expense. And who could deny that Philadelphia was the creation of William Penn, aided by his surveyor general, not the people who lived there.

Yet when grievances were presented to Penn in the "Humble Remonstrance & address of several, the Adventurers, Free holders & Inhabitants and others therein concerned," he responded to the objection that there was no town charter: "Tis the People's Fault, not mine. . . . I was not to wait on them with Draughts." Still, he was willing to have a city charter, though he was hurt and offended by the charges leveled at him, especially since the chief complainers were the large purchasers whom he had favored. His impending departure for England in mid-1684, which had been responsible for precipitating the grievances, made it impossible for him to do more than reach agreement with several of the merchants at that time.

The "Humble Remonstrance" was only one sign of a growing disaffection between proprietor and colonists, however. Disputes had arisen as early as 1682. Shortly after his arrival Penn summoned a convention of delegates from the three counties of Pennsylvania (Philadelphia, Chester, Bucks) and the Three Lower Counties (Kent, Sussex, New Castle) to approve the Frame of Government, the Forty Laws agreed upon in England, and about fifty additional laws. Instead of immediate and full endorsement, there was lengthy debate and dissent. In the end, nineteen laws were rejected, and it was proposed that "any Member may offer any Bill, publick or private, tending to the publick Good, except in case of levying Taxes," a clear violation of the Frame of Government, which specified that legislation could originate only from the governor or Provincial Council.

In March 1683, the Council and Assembly convened for the first time, the former dominated by friends of the proprietor, the latter a disparate array of recently arrived English Quakers and older residents of the Delaware Valley, many neither Friends nor English. The size of these two bodies was drastically reduced (from seventy-two to eighteen and from two hundred to thirty-six, respectively), but there was little agreement on other innovations. Rather, a new Frame of Government emerged as a compromise. The proprietor argued successfully for the right to veto all legislation, claiming that the royal charter specifically assigned this power to him. In turn, he agreed not to take major legislative action without the "advice and consent" of the Council. The Assembly, intent on gaining the right to initiate bills, was temporarily, but only temporarily, satisfied with the

"Privilege of conferring" with governor and Council on law making.

The aspirations of the Assembly did not simply represent an inevitable growth of democratic institutions on American soil. Tangible interests and specific grievances were involved, the most obvious of which were the complaints of the Three Lower Counties. Granted parity in the lower house through the Act of Union of 1682, inhabitants of this region could there express resentment against Quaker intrusion, and they refused to be mollified by the Naturalization Act of the same year, which guaranteed personal equality regardless of national background. Maryland still laid claim to the area, and agents of Lord Baltimore actively recruited the allegiance of its residents. Transforming disloyalty into simple disaffection sometimes provided Penn with a task in itself.

The proprietor wanted to dominate the lower Delaware for commercial reasons, but trade proved to be a divisive force among Quakers as well as between them and the older inhabitants. The merchants who were living along the river previous to the settlement of Pennsylvania reaped great profits by provisioning the arriving colonists. The lure was great enough to draw traders from other parts of America, such as Samuel Carpenter, a Quaker merchant in the West Indies. Thus, before the Free Society of Traders favored by the proprietor could get into operation, the commercial initiative had been taken. Not surprisingly, the Society was opposed by individual merchants. Nevertheless, the Society did make its bid for a monopoly of the provincial trade, only to founder on undercapitalization, litigation, and the apathy or selfish interests of its members. Finally, its members made a last-ditch effort to stave off failure through the use of political influence. Although the attempt was abortive, it produced further friction in the colony, among the merchants, and between some of the merchants and the proprietor. The quarrels over land policy in Philadelphia, in which Penn was accused of opportunism as well as favoritism, accentuated these divisions.

Nor were unity and harmony likely to result from the arrival, in the late summer of 1683, of Francis Daniel Pastorius of

Frankfurt with a small band of settlers, followed in October by thirty-three Germans from Crefeld, a city on the lower Rhine near Holland. These two separate groups, who were brought together in America, had become acquainted with Penn during a preaching tour which he made through Germany in 1677 with Benjamin Furley. After the royal charter for Pennsylvania was issued, the two Quaker leaders encouraged the German converts to leave for the New World, at which point the role of Pastorius became vital.

Like Penn, Pastorius possessed a solid academic background, was trained in the law, and could have anticipated a successful worldly career. But his serious turn of mind attracted him to a group of Pietists in Frankfurt. Having taken a two-year tour of Europe in the company of a frivolous nobleman, he returned to the city in November 1682 to find his religious friends talking excitedly of Pennsylvania. He later recalled that at this point, "I withdrew into the retirement of my chamber and recalled to mind everything which had passed before my eyes on the stage of the world, and could not find any enduring pleasure in anything." Despairing of change in his homeland, Pastorius decided "to teach the learning which I had received by grace from the highest Giver and Father of Lights to the new-found American peoples of Pennsylvania." As agent for the Frankfurt (or German) Company, he traveled to London in the spring of 1683 to purchase 15,000 acres, then sailed for Philadelphia. At approximately the same time individuals from Crefeld bought 18,000 acres.

When Pastorius arrived in the Quaker colony, he found Penn reluctant not only to give him title to land in Philadelphia commensurate with the company's outlying holding—the proprietor had reserved this bonus for first purchasers—but also to assign him 15,000 acres in one tract or barony. Pastorius prevailed in both instances, arguing in the latter that it was unfair for Germans to have to settle among the English, a sentiment that did not vitiate his desire for land in the city. Penn agreed to the second request on the condition that families would quickly be settled in each of the townships created. When the

Crefelders arrived and Frankfurters doggedly stayed home, Penn combined equal shares from each grant into a township called Germantown, organized by Pastorius and settled by the low Germans from Crefeld.

Germantown was not the only ethnic conclave in Pennsylvania. Quakers from Wales were early attracted to this New World haven. Delegates from six Monthly Meetings traveled to London in May 1681 to interview Penn, and they left with the impression that land purchased by Welsh Friends could lie in one barony "within which all causes, quarrels, crimes and disputes might be tried and wholly determined by officers, magistrates, and juries of our language." (Soon after the establishment of Germantown Pastorius wrote: "I could wish for my small part that we receive a small separate province, and be so much the better able to protect ourselves from oppression.") These expectations, complemented by the proprietor's promised liberalism and a heavy dose of promotional literature, enabled the delegates to dispose quickly of 30,000 acres in 5,000-acre bundles to "companies." Since Penn's idea was that 5,000 acres constituted a perfectly sized township, half the Welsh land was transformed into Merion, Radnor, and Haverford townships by proprietary fiat. But it was several years before Penn consented to survey the Welsh Tract, at that time encompassing 40,000 acres including Merion, Radnor, and Haverford, and he refused its inhabitants the special privileges they expected.

Although Penn reaped the consequences of this denial in local politics, the conflict over the barony was not an outright contest for power but a disagreement arising from the different intentions of the parties involved. While Welsh or German settlers saw security in segregation, an attitude deriving as much from insularity in the Old World as uncertainty in the New, Penn had no intention of letting his province degenerate into an aggregation of loosely knit principalities. Yet his enthusiasm to dispose of land may well have disguised this fact to prospective buyers.

Penn and the early Pennsylvania settlers simply had different perspectives on the "holy experiment." The proprietor expected gratitude and harmonius cooperation from people for whom he provided a religious haven, economic opportunities, and political liberty. To achieve his aims, he acted alone, not only because his course, if publicized, might offend London officialdom but also because he believed that he had the well-being of the immigrants at heart; and, probably, he wanted to avoid repetition of the New Jersey confusion of leadership. To men and women who had suffered at the hands of authority, he depicted Pennsylvania in utopian terms. Yet to underwrite the cost of settlement and ensure its later prosperity, he made concessions to some colonists and not to others.

The new settlers were Quakers, with few exceptions. Their monolithic response to Penn's invitation reflected the recently imposed group discipline in the Society of Friends, and especially the communications made possible by the hierarchy of meetings. Apparently, though, there was resistance to the exodus. Persecution, certainly a motive for migrating, was not considered sufficient cause in itself. Thus one meeting, objecting to the loss of a member, declared: "He hath given us no satisfactory reason for his removing, but our godly jealousy is that his chief ground is fearfulness of sufferings here." There were even reported instances of Quakers being released from jail on the condition of migrating. A separate but related argument, that settling in America "may lessen the number of Friends here, and so make them the more unable to assist each other in a suffering day," was considered important enough to be cited and refuted in *Plantation Work the Work of this Generation*, a tract favoring the exodus.

If Quakers who sailed to Pennsylvania had to overcome opposition to their leaving within the Society, it is more than likely that they fastened on Penn's promotional literature with an inflexible tenacity. The concessions which Penn made to economic realities could also be viewed as betrayals. In the very act of taking individual command over the fate of Pennsylvanians, Penn was challenging the antiauthoritarian tendencies of Quakers who had, at least recently, been acting on the basis of consensus. Indeed, implicit in colonization was a rejection of civilization for a better world. Penn's own expectations had to be scaled down (quite actually, as in the size of Philadelphia and of the Council and Assembly), a situation to which he could reconcile himself. His misfortune was not to be able to reconcile many of the settlers nor even understand their discontent.

3

FIRST SHOOTS: IMPERIAL AND PROVINCIAL POLITICS IN THE LATE SEVENTEENTH CENTURY

Political development during the first two decades of Pennsylvania's existence demonstrated a steady drive toward autonomy but a rather confused search for local authority until, in 1701, the Assembly became the dominant institution. This was also a period of increasing imperial control, as the policies of James II, William and Mary, and Parliament not only rationalized administrative procedures and commercial regulations but also attacked the charters of private colonies. William Penn, who played the difficult role of mediator, lamented after almost two decades of buffeting: "You cannot easily imagine the difficulties I lie under, what with the King's affairs, those of the Government, and my Proprietary ones . . . 'tis I that pay the reckoning." Proprietary power declined, even as the colony prospered, developing in some directions that Penn never imagined. He had not been able to supervise the "holy experiment" with a firm hand. Having sailed from his homeland in the autumn of 1682 with the intention of passing the rest of his life in his New World haven, he remained in Pennsylvania less than two years. His return to England was prompted by a controversy with the proprietor of Maryland over control of the Three Lower Counties, which both men viewed as crucial to the commercial lives of their respective colonies. The matter would be handled in London by the Lords of Trade, a committee of the Privy Council recently established to deal exclusively with colonial affairs, and a committee where Penn could make his influence at court felt. His necessary concern with a transatlantic world of imperial issues, while most of the Quaker colonists transacted their business in a smaller sphere, accentuated differences between him and his people.

Penn was not without friends in Pennsylvania. They were usually tied directly to proprietary government: such as his kinsman and former deputy, Robert Markham; surveyor general Thomas Holme; members of the Board of Propriety, created to sell or allocate land in his absence; provincial treasurer Robert Turner; Thomas Lloyd, master of the rolls. Or they were merchants who dealt in the transatlantic world, sharing Penn's mercantile mentality and, from their estates in Chester or Bucks counties, his aristocratic predilections. James Claypoole, for example, a London merchant who had "a great drawing in my mind to move my family thither" to Pennsylvania, left not for reasons of persecution but rather because of personal indebtedness and the promise of the Free Society of Traders. In Penn he recognized a man who was "so much my friend that I can have anything in reason I desire of him." Other merchant-supporters of the proprietor included Samuel Carpenter, James Harrison (also proprietary steward), and Nicholas More, chief justice of the Provincial Court, created in 1684 to hear appeals in both criminal and civil cases not determinable in the county courts, which were administered by large landholders. More's four associate justices were drawn from among wealthy Quaker advocates of the proprietor.

These men controlled the Provincial Council as well as the courts. The fact that such men were elected is evidence that colonial Quakers concurred with the proprietor's hierarchical view of politics, though Penn had earlier attempted to impose a law allowing him to appoint Council members. As he departed the colony, Penn delegated executive power to the Council and, through President Thomas Lloyd, admonished the inhabitants: "Oh, now you are come to a quiet land, provoke not the Lord to trouble it . . . Truly, the name and honour of the Lord are deeply concerned in you, as to the discharge of yourselves, in your present stations; many eyes being upon you."

Penn was to remain in England for the next decade and a half, through the turbulence surrounding the reign of his close friend James II; through the Glorious Revolution and the ascendancy of William III, never Penn's ally; through the years of imperial reorganization in the 1690s. Always his plea would be for stability and quiet in Pennsylvania's politics, a condition that would lighten his load as defender of the "holy experiment" in England. Thus, he attempted to control the province with what appeared to be an increasingly heavy hand, alienating his friends as well as confirming the judgment of his opponents.

Antiproprietary feeling came easily to the non-Quaker inhabitants of the Three Lower Counties, whose settlement predated Pennsylvania, while Quakers in the upper counties who were not beneficiaries of proprietary largesse became increasingly resentful, expressing more and more their point of view through the Assembly. This body, chafing at its restricted functions, asserted at its first meeting after Penn's departure the right to debate and vote on bills "without the least restriction by the Council." It also attempted to impeach two proprietary appointees, Chief Justice Nicholas More and Provincial Court Clerk Patrick Robinson.

But it was Penn's well-to-do allies who held the upper hand during the first decade of the colony's existence. Working through the Council, these men affixed to Penn's grant of executive power certain judicial and legislative functions which had been reserved to the proprietor, appointing judges to county courts and to the Provincial Court, and submitting laws on the Council's authority for the Assembly's approval. Indeed, as they held power, the proprietor's friends became his uneasy allies, jealous of their newly gained prerogatives and, thus, wary of instructions from England. And from their position of economic advantage, they were dissatisfied with Penn's land policy: it barred speculation, which was financially stifling; and it was inconsistently applied, especially regarding the proprietor himself, who retained one-tenth of the colony's estates, mostly idle, and of course did not pay the quitrents which were to be exacted from all other real property.

From afar, Penn was less worried by, or perhaps was unaware of, the developing disaffection and will to power of his friends than by the reports of real or potential political turbulence. In 1686 William Markham wrote of a conference between Council and Assembly on "the privilidg of the people, a Dangerous thing to Dispute in the face of such a Congregation," and he warned that "if such Disputes be allowed it will hazard the over throw of the Government, for what ever privilidg you once grant you must never think to recall with out being Reflected on and Counted a great oppressor." An angered Penn threatened to "keep the Power & Privileges I have left, to the Pitch, & recover the rest," but instead he attempted to strengthen his hand by shifting the executive function from the Council to a Commission of State composed of Thomas Lloyd, James Claypoole, Nicholas More, John Eckley, and Robert Turner who, along with Markham, Thomas Holme, and a few other stalwarts, remained true to Penn.

When the Commission had no more success than the Council in curbing factional quarrels and unseemly noise from "an infant Province whose steps are numbered and watched," Penn decided to invest executive control in the hands of one man. Thomas Lloyd, the Welsh Quaker and Oxford graduate who had benefited more than any other man from the distribution of provincial offices, refused the appointment, a bad omen, so the job of deputy governor went to an outsider, John Blackwell, formerly an officer in Cromwell's army. If his Puritan background demonstrated Penn's continuing Protestant allegiance despite service to the Catholic James II, Blackwell's military training was not only inappropriate to Quakerism but also to a situation where Penn should have been striving for adaptation rather than discipline. It was a case of poor judgment, compounded by instructions and explanations which assigned Blackwell virtually impossible tasks while simultaneously undermining him. "Lett him see what he can do awhile," wrote Penn to the Commission of State in a letter describing the deputy governor and promising that he would be "layd aside" if unsatisfactory. Meanwhile, Blackwell was charged with suppressing "the animosities" in the province, checking the aspirations of the Assembly, and collecting the quitrents.

It is doubtful that Blackwell could have carried out his duties under the most favorable conditions. Instead, adversity was his lot. No response came to his announcement that he would land in New York, and finding his way to Philadelphia was only slightly more difficult than locating his Council members. When they finally appeared, President Lloyd performed in his most quibbling and contentious manner, even claiming that Blackwell's commission was invalid because it did not bear the great seal, which only Lloyd, as keeper of the seal, could affix. Constantly goaded in this manner, Blackwell responded with humor that barely concealed his contempt (about the Quakers: "each prays for his neighbor on First Days and then preys on him the other six") and with a zealous assertion of authority that exceeded Penn's instructions. Although his challenge to the legislature that "you, when chosen, are his, vizt. the Proprietors; not theirs, vizt. the peoples. . . . He may Reject your Councills, & take such others as will answer the Ends of the Kings just Expectations, or act therin without you" reflected Penn's sentiments, and his attempt to impeach Thomas Lloyd may have mirrored Penn's desire, still Blackwell was scolded by the proprietor for stirring up controversy, and his resignation in 1689 was quickly accepted.

Executive power now slipped back into the hands of the Council. Lloyd and his followers boldly removed proprietary supporters from office while Penn, suspect after the Glorious Revolution because of his earlier association with James II, was in no position to aid his allies or enforce his policies. His one major act at this time, the incorporation of Philadelphia, only served further to strengthen the merchant elite, who took over the extensive powers of city government. But discontent with this leadership was clearly demonstrated when the Council proposed a modest property tax in 1692. Two hundred and sixty-one Philadelphia freemen signed a petition of protest, an opposition that went well beyond a small core of proprietary supporters to include disaffected merchants, smaller entrepreneurs, shopkeepers, and artisans, as well as non-English inhabitants such as Francis Daniel Pastorius of Germantown. The Assembly refused to pass the tax bill. Thomas Lloyd and his followers, men whose economic status made them the most likely candidates for playing the role of reigning gentry in the English tradition, were having no more success in establishing authority than William Penn enjoyed.

Quakers, of course, were not known for their submissiveness, and it is likely that those least sympathetic to group discipline in England immigrated to America. Their Old World experience with government, as with organized religion, had been as adversaries. Where they were not indifferent they were hostile to form, structure, and institutions, the very stabilizing forces of society. Some Quakers worried about these tendencies, causing Penn to warn the magistrates of Philadelphia: "There is a cry comes over into thes parts agst the number of the drinking houses & Loosness that is committed in the caves" along the Delaware, the primitive domiciles of the first migrants. Laws were passed in Pennsylvania to prevent "Clandestine Loose, and Unseemly proceedings" and to license ordinaries or drinking houses. But political excesses went unchecked. Personality proved a more pertinent rallying point than abstract ideal or tangible institution, a logical development among individualists. For one man could sound the grievances of disparate peoples. As Thomas Lloyd moved into the power void left by William Penn, the center of contention was taken over by George Keith.

Keith had crossed the Atlantic in 1685, restless, dissatisfied, in search of broader opportunities which were not to be found as surveyor general in the wilds of East New Jersey. When invited to Philadelphia as master of the newly established Quaker school in 1689, he readily accepted. Keith was intellectually if not temperamentally suited to the post. Although he had once denounced all universities as "the stews of anti-Christ," he earned a degree from the University of Aberdeen. But the excess of his language was characteristic. Keith was always a controversialist, fighting battles against himself as well as others. His conversion to the Society of Friends was not an emotional experience as it had been for Penn, whose formal learning rivaled Keith's but whose disposition was entirely different. Rather, it came as an effort of rationalization and introspection.

Scottish Quakerism was more doctrinal than the English variety, and Keith accentuated the divergence. Dogma became crucial; therefore, teaching was essential.

Henry More, the Cambridge Platonist whose work influenced Keith, referred to him as "the best Quaker of them all" but "rudely and unjudicially schismatical." Keith argued and wrote, preached and taught, traveled with such luminaries as Penn and Quaker theologian Robert Barclay, and, within the Society, raised some doubts as to his own orthodoxy. His acerbic, disputatious demeanor was also frowned upon, but it could be excused as a zeal for the truth, an enthusiasm which propelled him into the New World. Here he found himself surrounded not by his intellectual peers but by rustic Friends who, while they were willing to pay him deference, remained impervious to his doctrinal, logical approach to religion. Appalled by this attitude, certain that the wilderness fostered a laxness which could undermine orthodoxy, Keith became convinced that only a rigid definition of Quakerism could salvage the situation. His conservative reaction to the new environment was opposite to that of many Friends.

Arriving in Philadelphia in 1689, he devoted his time not to teaching but, as he later recalled, to "Reading, Meditation, Visiting Meetings and answering the Conscientious Doubts and Questions of many People." His plan was to build Quaker unity on the rock of doctrine; instead, he ultimately split the Society. In 1690 he presented to the Yearly Meeting for Pennsylvania and West New Jersey a proposal for church government and discipline which would have undermined the freedom of spiritual expression unique to Quakerism. Rebuffed, Keith set forward a creed defining the faith, only to be turned down again. His interests were now ranging beyond the policy and theology of the Society to its relationship with the larger community. He began to ask whether a Friend, because of his belief in nonresistance, should hold civil office and, if he did, how he should carry out his duties.

Roger Williams had raised a similar question in Massachusetts, to the discomfort of the magistracy, and Keith's probing was no less upsetting to the Quaker establishment. Fortuitously, there arose at this moment an incident which underscored the relevance of his questioning. A band of smugglers stole a ship in Philadelphia and brazenly looted along the riverbank, believing the Quakers would look on passively. Instead, a group of men was commissioned and armed to deal with the situation. Keith seized on this violation of pacifism to launch his own attack. Given the political division in the province, he did not want for followers.

Thus, when he was charged with heresy at the Yearly Meeting in 1691, the whole Quaker community became embroiled in a controversy which had political as well as theological implications. The Monthly Meeting in Philadelphia, dominated by Lloyd and his followers, was at first inclined to drop the matter. But Keith, righteous and contentious as ever, insisted on airing the conflict. A fiery exchange took place between Lloyd and him, followed by charges and countercharges traded between orthodox and Keithian (called Christian) Quakers. When English Friends failed to effect a reconciliation, Keith was read out of the meeting, which only increased his zeal and inflamed his rhetoric. "Fools, idiots, silly souls, hypocrites, heathens, rotten ranters, Tyrants, Popes" were the labels he affixed to his opponents, who showed almost as little restraint in response. In 1692 there were more tracts published in Pennsylvania than in all the previous years combined.

When, in September of that year, the Council ordered the judiciary to clamp down on the press in such a way as to gag Keith, it was an acknowledgment that religious and political divisions were largely the same. "Alls a fire spiritual and temporal," Penn was informed by Robert Turner, long a proprietary supporter and now the only Keithian on the Philadelphia Court. The other seven Quakers on the Court took the orthodox side, as did members of the bench from Bucks and Chester counties, and the Provincial Court, as well as all nine Friends on the Council. Conversely, the Keithians were, in the main, opponents of Lloyd who used Christian Quakerism as a vehicle for their discontent. In Massachusetts Anne Hutchinson had gathered much the same sort of support; merchants who disagreed with the economic policies of the magistracy embraced the antinomian heresy. Mrs. Hutchinson, like Roger Williams, was exiled. But Keith remained until late 1693 to perpetuate the schism, accentuating the divisive tendencies in the province, and undermining the constituted leadership.

William Penn was by now only a shadowy figure in Pennsylvania. Having returned to England in 1684 to defend successfully his claim on the Three Lower Counties, he did not immediately leave again for his province as intended. Rather, with his friend the Duke of York crowned James II in 1685, Penn seized the opportunity to work in behalf of religious toleration. And James, recognizing the Quaker leader's influence among dissenters when his own popularity was declining among Anglican Englishmen, happily attached Penn to his short reign. It was a symbiotic relationship in which the Quaker was willing to believe that an increasingly authoritarian, Catholic monarch was a true advocate of tolerance, while the king harbored the thought that a peaceful Protestant dissenter would aid him in forcibly forging England into a Catholic nation.

Still, Penn was not entirely naive. His motives included the defense of Pennsylvania against the incursions of the home government, as Stuart policy abroad showed the same repressive instinct manifest in England. Between 1660 and 1673 Anglo-American commercial relations had been defined by a series of parliamentary acts aimed at excluding all but English ships and crews from the American trade, including colonial ones, while designating London the economic center of the empire. By 1675 efforts at establishing a central agency to handle plantation affairs had culminated in the creation of the Lords of Trade. The logical consequence of this attitude was interference in provincial politics, the most blatant example being the establishment of the Dominion of New England, a regional government administered from Boston which by 1687 included Massachusetts, New Hampshire, Plymouth, Rhode Island, Connecticut, New York, and New Jersey. Penn's friendship with James II served to protect the Quaker province; at one point the king suspended proceedings that probably would have brought Pennsylvania under the sway of the Dominion.

While the Glorious Revolution of 1688 marked the end of

James II's reign, it also signaled a victory for Penn's whiggish principles of republican government and religious toleration. But because of his association with the deposed monarch, Penn himself was suspect. The new king and queen, William and Mary, were never friendly to him; for the time being, he lost his allies in high places. And since the imperial policy of the Stuarts was not to be discarded, the "holy experiment" was in greater danger than before, without Penn to defend it. War proved to be the *bête noire* of Pennsylvania's autonomy. William III brought his anti-French foreign policy across the Channel, reversing the Stuart's pro-Catholic stance, and the two countries were engaged in conflict by May 1689. In the upper reaches of New York, the French and their Indian allies posed a threat which had to be met. But when the governor of New York requested troops of neighboring Pennsylvania, he was turned down by the Quaker politicians.

This refusal, supplemented by reports that Philadelphia merchants were trading with the French, put Pennsylvania in the limelight of imperial concern. The Lords of Trade recommended that the province be brought under royal control, in accord with William and Mary's policy toward Massachusetts, New York, and Maryland, where regional revolts had occurred in the wake of the Glorious Revolution. It was also recommended that the Quaker colony be annexed to an adjoining government, advice that demonstrated the continuing appeal of the dominion concept. Thus in late 1692, as the Keithian controversy was raging through Philadelphia, Benjamin Fletcher received a commission granting him the same governing power in Pennsylvania as he had recently received for New York. After a turbulent decade of self-rule, the colony was to be subject to the crown.

Fletcher's powers were extensive. In addition to appointing a deputy governor, he could name his own Council, adjourn and dismiss the Assembly, and veto its bills. He could establish courts, choose justices of the peace, and select provincial officers. And, of course, he was to undertake military preparations. Needless to say, he was not a welcome figure in Pennsylvania (he spent only a few weeks of his two-year tenure there), nor did he strive for popularity with the dominant Quaker faction. When Thomas Lloyd declined a place on the Council, Fletcher filled appointive offices with his opponents, including William Markham as deputy governor and several Keithians on the Council. But the followers of Lloyd had long experience in obstructionist politics, and Fletcher suffered many of the same indignities as had his Puritan predecessor, John Blackwell. Fletcher's attempts to get money for defense led to a small appropriation and much frustration; he finally referred to the minutes of the legislature as "a farce."

In the meantime, Penn's situation in England was changing. Several of his friends from earlier reigns joined William III's Privy Council, and by December 1693 the Quaker proprietor had emerged from his seclusion and could move freely through the country. He petitioned for the return of his government. Despite the protest of the Lords of Trade against the inaction of the Pennsylvania legislature, the province was put back into Penn's hands, not only as a result of his royal connections but on the assumption that he could accomplish what the royal governor could not. Penn promised to put before the Council and Assembly in person an order for "the supplying such Quotas of Men or the defraying their part of such charges as their Majesties Dominions in that part of America."

Penn's promise was not a model of pure pacifism, because in his own mind he distinguished between what a man owed to his state and to his religion, to an earthly ruler, and to God. Other Quaker leaders, such as George Fox, had made clear that while Friends would not personally bear arms, they would not bind their government to this position; indeed, they expected the protection of the government. Fox also characterized as sacred the duty of obedience to the state, since government was installed by God. If government obviously violated holy commandments, then passive resistance was allowable. Penn, unlike Fox, saw ruler and ruled bound together by social contract. The difference in point of view became important only with the founding of Pennsylvania: how would a Quaker government protect its citizens; did the peace testimony infringe on liberty of conscience by involving religion in politics; could the demands of the

English government be ignored, since the proprietor was granted powers to raise an army, declare war, and conclude peace? Penn, by theoretically restricting government to earthly matters and thus divesting it of sacred character, did not doubt that the Quaker leaders in Pennsylvania should respond to imperial demands through appropriations of a military nature. In fact, the Assembly in 1693 had made a gesture in that direction, though not sufficient to the royal governor's liking.

It is doubtful, however, that the Quaker politicians were as interested in theoretical arguments as in practical realities. The lower house had been willing to make a token grant of defense funds to Fletcher in 1693 and 1694 only in exchange for a concession of broader political power. The experience of William Markham, appointed deputy governor by Penn in 1695, was no different. The money bill which emerged from the Assembly in 1695 was tied to a so-called "Act of Settlement" that would have radically altered the Frame of 1683, under which the government was presumably operating. The number of representatives to the Council and Assembly was cut in half, to two and four members per county respectively, while the franchise requirements were changed to give Friends a greater edge over recent non-Quaker migrants. The Assembly was given its long-sought right to initiate legislation, as well as the power to determine its own adjournment and pass on the qualifications of its members. Markham turned down this political bargain in 1695 only to accept similar terms in 1696, with the realization that the proprietor had no choice but to satisfy the conditions on which his government was returned to him—in this case, a bill raising £300 for Fletcher in New York.

Markham's willingness to concede stemmed not only from his long experience with obstructionist Quaker politicians but also from a change in the attitude of the proprietor. Penn's personal troubles in England, the death of his wife, and the defection of his steward, Philip Ford, only accentuated his disappointment with the course of provincial politics. With his government returned to him, he ceased trying to direct political and economic affairs along the lines of his initial plans and asked simply for an adherence to the demands of the English government. As yet he had no definite plans for returning to Pennsylvania, believing that he could best preserve the proprietary autonomy of the province by cultivating his political connections at home.

It was clear enough that the Quaker colony had not developed in accord with the proprietor's original vision. When he mustered the support of Quaker merchants to help underwrite the founding of Pennsylvania, rewarding those who immigrated with political office, Penn thought he could establish an elite faithful to his interest. But challenges from outside the proprietary circle and defections within produced a coterie of Quaker politicians, wealthy merchants, and landowners led by Thomas Lloyd, who by 1688 controlled the government for their own purposes. Old friends of Penn and lesser merchants, small landowners, and city artisans and shopkeepers opposed the Lloydian group, rallied behind George Keith's challenge to the Establishment, and even lent support to Governor Fletcher. With the restoration of proprietary government, however, the Quaker elite returned to power, led now by the deceased Thomas Lloyd's distant cousin, David Lloyd.

Before he sailed to Pennsylvania in 1686, David Lloyd for three years had handled legal aspects of land transfer for Penn as well as selecting from the acts of Parliament laws pertinent to the colony's autonomy. Although he was not a Quaker, his knowledge of English law was needed in Pennsylvania, and for this reason Penn commissioned Lloyd his attorney general. Lloyd came from a lower-class background and, unlike his illustrious cousin, could lay claim to no land in America. But he was not long in the colony before his friendship with Thomas Lloyd and the rising Quaker elite led to appointments as clerk of the Philadelphia county courts and clerk of the Provincial Court. As attorney general he upheld the proprietor's authority in the judiciary, but he never challenged the increasingly aggressive behavior of the legislature. The reason for his silence may be found in his establishment of an identity independent of his sponsor. He was recognized by the leading politicians, received a small salary as deputy register of wills, and began speculating in land. By 1688 his lack of devotion to the proprietary interest lost him his job as attorney general; he was a zealous opponent of Governor John Blackwell. Probably Lloyd was ignorant of the political situation in England which led Penn to appoint Blackwell. His perspective had become provincial, for in Pennsylvania he quickly achieved the eminence denied him in the mother country.

David Lloyd continued to accumulate offices, including those of clerk of the Assembly and of the Council in 1688. He converted to Quakerism, barely in time to disown George Keith. When Governor Fletcher arrived, Lloyd battled against royal authority from a seat recently won in the Assembly, where he was elected speaker in 1694. A year later the freemen in Chester County sent him on a three-year term to the Council. He was a major architect of the Frame of Government reluctantly accepted by Deputy Governor Markham in 1696, by which time Lloyd had succeeded his cousin as leader of the Quaker political elite. In 1697 David Lloyd married Grace Growden, daughter of a wealthy landowner and active politician.

The rapidity of Lloyd's rise to power was indicative not only of personal ability but of a pervasive social mobility arising from the absence of anything like permanent stratification in Pennsylvania. Among the early settlers, probably half the adult males came as indentured servants, men who contracted their labor to reach the Quaker colony where economic and social ascent was open to the ambitious. Of the immigrants who did not come as servants, most (an estimated 80 to 90 percent) were from yeoman or artisan backgrounds, the case of David Lloyd. The few men who had genteel pretensions could hardly be distinguished from their more common neighbors in the wilderness. The contrast to England was striking. There, though the gentry was no more than 5 percent of the population, it owned most of the wealth and wielded virtually all the power. More than half of the population was economically nonproductive. The amount of mobility was quite modest and the direction was probably more often downward than up.

The unstructured, mobile quality of Pennsylvania was economically and politically stimulating. The merchants who were early attracted to Philadelphia simply rode roughshod over the monopolistic Free Society of Traders. The phenomenal growth of commerce was noticed in 1696 by Governor Fletcher, who observed that Philadelphia was "nearly equal to the city of New York in trade and riches." Even at Penn's departure in 1684 there were about 350 houses and 2,500 people in the city. The men who competed successfully in trade also contested for office, creating the political turbulence which so disturbed the proprietor. Penn was, of course, liberal in outlook by the standards of Restoration England, where his political experience lay. In Pennsylvania, however, the conditions of life produced a government based not on the rule of an acknowledged gentry but rather on an economic elite, freshly established, which sought political power corresponding to financial achievement. Yet the fluidity of society made it difficult for the ruling group to rest comfortably in control.

During the initial decade of Pennsylvania's existence, the Council represented first the interest of the proprietor and later that of the Quaker elite, while the Assembly was the seat of opposition. When Governor Fletcher came to Pennsylvania with the power to appoint a Council and veto the legislation of the Assembly, the Quaker leaders moved into the lower house, whose quest for power was institutionalized in the Frame of Government of 1696. (An added motive for transferring power to the Assembly was the fear that the Council might become appointive, especially if Pennsylvania again became a royal colony.) The Assembly thus became the agency of provincial political aspirations, a development not peculiar to the Quaker colony but common to the Atlantic seaboard settlements at this time. Pennsylvania had, however, arrived at this mature state more rapidly than her neighbors, and the accelerated ascent of the Assembly continued, despite the fact that the colony remained at the center of imperial concern even after Penn resumed control of it in 1694.

The advent of international war and the rebellions in several colonies in 1689 had heightened the interest of the English government in the American colonies. Military preparations and political stability achieved through royal control were the major objectives of imperial policy. By the mid-1690s, however, economic considerations were primary. The conflict with France disrupted English shipping, and colonial merchants did not hesitate to bite off a larger share of commerce in the West Indies, sometimes illegally, and the merchants at home grumbled that such activities were contrary to the purpose of colonies. Parliament responded to mercantile discontent in 1696 with an Act for Preventing Frauds, and Regulating Abuses in the Plantation Trade, intended to strengthen the previous Navigation Acts through more efficient enforcement. There were certain innovations as well, including the requirement that the crown approve colonial governors, who would give oaths to uphold the commercial acts, and the establishment of vice-admiralty courts, where violators would be tried without juries.

The commerce of Pennsylvania fit the pattern mercantilists complained of. The mainstay of Philadelphia's seaborne trade was the West Indies, involving pork, beef, lumber, and wheat products, especially flour, which became as valuable as the rest of the exports combined. The same goods were shipped outside the empire to Lisbon and the wine islands. The next leg of the trip was to England, carrying sugar, molasses, rum, wine, or simply ballast. Tobacco from the Three Lower Counties was shipped directly to England, as were skins and furs. Manufactured goods, primarily hardware and dry goods, were brought back to the Quaker colony. It was not simply the details of the rivalry with Pennsylvania merchants which reached the ears of the home government, but accusations of illicit trade. New Castle on the lower Delaware as well as Philadelphia were the scenes of this illegal activity, while pirates were to be found all along the river, according to accounts from Edward Randolph, the peripatetic and indefatigable civil servant whose earlier reports on Massachusetts had been primarily responsible for the Dominion of New England. Francis Nicholson, once lieutenant governor of the Dominion and currently governor of Maryland, a colony which was suffering from the competition of Pennsylvania merchants, joined Randolph in hurling charges. Supposedly, tobacco was moving from Maryland into the Quaker colony and, without customs being paid, shipped on to Scotland. This enumerated commodity was not to leave the empire; Scotland, not united with England until 1707, was considered a serious threat in commercial matters, and as early as 1684 Penn had been fined because Philadelphia merchants were trading there.

But violations of the Navigation Acts were seldom noticed on the Delaware, and convictions by local judges and juries were out of the question, according to the informers. In 1695 Nicholson had suggested that the king appoint an admiralty judge to try violations in Pennsylvania. And with regard to the provision of the Navigation Act of 1696 regarding colonial governors, Randolph later called it an effort "to bring the Governments of Proprietys to a dependence on the Crown." Penn, who was not consulted while the bill was in Parliament, called the act "darkly, & If I may say so, inconsistently worded" and informed Randolph that it "was made to ensnare honest men." The proprietor soon appeared before the Board of Trade to question the operation of the act.

The Lords Commissioners of Trade and Plantations, or Board of Trade as it was commonly known, was created in 1696 to replace the faltering Lords of Trade as part of the movement to rationalize colonial policy and strengthen its administration. The Board, mercantilist in outlook, supplied information and advice to the crown and its administrative agencies, as well as to Parliament, basing its recommendations on a steady stream of correspondence with the colonies. One of the first issues before the Board was a battle between Randolph, the civil servant who wanted immediate implementation of the act of 1696, and Penn, spokesman for the private colonies who resisted—unsuccessfully, as it turned out—both the creation of vice-admiralty courts to try violations of the Navigation Acts and the requirement of royal approval for appointments to the governor's post. In Pennsylvania's case, particularly, the official challenge to autonomy was continuously fueled by reports from America, telling of illegal trade and piracy along the Delaware. It did little good for Penn to warn Deputy Governor Markham and the Council that "the Accusations of one sort, & the reports of another that are come for England against your Govermt. not only attend to our ruine but our Disgrace." The hostility toward Pennsylvania was prompted by the mercantile success of Philadelphia, good or bad behavior notwithstanding. And the animating spirit in the Quaker colony itself was at cross-purposes with imperial designs.

Thus, when Penn was unable to block implementation of the act of 1696 in England, the Pennsylvania legislature, led by David Lloyd but encouraged by Markham, passed an Act for Preventing Frauds and Regulating Abuses in Trade, the purpose of which was to undermine rather than (as stated) to reinforce the act of 1696. Governor Nicholson of Maryland, commenting on this and other breaches of the home government's intentions, summarized his experience: "I Have observed that a great many people in these Colonies, especially under proprietors and in Connecticut and Rhode Island, think that no law of England ought to bind them without their own consent; for they foolishly say that they have no representative sent from themselves to the Parliament in England, and they look upon all laws made in England, that put any restraint upon them, as great hardships."

Nicholson was describing not the emergence of a New World freedom, antiauthoritarian and egalitarian in nature, but the development of provincial political stability through the establishment of semiautonomous governments. The common feature of these colonial structures was the rising power of the lower house of the legislature, a body controlled, in Pennsylvania as elsewhere, by the economic and social elite. Content to mimic the procedures of Parliament at this time, these men would ultimately consider their respective assemblies the equals of the House of Commons.

Such provincial pretensions were incomprehensible in London. Though David Lloyd might depict the vice-admiralty courts as a greater danger to popular liberty than the collection of "ship monie in King Charles the first's time," the historical analogy was lost on crown officials who believed implicitly in colonial subordination. In the summer of 1699 the Board of Trade, prodded by the Privy Council, prepared a detailed report on Pennsylvania, recommending not only that the Quakers' Act for Preventing Frauds be disallowed (which was promptly attended to), but also that Penn dismiss Deputy Governor Markham and Attorney General Lloyd and call for obedience to the vice-admiralty courts as well as to other provisions of the Navigation Acts.

Thomas Holme's map of Pennsylvania in 1696. *Historical Society of Pennsylvania.*

Realizing that he could best accomplish these demands in the province itself, where he might also silence the outcries against Pennsylvania at their source, the proprietor decided to carry out his long-promised intention of returning.

When Penn arrived in Philadelphia in December 1699, he found a city which had doubled in size since his departure fifteen years earlier. Its five thousand inhabitants, equal in size to New York and only slightly lagging behind Boston's sixty-seven hundred, were more commodiously housed and in better structures than previously. "They Build all with Stone and Brick now, except the very meanest sort of People, who Build Framed Houses with Timber," an observer noted. Wealth was founded on commerce. Penn, of course, had placed his city on the Delaware for its convenience to trade, and although seagoing commerce never supplanted agriculture as the fundamental economic activity in the Quaker colony, its social consequences were striking. The country folk of rural Philadelphia county, as well as Chester and Bucks counties, were mainly subsistence farmers who led simple lives in contrast to the Philadelphians, whose surplus wealth and economic mobility had already led to social distinctions.

Not only did successful Philadelphians possess such material endowments as linens and silver, fine houses and furniture, but they also held human goods: black slaves. As early as 1684 a shipload of a hundred and fifty Negroes was sold in the city, and blacks continued to be imported from the West Indies by Quaker merchants who engaged in the slave trade despite the misgivings of the Society of Friends and the protests of George Keith and some Mennonites in Germantown. Of the small villages surrounding Philadelphia, Germantown was the most notable. Daniel Pastorius, its founder, pointed out that "by virtue of the franchise obtained from William Penn, this town has its own court, its own burgomaster and council, together with the necessary officials, and well-regulated town laws, council regulations, and a town seal." But it had only one-seventh as many taxable citizens as Philadelphia and paid only one-fifteenth the tax, its inhabitants being (in Pastorius' words) "for the most part tradespeople . . . and linen weavers, tailors, shoemakers, locksmiths, carpenters" who were farmers and husbandmen on the side. The Germans, like the Africans, contributed to the heterogeneity of Pennsylvania, but their settlement was no match for Philadelphia.

The Swedes and the Dutch of the Three Lower Counties, virtually none of whom were Quaker, had not become an integral part of the colony's political life as Penn had hoped. Rather, they resented being dominated by the Quakers in the Assembly, and they came off second best in the commercial rivalry with Philadelphia merchants. In 1691 the Lower Counties broke away from Pennsylvania, with William Markham serving as deputy governor. Fletcher ostensibly healed the breach by appointing Markham deputy governor of Pennsylvania as well. But by rescinding all provincial laws in 1693 and not reenacting the Act of Union of 1682, which bound the two regions together, the royal governor provided a legal basis for separation if sectional tensions were not relaxed in the future.

Yet at the time of Penn's arrival it was not the problems arising from the ethnic or racial mixture of the province but the growing number of Anglicans in Philadelphia which was uppermost in the minds of Quakers. In 1695 Christ Church was built in the midst of the City of Brotherly Love, putting that label to the test. The political import of the Anglican presence was plain. Christ Church, in addition to attracting immigrants to Pennsylvania from New York, Maryland, and abroad, was the worship place of royal officials whose secular aims were as different from Quaker objectives as the chapel was from the meetinghouse. The fears of Friends in power were reflected in the frame of 1696, which redefined the franchise in terms of a two-year residency requirement and a change in the property conditions, making it easier for Quaker farmers and harder for urban immigrants to vote. Anglicans hastened to point out to the home government that they were being persecuted in Pennsylvania.

As Penn sailed up the Delaware he approached a scene about which he could be only ambivalent. His colony had undoubtedly prospered, especially in the area of commerce, yet he was arriving with the ostensible intent of imposing restraints on provincial trade according to the Navigation Acts. Pennsylvania

Christ Church, 1727. *From John F. Watson,* Annals of Philadelphia and Pennsylvania *(Philadelphia, 1845)*.

Friends Almshouse, 1729. *From John F. Watson,* Annals of Philadelphia and Pennsylvania *(Philadelphia, 1845)*.

was, as he had intended, a mixture of different people, a richer cultural blend than any other English colony, but variegation had fostered division rather than the harmony of mutual tolerance. The Quaker haven on the Delaware allowed Friends to live beyond the reach of persecution and develop their talents unimpeded. But now an elite group of them, guided by David Lloyd, ran a government which showed scant regard for the proprietor who made their New World existence possible.

But however ambivalent, Penn had made promises to London officialdom which he must keep if he was to retain his colony. His presence was commanding enough to be of aid in this mission. Soon after he landed in Philadelphia a special session of the legislature was called, which produced a bill so clearly censuring illicit commerce that vice-admiralty Judge Robert Quary was moved to commend Penn to the Board of Trade. "He is so far from countenancing what hath been done that he hath publicly shewn his resentment and abhorrence of it all," Quary wrote. "He hath given ample assurance to all the King's Officers of his favour and encouragement to them in all matters relating to the King's service." Yet Penn's insistence on rooting out piracy and illegal trade quickly depleted his personal political capital, even before he could implement a proprietary policy calculated to bring financial return.

In 1699 Penn was deeply in debt. His steward, Philip Ford, had systematically defrauded him and was now claiming that Penn owed £11,000 or must forfeit the province (Penn had unwisely given the charter to Ford in 1697). The crown was dunning him for £6,000 in rents and profits from the Three Lower Counties, the result of an agreement Penn had made with Charles II. Having invested more than the total of these sums in Pennsylvania, the proprietor felt he could fairly recover his losses simply by closing accounts on land sales and back quitrents. But when he established a special agency to carry forward this plan, he met a cry of outrage and almost total unwillingness to cooperate.

Finally Penn sent his secretary on an inspection tour of land titles and claims, empowering him to resurvey, sell, and assess land, examine titles, and determine and collect rents. It was not a way to pacify the restive populace, and Penn's secretary, even under more favorable circumstances, was not the man to undertake the job. James Logan, barely twenty-five years old, was the son of a Scotch Quaker schoolmaster who eked out a living teaching the children of impoverished, persecuted Friends in northern Ireland. Young James' boyhood was one of insecurity and fear, alienated as he was from the society about him, and he found in books the solace denied him in the real world. He had a mighty desire to rise out of his lowly station, which drew him from teaching into trade. Penn recognized Logan's intellectual abilities, and perhaps he also saw that Logan's respect for status was of the sort to make him a good servant to a great man. Indeed, Logan seemed to be an extremely competent and faithful administrator of proprietary affairs. In addition to being proprietary secretary, after Penn's departure in 1701 he served as provincial secretary, clerk of the Council, a commissioner of property, and receiver general. Yet he had as little appeal as the policy he was attempting to enforce. He was a cold and formal person, disdainful of provincial society and, particularly, of the political pretensions of its inhabitants. He wrote in 1704: "This people think privileges their due and all that can be grasped to be their native right . . . Charters here have been, or I doubt will be, of fatal consequence; some people's brains are as soon intoxicated with power as the natives are with their beloved liquor, and as little to be trusted with it."

This, the viewpoint of an aspiring aristocrat, was not acceptable to a rising bourgeoisie. Many Pennsylvanians could identify with David Lloyd; even Logan's political allies had difficulty tolerating him. Penn could easily discharge William Markham, his own kinsman and an Anglican. But Lloyd's dismissal was an affront to colonists who saw in his behavior the personal expression of political autonomy. Penn, whose vantage point on colonial affairs was English, fired Lloyd for that very reason. Yet he was not long in Pennsylvania before his perspective began to change, especially as he questioned the honesty and competence of royal officials who mixed public duty with private business, much to their own advantage. Nor were Anglicans in Philadelphia cooperative with the provincial government, reacting especially against the Quaker practice of abjuring oaths for a simple affirmation and informing the London authorities of their discontent. When a bill for uniting the charter and proprietary colonies to the crown emerged in Parliament in 1701, Penn knew where the blame lay. And he was so worried by the development that he decided to return to England, assuring James Logan that "no man living can defend us or bargain for us better than myself."

This sudden decision made the solution to major problems imperative. Whether the proprietor would come back to Philadelphia for further negotiations was questionable, and if he were to be unsuccessful in England, the question of institutional protection of autonomy was crucial. David Lloyd had already tried to convince Penn of a constitutional settlement involving not only an acknowledgment of the Assembly's increased power but also a political separation from the Three Lower Counties. The popular leader, who had frightened away a number of his wealthier supporters through his unrestrained (and, it was said, disloyal) attacks on the vice-admiralty courts, now drew support from the city artisans and shopkeepers who had followed George Keith a decade earlier. They signed a petition concerned with the critical matters of land and government, which Lloyd presented to the Assembly that convened in mid-September 1701.

With regard to real estate, it was requested that Penn grant "Such an Instrument as may Absolutly secure & Defend us in our Estates & Propertyes from himself his heirs & assignes forever," as well as demands for reform in the method of granting land, for the handling of property disputes by the provincial courts rather than the Board of Propriety, and for the abolition of quitrents in Philadelphia. Although a law confirming the property rights of the colonists had been passed a year earlier, Penn had already shown a disposition to interpret its ambiguous terms in his own favor. Furthermore, his attempts to collect money due on back rents and sales, resurvey and assess land, and examine titles had inclined the colonists to suspect his intent. This feeling was confirmed by Penn's response to the petition. While he promised the "Instrument" requested, he agreed in substance only to minor administrative changes in land policy and not to the major points concerning adjudication and quitrents. Since most members of the Assembly, including many not attached to Lloyd, were dissatisfied with Penn's land policy, his response was unacceptable.

The petition laid before the lower house in September also called for a new frame of government. Penn was no happier with this prospect than he had been with the request for a reformed land policy, but some change seemed inevitable. He sent to the Assembly the "Heads of a Frame of Government," a compromise measure from his point of view, only to encounter the obstinacy of Assembly members offended by his response to the property provisions of the petition. The lower house had a plan of its own, the genesis of which Penn later explained to Logan: "The Charter was never altered by me, but by the suggestions of . . . David Lloyd, to my regrets, as my letters before and my conduct after plainly showed." The proprietor was forced to concede to a scheme of government which differed little from the one Deputy Governor Markham was obliged to accept in 1696, later denounced by Penn. The Frame of 1701, usually known as the Charter of Privileges, represented a rejection of the Quaker leader's thinking on the nature of political institutions. The devices found in the Frames of 1682 and 1683—a bicameral legislature with a powerful upper house, the ballot, indirect election, rotation—were omitted from the new instrument of government. Thus, the Pennsylvania Assembly became the only such unicameral body in the British Empire, with the right to initiate legislation, elect officers and appoint committees, and decide who could sit and the length of the session. The Council would be appointed by the proprietor but have no role in the legislative process. Although Penn had earlier tried to preserve the power of his Board of Propriety, he now consented to having all matters of property handled in provincial courts. Although he did not approve of the new Frame, he noted later that "it was carried by so great a majority that I see no blame." He also justified his concessions on the grounds that the colonists deserved greater autonomy in case he lost his government to the crown. The Frame of Government of 1701 lasted until 1776.

To this Charter of Privileges Penn attached a clause providing for the political separation of the Three Lower Counties from the province of Pennsylvania. He did so with great reluctance but, again, because there was no apparent alternative. The Act of Union of 1682 was considered no longer legally binding by leaders from the Lower Counties who, feeling the disadvantage of their situation, proposed in 1700 to reconfirm the act only on the promise of parity of representation in the Assembly. This was rejected by politicians from the province, despite Penn's attempts at compromise. In the 1701 session the men from Philadelphia, Chester, and Bucks counties so offended their southern neighbors that the representatives from the Lower Counties left the Assembly in anger. By confirming this rupture Penn eased the burden of the Quaker politicians but weakened his own hold on the region along the lower Delaware.

As he was signing the Charter of Privileges, on October 28, 1701, only three days before setting sail for England, Penn also approved passage of a Judiciary Act which, more certainly than the frame of 1701, was the handiwork of David Lloyd. The popular leader's great contribution to the judicial history of the province was to define for the first time original and appellate jurisdictions and to describe fully the functions of each court in the system. Considering the complicated background of the judiciary in Pennsylvania, this was a major achievement.

The first courts of justice along the Delaware had been established by the Swedes in 1643, but they were of less influence on future development than the Dutch courts which began functioning in 1655. When the English took charge of the region in 1664, both Swedish and Dutch magistrates were allowed to remain, and they did so long after Penn's arrival. The establishment of English jurisprudence was a gradual process, as compromises with already settled customs and practices were worked out, magistrates educated in English court practice, and the common law modified to suit conditions. The colonial tendency toward codification of the law—the creation of a perfect society by statutory fiat—was carried out through a code known as the Duke of York's Laws, which drew heavily on the example of New

England. Courts were organized similar to Dutch practice, with borrowings from older English colonies. The general court of assizes, meeting annually and attended by governor (presiding), Council, city officials, and justices of various courts of sessions, was the principal judicial institution. Courts of sessions, held three times a year, were established in districts corresponding to counties. There were town courts as well, in deference to the desires of New England settlers.

Thus, Penn did not discover a legal wilderness in the New World. He did, moreover, arrive equipped with certain ideas about the law, based on his short training at Lincoln's Inn and his experience as a defendant in English courts. Like his contemporaries, he viewed the judiciary as a subordinate branch of government. As a Quaker, hounded into court and harassed by legal technicalities, he believed in simplicity and individual rights. In the "Laws Agreed Upon in England" it was stated: "That in all courts all persons of all persuasions may freely appear in their own way, and according to their own manner, and there personally plead their own cause themselves, or if unable, by their friends. . . . That all pleadings, processes, and records in courts, shall be short, and in English, and in an ordinary and plain character, that they may be understood, and justice speedily administered." These provisions, approved by the Pennsylvania legislature, were supplemented by others in the same vein.

Adaptation rather than simplification was the principle governing the erection of courts. Pennsylvania was divided into three counties immediately after Penn's arrival in 1682, and courts were set up in each of these as well as in the Three Lower Counties. Following the procedure of the earlier courts of sessions, these county courts were presided over by justices of the peace and their purview corresponded to that fixed by the Duke of York's Laws: actions involving small sums of money, preservation of the peace, trial of petty offenders, and grant of licenses and letters of administration. They handled criminal cases except for treason, murder, and manslaughter and, after 1693, burglary, rape, and arson. Jurisdiction, however, was more vague than these terms would suggest, and attempts at a more careful definition suffered the effects of political turbulence in the 1680s and 1690s.

These effects were even more evident in the Provincial Court, created in 1684 to hear appeals from the county courts, formerly a function of the Provincial Council and, before 1682, of the court of assizes. Five judges, any three of whom composed the Provincial Court sitting twice a year in Philadelphia and two of whom rode circuit twice a year in every county, were appointed but assigned irregular terms and were inadequately paid. It was, however, political dissension which hurt the court from the start as Nicholas More, the first chief justice, was impeached by the Assembly within a year of his appointment. Meanwhile, the Provincial Council continued to exercise judicial functions. And, as specified in Penn's charter, the court of last resort was not even in the province; ultimately, appeals could go to the crown.

In 1698 Gabriel Thomas, a Welshman who had lived for fifteen years in Pennsylvania, wrote in a description of the province: "Of *Lawyers* and *Physicians* I shall say nothing, because this Countrey is very Peaceable and Healthy; long may it so continue and never have occasion for the Tongue of the one, nor the Pen of the other, both equally destructive of Mens Estates and Lives." Dedicated to William Penn, Thomas' tract duplicated the enthusiasm and the information of the proprietor's promotional literature, and its naiveté as well.

Another Welshman, David Lloyd, held a different view of the judicial situation. From the perspective of his own thorough legal training he saw the need for a detailed definition of the jurisdictions and functions of Pennsylvania's courts. As a provincial politician he spied an opportunity to weaken the hold of the proprietor and the crown on the judiciary. The result was the Judiciary Act of 1701, which enlarged the scope and power of the county courts, notably in equity cases but also in maritime actions, the latter being another attempt to undermine the vice-admiralty courts. By extending the original jurisdiction of the county courts, judicial authority was decentralized and, thus, made less amenable to proprietary or crown control. Appellate jurisdiction within Pennsylvania was granted to the provincial court alone, thereby eliminating the Council from the judiciary altogether. The Provincial Court retained its earlier-defined powers of original jurisdiction. By carefully describing the duties, procedures, and meeting times of the courts as well as other details in a legislative act, the Assembly gained greater control over the judiciary.

The politicians in Pennsylvania enhanced their power not only through provincial changes—the new frame of government, the separation of the Three Lower Counties, and the reorganization of the judiciary—but by way of municipal alterations as well. The Stuart attack on city charters in England had fostered the belief that a strong municipal corporation was a bastion against executive encroachment. As early as 1684 a "Humble Remonstrance" presented to the proprietor by inhabitants of Philadelphia complained that "they were only a nomenall citie haveing no Charter to incorporate them." But Penn disclaimed responsibility for establishing a city government, though he was less indifferent than opposed to granting a charter which might loosen his control over land policy in Philadelphia. In 1691, however, when the proprietor was incapacitated in England, a charter of incorporation was issued by Deputy Governor Thomas Lloyd, who placed his supporters in key municipal offices. That this government ever functioned is uncertain.

But the desire for an operative municipal polity remained as vital as the issues which fostered it. Grievances over land grants and quitrents in Philadelphia, cited in the petition presented by David Lloyd to Penn in 1701, were an important source of conflict. And no agreement on a provincial property law had yet been reached. In addition, the changing composition of the city's population, increasingly non-Quaker, stood as a threat to the reigning politicians. Finally, questions concerning the regulation of commerce had arisen. The charter for Philadelphia of 1701 was a response to this situation. Following the English model of a corporation, in which mayor, recorder, sheriff, clerk, aldermen, and councilors were the officials of a closed, self-perpetuating organization (that is, vacancies would be filled by choices of the corporation members), the new municipal government would have the powers to regulate markets and trade, to make laws and ordinances, and to act in a judicial capacity. Mayor, recorder, and aldermen served as justices of the peace, and the city court handled all civil and criminal actions. Franchise qualifications—a two-year residency and an estate of £50—would bar the newer (and poorer) non-Quaker city dwellers from voting.

In a corporation of this type, in which the mayor was chosen from the aldermen and the aldermen from the councilors, the initial appointment of officials would be crucial. Although Penn named the four principal officers from among his supporters, fourteen of the twenty aldermen and councilors chosen had signed Lloyd's petition of protest. Perhaps the proprietor viewed this as a necessary compromise, but it is also possible that he doubted the viability of municipal government. For in the Charter of Privileges the Assembly had been granted the power to regulate cities, and Penn knew from hard experience that the legislature would not be thwarted in its exercise of power.

The final and most far reaching concession that David Lloyd and his partisans tried to wring from the departing proprietor was a Charter of Property. Just as Penn was to set sail for England he received Lloyd's draft of this document and, without time to read it carefully, gave it only tentative approval. On closer inspection he realized that Lloyd proposed to transfer ultimate authority over the land from him to the Pennsylvanians, largely by means of a general court. This body, comprised of eight men appointed by the proprietor and thirteen elected by the colonists, would settle estates, probate wills, and handle all legal suits relating to the land. Additionally, it would create courts of record, equity, and others "necessary for the administration of justice," a broad power indeed, transcending the scope of property affairs. Finally, the general court was to play a key part in the political organization of western lands in the province, a duty not unrelated to the real estate speculation Lloyd carried on through the Susquehanna Land Company.

In the end, Penn refused to consent to the Charter of Property. He felt he had already conceded too much, as his bitter message to James Logan in January 1701/2 made clear: "God forgive those wretched people who have misused me so." Penn did not fully understand the changes that were taking place in his province. In attempting to reconcile the views of London officialdom and colonial politicians, he vigorously defended the rights of the Pennsylvanians, while cautioning them to proceed more quietly, before the Board of Trade and Parliament. But his defense rested not on the concessions that must be granted a maturing society; instead, he constantly made reference to the terms of his charter from the crown. He was unable to mute his role as proprietor, even though the colonists were becoming less willing to concede him the traditional privileges of his position. Opposition in the 1690s found its voice in the Assembly, a body which generally spoke for the emerging economic and social elite of the colony. Penn was hardly friendless in this political situation, being able to draw numbers of prosperous merchants and landowners to his interest. But even their support could not always be counted on when provincial autonomy was pitted against proprietary privilege, as the numerous concessions forced on Penn in 1701 amply demonstrated.

4

EARLY GROWTH: POLITICAL, SOCIAL, AND ECONOMIC STRUCTURE IN THE EARLY EIGHTEENTH CENTURY

If Penn had constantly to superintend his political fortunes in Pennsylvania, the same watchfulness was no less true in England. The Board of Trade, which in the years following its founding in 1696 had shown no special antipathy toward private colonies, even agreeing that Penn should police his own province in 1699, became notably hostile at the turn of the century as a result of changes in its personnel, inflammatory correspondence from the colonies, and intractability on the part of the proprietors. Furthermore, the Bishop of London and other influential Anglicans were agitating against independent charters, especially Penn's, bewailing conditions in those colonies, as one of them observed, "abandoned to Atheism; or, which is much at one, to Quakerism, for want of a settled clergy among them." The belief that violation of the trade acts and even disloyalty to the crown were common in the chartered colonies gained currency, as did the solution—proposed by Edward Randolph and Robert Quary from America and advocated by William Blathwayt on the Board—that these colonies must be brought under the king's control. Pennsylvania bore the brunt of the Board's attacks because of Penn's prominence, Robert Quary's tenacity, and the central position of the province with regard to matters of primary importance: trade, warfare, and religion. A bill to reunite the private colonies to the crown, introduced into the House of Lords in 1701, was successfully combated by London Quakers. But

Penn was enough alarmed by the Board's efforts to return to England.

Just as he arrived the proprietors of East and West New Jersey were surrendering their rights of government to the crown, an act which Penn characterized as "an ugly preface." Anticipating the Board's intention of again pressing for legislative action, he submitted a bill of his own, which would have given the king control of military, admiralty, and customs matters in the private colonies, as well as the right of veto over all laws, while leaving the civil governments in the hands of the proprietors or corporations. The Board naturally objected to this scheme, which avoided the central problem of enforcement of royal orders and only proposed what was already the official, if not the actual, situation in Pennsylvania. The Board's own bill did not reach Parliament, however, as the death of William III brought the session to an untimely close in March 1701/2. Penn still had to fear the damage which might be done by Robert Quary, judge of the vice-admiralty court in Pennsylvania, who arrived in London that spring armed with evidence of the wrongdoings of the Quaker colonists. But by rebuilding his connections with men of power and influence, Penn was able to put Quary and his Board sympathizers on the defensive and even, though only temporarily, have Quary discharged from his judicial position. When Quary later returned to the province he wrote that it was "the General discourse of the Quakers that the Lords of Trade and Plantations are Mr. Penn's Enemies, but that he values them not, having a greater interest than all of them, and shall be able to Carry on all his designs in spite of them."

But for Penn the personal sacrifice demanded by his political activity was becoming an unbearable burden. "Never had a poor man my task," he lamented to James Logan in June 1702, "with neither men nor money to assist me . . . besides, my uncomfortable distance from my family, and the unspeakable fatigue and vexation of following attendance, draughts of answer, conferences, council's opinions, hearings, &c. with the charge that follows them." Now almost sixty, age was taking its toll on Penn. Financial pressures were nothing new to him, but the son of his steward, Philip Ford, Jr., was still holding him to account for the

William Penn at age fifty-two,
a portrait by Francis Place.
Historical Society of Pennsylvania.

Hannah Penn, a portrait by
Francis Place. *Historical Society
of Pennsylvania.*

sum of £11,000. His own son by his first marriage, William, Jr., was proving to be an emotional as well as an economic burden. The measure of the proprietor's waning spirit was his disclosure to Logan that he was considering "bargaining with the crown for my government."

Indeed, Penn had often spoken of the unbreakable link between power and property, arguing that the latter was of little worth without the former. Now the selling of the polity of Pennsylvania became plausible because Penn was finding it increasingly difficult to summon the energy and resources necessary to defend his proprietary privilege, and not only from the home government, since his prerogatives in Pennsylvania had been severely curtailed by the Frame of 1701. Perhaps he had even discussed selling the province before departing for England, since he had hardly posted his letter when he received from Logan a message approving this new course of action. The belief was widespread, the provincial secretary noted, that war would oblige Parliament to annex the private colonies to the crown. "Nor can I find any, even of our friends, desirous that it should be otherwise, provided thou canst make good terms for thyself and them; for they seem both weary and careless of government."

With his conscience eased respecting the Pennsylvania Quakers, with the Board continuing to press for legislative action and thus putting constant demands on his vigilance, Penn might have been expected to dispose of his government quickly. Yet he was understandably reluctant to part with an experiment which had demanded his most creative energies and, despite the many alterations, embodied his deepest beliefs. But, with his typical ideological inconsistency, Penn wanted to be compensated for relinquishing his government to the crown with "some honorary mark, as a founder of the colony, viz., as the first-hereditary-Privy Councillor or Chief Justice or the like." Since his friends in England and America urged him to bargain for the best terms, this became the rationale for drawing out the negotiations, which were not even begun until June 1703. At that time he laid a proposal before the Board of Trade stating the conditions of sale. Some of these were reasonable, for example, that he retain all rights to the land as distinct from the government. The price, £30,000, was negotiable; Penn claimed it represented his investment in the colony, but he did not mention his involvement with the Fords. He wanted a patent for the Three Lower Counties, which would have been tantamount to underwriting his quitrents from that region. Two of the conditions were such that Penn could hardly have expected them to be accepted: that the "Laws and Constitutions thereof be confirmed by the Queen, except such few as I shall object against," and that he be allowed to nominate several persons from whom the crown would choose the governor. The Board balked at both of these clauses, and negotiations broke off, only to be periodically renewed by Penn during the ensuing decade.

The Board's sustained efforts, through 1706, to obtain a reunification bill and Penn's repeated attempts to sell his government were related to two issues which frequently generated friction between the home government and the Quaker province: military defense and the public administration of oaths. The growing Anglican community in Philadelphia, often in cooperation with churchmen in England, was not above using such issues to exacerbate antagonisms. Thus, after war was declared on France in 1702 and the proprietor was ordered to put the province in a state of defense, which the Assembly refused to do, the deputy governor attempted to raise a militia without legislative aid. The greater opposition to this activity came not from Quakers but from Anglicans, whose obvious purpose was to discredit the Pennsylvania government. In 1703 Penn appointed John Evans deputy governor, instructing him to placate the Anglicans and ensure that "nothing may lie at my door in reference to the Defense of the Country." But from 1704 until he left the colony in 1709, Evans was in constant conflict with the Assembly over military appropriations while the Anglicans continued to obstruct efforts to raise a militia. Finally Evans, an impulsive and unstable man, spread a false alarm that a French fleet was sailing up the Delaware, throwing the province into a panic and highlighting its defenseless condition.

Pacifism was an issue only in time of war, but the matter of taking oaths could be raised whenever the Quakers' adversaries chose to do so. The literal acceptance of Christ's injunction, "Swear not at all," underlay Friends' insistence on giving a simple affirmation rather than invoking the Almighty through an oath, though swearing was considered necessary to office holding and court testimony by most Englishmen. Consequently, Quakers in England were denied civil and political rights and subjected to fines and other penalties for the practice of their belief. During the settlement years in Pennsylvania, however, they could embody their principles in statutes without fear of local reaction. According to the Great Law passed in Chester in 1682, employees of the government were not required to give an oath of office but simply to profess a belief in Christ and fidelity to the proprietor (a year later allegiance to the crown was added), while witnesses in court were to promise "to speak the truth, the whole truth, and nothing but the truth."

No complications arose until the 1690s. When Benjamin Fletcher became royal governor in 1693, he was faced with a conflict between Quaker principle and a parliamentary act of 1689 requiring an oath of fidelity and allegiance to the king. He allowed the affirmation to be taken, and the Frame of Government of 1696 followed his example, recognizing the act of 1689 but permitting an affirmation in lieu of an oath, except where swearing was specified in acts of trade and navigation. Since the Navigation Act of 1696 required oaths from merchants and shipowners, however, some Friends were again trapped between conscience and the law. When David Lloyd informed Edward Randolph that this provision of the act "was never intended to be observed in Pensilvania," the surveyor general immediately warned the Board of Trade that the Quakers were asserting their independence of the crown, thus obliging the Pennsylvania Assembly to make a specific declaration of loyalty to William III.

But the lower house was seldom this conciliatory, and as the number of non-Quakers in the province increased, the issue of oaths became a greater source of friction. In 1700 the Assembly reconfirmed the use of the affirmation as specified in the Great Law of 1682. Although it was not the intent of the new law to force Quaker practice on those outside the fold, the result, given the number of official positions held by Friends who could no more administer than take an oath, was often just that. Anglicans, who doubted the binding nature of an affirmation, also protested against its use in criminal cases and for juries. The Board of Trade took up their cause, asking the crown to require that all persons who "are obliged and are willing to take an oath in any public office or judicial proceeding, be admitted to do so by the proper offices and judges." When an Order in Council was issued in response to this request, Penn intervened, arguing that Quakers would thereby be blocked from many government positions and, furthermore, that the order violated his royal charter, which allowed such action only to the provincial legislature or Parliament.

But the order was sustained, and Robert Quary was determined to enforce it. It was questionable whether the courts, as they were then staffed, could function under these conditions. Penn hoped to ameliorate the situation by unseating Quary from his post on the vice-admiralty court, but this proved to be a temporary expedient at best. Deputy Governor John Evans made a special effort to placate the Anglicans, even, apparently, appointing them to high judicial office. But he came into conflict with the Assembly, which was determined to resolve the issue through legislation allowing the affirmation rather than the oath in all cases, regardless of the Order in Council or royal disallowance of the Act of 1700. Ironically, the attorney general in England, whose opinion was solicited by the Board, took the side of Penn and the Assembly: "The greatest part of the inhabitants are Quakers, the Proprietor being also a Quaker, and Quakers by the laws there may have judicial places, I do not see but the Law [in this case, the Act of 1706 which was a copy of the repealed Act of 1700], which is made with the Spirit of the Quakers, may be allow'd them." Despite this opinion, the Board drew upon the strong objections of the Bishop of London and Pennsylvania Anglicans to attack the law, which was finally disallowed.

The issue, seemingly insoluble, continued to be a source of contention in provincial and imperial politics as Isaac Norris, a young Quaker merchant and politician sympathetic to proprietary interests, informed Penn in 1710: "We say our principles are not destructive or repugnant to Civil Government, and will admit of free liberty of conscience to all; yet to me it appears, according to the best scheme I can form, from the opinions of many Friends, to be concerned in Government and hold them, we must either be independent and entirely by ourselves; or, if mixed, partial to our own opinion, and not allow the liberty to others, who make conscience, they say, to have an oath, we desire from them; or be, as thou used to express it, 'Dissenters in our own country.' "

Norris neglected to mention, however, that there was no perfect harmony among Quakers themselves. Although Anglicans took every opportunity to disrupt the government and foster antagonisms where they existed, tactics which had strong support from politicians in the Three Lower Counties who had long resented the Quakers and opposed proprietary land policy, the main source of political turbulence in the decade after Penn's departure in 1701 was not opportunism or resentment manifested by non-Quakers. Rather, it was David Lloyd's campaign for greater provincial autonomy. The popular leader carried on a constant battle against proprietary authority, hotly arguing that government in Pennsylvania must reflect the desires of the people, whether through the Assembly or the corporation of Philadelphia. The general expectation that the crown would soon annul Penn's charter also inspired support for Lloyd's cause, as did the economic slump in the first years of the eighteenth century, which produced widespread discontent and, as Penn pressed Logan to exact back rents and taxes, dissatisfaction with the proprietor.

The situation was uncomfortable but ironic. The war which spotlighted Quaker pacifism, thus making more difficult the defense of the colony against royal intervention, also led to the decay of the West Indian trade, leaving merchants and farmers without funds to pay proprietary fees which Penn needed to combat hostile officialdom in London, not to mention the Ford family. While Pennsylvanians listened to rumors that the proprietor had carried large amounts of specie back to England in 1701, Penn attempted to sell the province he could not afford to protect. Logan, whose position in the colony as proprietary representative might have encouraged him to mediate between the Quaker settlers and Penn, alienated himself from the former by his officious manner.

Logan had, at least, the virtues of strong character and intellect, which was more than could be said for John Evans, who served as deputy governor of the province during the greater part of the decade after Penn's departure. The executive office had been filled briefly by Andrew Hamilton, formerly governor of both East New Jersey and West New Jersey, and by the Provincial Council until the twenty-six-year-old Evans arrived in Philadelphia in February 1703/4. Appointed because of his father's friendship with the proprietor and accompanied on his voyage to Pennsylvania by the ne'er-do-well William Penn, Jr., Evans had the proper connections but no executive experience. It is doubtful that Penn could have employed a governor whose political talents matched David Lloyd's, but by sending the untested and impulsive Evans into the fray the proprietor was virtually conceding defeat. Penn's emphasis on the youthful deputy's strong church background (his uncle was Bishop of Bangor) was calculated to appease Anglicans in the province and on the Board of Trade but hardly recommended him to Quakers, even those normally sympathetic to the proprietary cause. Indeed, there was no well-organized proprietary party upon whom Evans could depend for support, nor did the deputy governor's office afford him a shield behind which he could take cover.

Politics in Pennsylvania were unstructured, although in the early 1690s it had appeared as though a framework was forming. John Blackwell, like Evans a stranger to Pennsylvania, had roused an opposition which crystallized around Thomas Lloyd and represented an emerging economic elite. The Keithian controversy had fostered the division between an upper crust and lower, discontent levels in society. While the latter were politically inarticulate, the demands of the parvenu merchants and landowners were voiced through the Assembly.

David Lloyd replaced his distant cousin as the spokesman for this group, but by the turn of the century his intemperate statements and aggressive behavior had scared off the plutocrats aspiring to gentility, who were now attracted to Penn's interest, unappealing as they found James Logan. Lloyd had to attract new support, which was found among artisans and shopkeepers in the city and less wealthy farmers in the surrounding country-side. He was also ready to lure Anglicans into his camp when expediency so dictated and circumstances allowed. Thus, in 1702 he accepted an appointment to the vice-admiralty court which he had attacked only a few years earlier.

By reversing his field in this manner Lloyd showed that his hostility toward the crown was not undying; other actions demonstrated that his rancor was redirected against the proprie-tor and his friends, especially against James Logan. More fundamentally, however, Lloyd's changing loyalties revealed a man who, for all his solid skills as a lawyer and politician, was vindictive and volatile. He apparently never forgave Penn for removing him from office in 1699, his pride was pricked, and his attacks on proprietary privilege often were as intemperate as his assaults on royal control.

That he was a self-styled enemy of authority was largely responsible for Lloyd's popularity among Quakers whose memo-ries of persecution in England and hard-fought battles against the wilderness in America inclined them to resent any outside interference. Lloyd's antiauthoritarian arrows did not want for likely targets: Penn, who recognized the pitfalls of this individu-alistic self-importance and remarked on it perhaps too often for comfort; Logan, who haughtily contrasted his cultural prefer-ences to the homespun attainments of the Pennsylvanians; prosperous merchants and landowners who, in a land where the range of wealth was narrow and most settlers had only the essentials of existence, thought their economic success entitled them to political eminence. Lloyd's personality coincided with and fostered a political situation which had existed in Pennsylva-nia since its founding; now he accentuated antagonisms in the name of popular rights.

While Lloyd's tactics nurtured divisiveness in an already atomistic society, he was simultaneously responsible, by the very act of institutionalizing the rights he so loudly proclaimed, for building structure into provincial life. This was evident as early as 1696, when in the Frame of Government he gave official form to the *de facto* prerogatives of the Assembly, and became even more pronounced in 1701 through the incorporation of Philadelphia and the reorganization of the judiciary. The Charter of Privileges was more a change than an introduction of structure, though by recognizing the speaker as embodying the authority of the Assembly, Lloyd was given the power of even greater accomplishment, since he served in that capacity almost continuously from 1703 to 1710, as well as in the sessions convening in 1714, 1723, and 1725. Furthermore, it was in 1701 that provincial laws began to be printed, while in 1703 the procedure for qualifying members of the Assembly was formalized and the rules of that body, which remained in force with some amendments until 1776, were adopted.

Thus, Lloyd presided over a legislature whose methods of operation were fairly well established, no small tribute to his efforts. Unlike the first assemblies, which met for only nine days annually to discuss bills issued by the governor and Council, the lower house, in conjunction with the chief executive, now was the sole lawmaking body, determining the length of its own sessions. It convened in a private house or city hall on October 14, at that time electing a speaker, qualifying its members (eight delegates from each of the three counties and two delegates from Philadelphia), choosing its officers and standing committees, ordering the preparation of reports, and listening to the governor's recommendations. After a few days the Assembly adjourned to late December or early January, sitting then a month or two and recessing again until early May, when a meeting of three to four weeks could be expected. (In fact, there was a considerable variation in the number of sittings, the crucial concern of most members being to return to their farms.) At these sessions the bills originating by petition, by the governor's recommendation, or, most often, by the motion of a member or the resolution of a committee were considered, being subject to three readings (and, frequently, amendment) before going out for the governor's approval. The last sitting of the Assembly after harvest in late August or early September was spent terminating the year's business (ordinarily no new business was introduced at this time) and settling provincial accounts.

No man during the colonial period in Pennsylvania had a more profound influence on provincial legislation than David Lloyd. From the early 1690s he played an important part in framing almost all of the colony's laws, exercising a skill which even James Logan acknowledged. The frequent dependence on English legislation as a model for the Assembly's bills lent a special significance to his early legal training. His intimate knowledge and understanding not only of law but of legislative procedure, supplemented by personal characteristics used to best political advantage and his powerful position as speaker, left no doubt as to the primacy of his influence. And as chief justice from 1719 until his death in 1731, he was able to interpret the very laws he helped frame. Always he moved in the direction of undermining proprietary power.

In the legislative session of 1703–4 Lloyd's strategy was clearly revealed. The strengthening of the speaker's powers, one innovation among several introduced into the rules of parliamentary procedure at that sitting, was quickly put to use as Lloyd convened the Assembly into a committee of the whole in order to mount a successful attack on the proprietor's veto power as it was described in the commission of the recently arrived deputy governor, John Evans. Furthermore, Lloyd was able to quash Penn's efforts, embedded in Evans' instructions, to effect a legislative reunion between the province and the Three Lower Counties, even though Logan and the Council fully supported a reconciliation for commercial as well as political reasons. At that time the speaker asserted that the Pennsylvania members of the Assembly "were a House of themselves, & it might they feared infringe their Priviledges to admit any other."

Gaining momentum, Lloyd introduced bills "for Confirmation of the Charter of Privileges" and "for Comfirmation of the Charter of the City of Philadelphia," both of which were more ambitious than their titles indicated. The former would have allowed the Assembly to determine its own adjournment or dissolution, heretofore a proprietary privilege used to check the lower house. The latter aimed to enhance the power of municipal government, especially the courts, at the expense of the county of Philadelphia, thus removing the city from proprietary power; it passed the Assembly with an additional clause providing for the universal use of the affirmation, despite the royal order that all government officers must take an oath. And since Penn had also refused Lloyd's proposal in 1701 for a Charter of Property, the speaker put these ideas into legislative form again. Deputy Governor Evans blocked all these bills, but Lloyd held Penn responsible for their failure. With the aid of a few cronies he drew up a Remonstrance, supposedly the work of an Assembly committee, which lashed out against Penn as a "Tyrant" who had violated every frame of government since 1682 and appointed placemen who obstructed the smooth flow of government, not to mention Penn's failure in getting royal confirmation of provincial laws. Still, recognizing the implications of crown control, Lloyd and his partisans asked the proprietor not to surrender his government.

Though Lloyd's legislative program was not successful, he did manage to focus attention on conflict between the proprietary interests and his own and to portray the latter as identical with the public concern. In eliciting popular sympathy he was aided by Deputy Governor Evans, whose behavior was often offensive to Quakers. Evans' habit of carousing through Philadelphia with William Penn, Jr., invited disapproval and, finally, in the summer of 1704, brought arrest. Less than two years later, when tempers were hot as a result of the Remonstrance and the Council's consequent attempt to examine the Assembly's journal, one of Lloyd's lieutenants was heard to say, by Logan's account, that Evans "is but a boy; he is not fit to be our Governour. We'll kick him out." The deputy governor filed suit and won £300 in injuries, which the defendant could not pay without selling half his farm. Instead of generously excusing the man and thereby currying public favor, Evans pressed for payment and even had his adversary imprisoned for a month. His false warning of an impending French attack, also in the spring of 1706, only compounded his unpopularity.

From this weak position Evans submitted a bill to the

Assembly for reorganizing the courts, the main feature of which was the transfer of equity jurisdiction from the counties to a special body which he would appoint. Royal disallowance of Lloyd's Judiciary Act of 1701 had brought court actions to a sudden and inconvenient halt throughout the province, and some action was clearly necessary. But it was a token of Evans' lack of touch with reality that he thought a bill underwriting increased proprietary power could command support in the Assembly or even in the province in 1706. The legislature countered with an act retaining features of the 1701 law but also allowing itself the privilege of removing unfit judges from the bench. Evans' announced intention—to establish courts by executive decree—was finally carried out in February 1706/7, after heated charges were made by both sides, joint conferences between the Council and Assembly failed, and James Logan was threatened with impeachment.

Evans was no match for the antiproprietary forces, but Logan was a rock of resistance. In the Assembly sessions of 1706–7 and 1707–8 Lloyd's pursuit of Logan became almost an obsession, with little other business conducted. The charges leveled against Logan, among them violation of the Charter of Privileges and maladministration of land policy, and his detailed responses were more symptomatic than substantial. Lloyd's failure to achieve his antiproprietary legislative program was, clearly enough, a motive for his attack on Penn's provincial secretary and stalwart supporter, but the feud was personal also. Both Logan and Lloyd were self-made men who had risen to power, proud to the point of arrogance and, when offended, prone to intemperate reaction. The strength of their personalities made them obvious rivals in the battle of Pennsylvania politics, as did their ideologies. Although they apparently represented opposite points of view— Logan the aristocratic defender of an anachronistic scheme of government, Lloyd the zealous crusader for an indigenous democracy—in fact the intensity of their conflict derived in part from their common political heritage. Both believed in Penn's whig philosophy, though emphasizing different aspects of it, and they viewed one another as apostates.

The biases of the two men were logical enough. Logan's

attention to balance in the political system was attuned to the proprietary interest, just as Lloyd's drive for legislative supremacy reflected the aspirations of his constituents. That Lloyd deviated farther from pristine whiggery was owing to the practical dynamics of the situation. The popular leader broadened his appeal to include previously apolitical members of the community, facilitating their exercise of the franchise by advertising forthcoming elections and substituting oral voting for the secret ballot in cases of illiteracy. He thereby brought into the arena a segment of the population unanticipated by liberal theoreticians, who linked liberty to property and voting to reason in a way that consigned landless artisans and untutored farmers to second-class citizenship. Lloyd's constituency also included many of Pennsylvania's malcontents: Anglicans, former followers of George Keith (who had returned to the province as an Episcopalian and, in the winters of 1702–3 and 1703–4, stirred the embers of dying conflicts), and restless members of the second generation of Quakers. Logan wrote in 1707 that Lloyd was "a close member among Friends, he is a discordant in their meetings of business,—so much so, that he expects a separation and a purging. This arises out of divisions in the government,—the young push for rash measures,—the old for Penn's interest."

A major function of the business meetings (or Meetings for Discipline) was, as in England, to regulate the behavior of the members. The Inner Light inspired conduct but the meeting judged it. No private affairs were closed to supervision and even interference, at least in the realm of economics. But politics were, apparently, another matter. Although William Penn considered government "a part of religion itself, a thing sacred in its institution and its end," provincial affairs were not always managed in friendly fashion. While the meeting was run on the principle of consensus, the majority ruled in the Assembly, where Quakers clashed head on in search of political victory. Agreement could not always be reached on such fundamental beliefs as pacifism and oath-taking. Nor was there a clear distinction between good and bad Friends. Fomenters of dissension, such as Lloyd, were truer to the original tenets of the faith than advocates of harmony, such as Logan.

Given this confusion of values, accentuated by the division between old and young ("that corrupt Generation here," in the words of a prematurely aged Logan, now in his early thirties and two decades Lloyd's junior), the political role of the Meetings for Discipline was uncertain, a situation hardly eased by the influx of outsiders who complained of Quaker influence on public affairs. Only a week before the provincial and county elections were held the Yearly Meeting convened. Attended by the most influential Friends in Pennsylvania, whether conservative farmers from the Monthly Meetings in the outlying counties or more liberal Philadelphians, the annual gathering could not ignore political issues. Indeed, in the first years of the century it had rebuked unnamed, but certainly not unknown, Quakers who had "by their Seditious Words, Insinuations, and Practices, disquieted the Minds of others, to the making of Parties and Disturbances: and some under the Fair Colours of Law and Priviledges, have promoted their Sinister Ends, when indeed it was but to take Vengeance, against those whom they had taken disgust against." If the creation of faction was seen as a more serious offense than infringement on principle, then David Lloyd would be less favored than James Logan.

Lloyd's attempts to hound Logan out of the Council may have appeared effective when the provincial secretary's steadfast defender, John Evans, was removed from office in 1709, but such was not the case. In Evans' place Penn appointed Colonel Charles Gookin, who unfortunately matched his predecessor in lack of administrative experience. As a former military man he came to Pennsylvania to carry out the proprietor's orders and obey the crown. He not only refused Lloyd's immediate demand that Logan be removed from the Council but countered the speaker's persistent assaults on proprietary policy, particularly as it was administered by Logan, with an attack on the privileges claimed by the Assembly. Whatever virtues these tactics had as a military maneuver, as a parliamentary ploy they served only to perpetuate the legislative impasse of the Evans administration. Government continued inactive in the Quaker province as deputy governor and Assembly engaged in a cold war of words, the latter vigorously arguing for its accumulated powers while

The proximity of the Friends' "Great Meetinghouse" to the Old Court House in the early eighteenth century (above), as well as the caricature of Quaker politicians in front of the Court House in 1765 (below), shows the continuing intimacy between religion and politics. (above) *From John F. Watson,* Annals of Philadelphia and Pennsylvania *(Philadelphia, 1845).* (below) *Historical Society of Pennsylvania.*

Gookin tried to raise funds for an intercolonial expedition against the French.

Lloyd's victory in the election of October 1, 1709, and Logan's announcement a month later of his impending departure for England, where he would surely give Quakers a one-sided account of political combat in Pennsylvania, brought on a test of strength in battle. In response to the volley of charges leveled at him by the Lloydians, Logan had returned some reckless accusations of his own. The Assembly challenged him to substantiate these before leaving and to account for all the money he had handled as provincial secretary. Logan refused, and when the Assembly failed to impeach him, it attempted to imprison him. At this point Gookin and the Council intervened, the legislature backed down, and Logan sailed for London.

This small victory for the proprietary forces was followed by a more substantial triumph: the defeat of Lloyd and every other member of the previous Assembly in the election of October 1, 1710. Some of the credit for this upset belonged to Isaac Norris, son-in-law of the late Thomas Lloyd, sometime mayor of Philadelphia, judge, Council member, merchant, and weighty Quaker. In 1710 he authored a tract, *Friendly Advice to the Inhabitants of Pensilvania*, which was published by order of the Yearly Meeting. Pointing to the painfully obvious fact that in recent years little public business had been accomplished because of persistent factionalism in the Assembly, Norris called for constructive change through the election of substantial men who sympathized with the proprietor rather than those who "Combat every thing 'tho never so well designed." Support of the government, he argued, was consistent with liberty, indeed was basic to it. For the alternative was royal control and higher taxes.

The men elected in 1710 represented a vote of confidence in the proprietor. Most of them were men of property, responsive to the program of stable and constructive government which Norris, himself a member of the new Assembly, advocated. A letter from William Penn, which arrived in November and contained a forceful statement of the proprietor's attitude toward balance in government, enhanced the position of the newly elected legislators. Contention gave way to action as an array of bills was passed dealing with such sensitive issues as the judiciary, public debts, and defense. (Norris, who lamented to Penn in November 1710 that there was no real solution to the controversy over oaths, was the leader of an Assembly which voted £2,000 for military purposes in 1711.) Council and Assembly got on smoothly, since the same sort of men or, as in the case of Norris, the same men served in each. Simultaneously, these politicians were infiltrating the Corporation of Philadelphia. As for David Lloyd, he settled into Chester County and tended to his private affairs for four years, not returning to the Assembly until 1714.

For the next decade or so, provincial politics in Pennsylvania was relatively subdued. Although Governor Gookin was at war with the Assembly from 1714 until his removal in 1717, these confrontations were mere skirmishes in view of the battles of earlier decades. Indeed, it was the coalescence of so-called popular and proprietary interests, symbolized and given substance by the fact of Assembly and Council working in tandem, which had this pacifying effect. Gookin, mistakenly believing that the sale of the province to the crown was assured, catered to resident Anglicans in hopes of being chosen royal governor, thus deserting the proprietary as well as the popular forces. Gookin's many other intemperate or ill-advised moves, including an attack on the characters of Isaac Norris and James Logan, caused Pennsylvanians to question his sanity and the Assembly to request his removal. On the recommendation of Logan and the Council he was replaced by Sir William Keith, a Scot who had served for several years as a customs official in America.

Logan received confirmation of Keith's appointment in 1717 from Hannah Penn, the proprietor's second wife who since his incapacitating stroke in 1712 had taken over his duties and allowed Logan even more power than he previously possessed. Hannah had visited Pennsylvania with her husband, sailing over with him and Logan in 1699 and giving birth to her first child, John, in Philadelphia immediately after her arrival. At that early date it was clear that she was interested in and capable of taking the initiative on proprietary affairs. She returned with her husband to England, where she bore him three more children who lived past infancy: Thomas, Margaret, and Richard. She also managed to handle the thorny relations with his surviving children by his first marriage, Letitia and William, Jr., the offspring of Gulielma Penn who had died in 1694. (Letitia had married a man whom the gentle Hannah characterized as a "muckworm," while William, Jr., was a disappointment to everyone.) After William, Sr.'s stroke, Hannah continued negotiations for the sale of the province, armed with the knowledge that she would be sole executrix of his will and that Pennsylvania would be left to her family rather than Gulielma's children, although William, Jr., was heir at law and jealous of her command. It was she who dealt with the Quaker merchants who bailed the proprietor out in 1708, when the Ford family agreed to a deed of release on their claims to the province; these men now served as mortgagees of Pennsylvania and had to be paid from the American income. She was in frequent contact with Logan, and her concern was to maintain the status quo until her husband recovered or died.

Unfortunately, the governor appointed in 1717 was not to prove compatible with her aim, though this was not initially apparent. Keith had hardly arrived in Pennsylvania before he confronted his predecessor and extracted an admission that Gookin's wilder charges had been the "effects of his passions." He already had an ally in James Logan, and he made another by naming David Lloyd to be chief justice of the Supreme Court. He cultivated the Assembly with statements of his desire to serve the people, emphasizing the harmony of his interest and theirs, and the legislature responded with a handsome financial sustenance. Nor was Keith's popularity a matter of grand gestures only. He recognized the shambles in which Gookin left the judicial processes of the province, showed his desire to reestablish law and order by personally overseeing a murder trial in Chester County, and then confronted the conflicting claims of Assembly, proprietor, and crown concerning the instituting of courts, their powers, and the qualifications of their personnel.

In 1718 an Act for the Advancement of Justice brought Pennsylvania's criminal code into greater conformity with England's, but at the same time provided for taking an affirmation rather than an oath, thus satisfying the Quakers. And, rather than following his predecessors' practice of establishing courts by ordinance, when the crown disallowed the Judiciary Act of 1715 Keith got the Council to agree to a substitute measure acceptable to the Assembly. In 1722 he signed an Act for Establishing Courts of Judicature, the only such legislation not repealed by the crown. Keith was so greatly respected that the Assembly even agreed to his plan for a voluntary militia. His handling of Indian relations was roundly applauded in the colony, while the Board of Trade enthusiastically received his recommendation for a more aggressive imperial (i.e., anti-French) policy in America.

But in his attention to the Assembly and the crown, Keith betrayed his lack of regard for the proprietor. Like Charles Gookin, Keith expected Pennsylvania to be sold to the crown, and his behavior mirrored his belief. He brought the constitution and provincial laws closer to England's, he suggested that judicial commissions be issued in the king's name, a practice he followed after Penn's death in 1718, and he denied constitutional status to the Council. Finally, in 1722, he got into a dispute with the commissioners of property, in essence denying their authority —that is, the right of the proprietary to the soil of Pennsylvania! —a stance which could only earn him the enmity of Logan and his followers.

Simultaneously, Pennsylvania was moving into a severe economic depression, a result, at least partly, of the drain of gold and silver to England in the wake of the South Sea Bubble collapse. Since specie was Pennsylvania's only legal tender, shipping and inland trade declined precipitously for want of a means of exchange. Keith encouraged the Assembly to pass legislation dealing with the slump by reviving trade and encouraging home consumption. Finally, he supported the issuing of paper money, even advocating this solution to the Board of Trade. Logan and Norris, however, were worried by the latter measure, fearing a "leveling spirit" and a loss of return to the proprietor. (Penn, however, on at least two occasions had advocated paper currency when specie was scarce.) The Assembly passed not only a paper money bill which, ironically, played a large part in Pennsylvania's remarkable economic recovery from 1723 to 1726, but other legislation easing the debtor's situation, as well. For Keith, the paper money issue was not simply a solution to a pressing problem but the symbol of a struggle between the common people and the moneyed elite. To Hannah Penn, the governor's encouragement of this legislation was only another instance of behavior hostile to the proprietor.

Yet Hannah was temporarily in a poor position to retaliate against her deputy. William Penn had died on July 30, 1718, leaving Pennsylvania's government, but not the land, in trust to John, Earl Poulet, and Robert Harley, Earl of Oxford, so that they could complete negotiations for the sale of the province to the crown. William Penn, Jr., disappointed to find that he had inherited only his father's Irish property, had formally objected to probating the will on the grounds that his father could not separate the land from the government (both of which should belong to him) and, therefore, the sale of the province could not be carried out. Although the will was probated and William, Jr., died in 1720, his son Springett, who was the age of Hannah's son Thomas and had lived in Hannah's household since he was eight, persisted in attempting to break his grandfather's will. It was Logan who strengthened Hannah's hand in Pennsylvania. In late 1723 he went to London, appraised Hannah of Keith's high-handed behavior, got letters of support for himself from Springett and the mortgagees as well as Hannah, and returned to Philadelphia equipped to shore up the proprietary interest.

While the provincial secretary appealed to the merchant interests, Keith took his case to the people, putting together a coalition of Philadelphia tradesmen, recently arrived immigrants, and backcountry Quakers. With strong support in the Assembly, Keith also made a bid to David Lloyd, causing Logan to lament: "Now Pilate and Herod are friends for the same goodly purpose—the Governor has all the proprietors rights— the chief justice expounds the law of which the other now says he is an oracle." But Lloyd's support for Keith was ambivalent, for he saw in his erstwhile ally a popular rival. And Logan prevailed on the proprietary family to remove Keith, only to see the undaunted ex-governor running for the Assembly in 1726. Here, however, Keith overstepped the bounds of political wisdom, challenging Lloyd for the speakership and thus losing his backing. Yet Logan's efforts to bolster Lloyd's forces ("Of two evils, one would choose the least," he wrote) did not bar Keith from reelection to the Assembly in 1727, though after his second unsuccessful bid for the speaker's chair he sailed for England, leaving others to cope with the bitterness he had done so much to provoke.

Keith's actions as deputy governor and his desertion of the Penns for the interests of "the people" while he kept a weather eye on Whitehall testified, as did his behavior in the Assembly, to a capriciousness of character which had limited his political durability. Yet his inconsistency could not be simply chalked up to the peculiarity of the man. Rather, it had to be understood also in terms of the office he occupied. Conflicting claims were made on his loyalty by the crown, the proprietor, and the Assembly. By the Navigation Act of 1696 he needed royal approval before assuming office, in addition to taking an oath to carry out the acts of trade. During his tenure he received instructions from and was expected to provide information to various departments in England. Much of his enforcement work was entrusted to a naval officer, whom he appointed. Other royal officials—the customs collector, the comptroller and surveyor general, the postmaster, the vice-admiralty court officers (judge, register, marshall, clerk, advocate)—were appointed by the Customs Board in London, though the governor derived some patronage advantage from recommending these appointments.

But his major sustenance came from the proprietor who appointed him and the Assembly which voted part of his salary, and the division of these allegiances was the source of confusion and discord. As a proprietary agent he was charged with carrying out private duties and public functions, including those tasks which a Quaker could not fulfill. Although the proprietary secretary (James Logan's post from 1701 to 1747) handled the bulk of the Penns' land transactions, the deputy governor was also involved, or implicated. As to his handling of intercolonial relations and Indian dealings, the Assembly showed little interest before the middle of the century. But the legislators constantly watched over domestic affairs, jealously guarding their prerogatives and infringing on his whenever possible, as illustrated in appointments to and payments for office.

The deputy governor designated an attorney general, responsible for prosecuting criminals and giving legal advice to proprietary officials and judges, who like the chief executive suffered the problem of collecting part of his salary from the Assembly. Although the legislature created the office of register general in 1705 to probate wills and grant letters of administration, the salary for this post came from fees, which was true also of the office of keeper of the great seal. Finally, the deputy governor appointed the clerk of the Council and a number of lesser officials. Until 1714, the proprietor appointed the provincial treasurer; in 1715 the Assembly passed an act providing for a treasurer responsible to the legislature, although full control of the office was two decades away. The Assembly established a provincial bank or loan office in 1723 and appointed from the legislature its trustees to deal in bills of credit. In this manner, the Assembly gained almost complete control over spending at the provincial level of government by the middle of the eighteenth century. The speed of this take-over, a process which occurred but took longer in other colonies, was partly owing to the lack of competition from an upper house.

The Assembly also gained power, largely at the expense of the proprietor, thus directly affecting the deputy governor—and, especially, Keith—because the rising eminence of its speaker and the increasing organization of its procedures enabled it to act with determination. By the charter of 1701 the Assembly gained the right to choose its speaker, enacted into law in 1705; and by the legislative rules of 1703, put into final form in 1720, the speaker was empowered to limit or terminate debate, control the members' entrance to and exit from the house, and name persons to committees, not to mention signing letters and petitions of the Assembly, bills, money orders, and the journal at session's end. The speaker of the House of Commons had similar powers, but as Parliament ceased using standing committees in the eighteenth century, his strength declined, unlike the situation in the Pennsylvania Assembly and the lower houses of the other colonies as well. Indeed, the power of a typical speaker extended well beyond the legislative halls into economic and social affairs, testimony to the intimate connection between politics and all other areas of colonial life, a fact which distinguished America from England and led to serious misunderstandings when comparisons of the two systems were made.

Organizationally, the Pennsylvania Assembly exercised increasing control over itself and, hence, other government agencies. It chose a clerk, a sergeant at arms, and a doorkeeper. It appointed a committee to audit the accounts of the loan office and the treasury, as well as two other, and less important, standing committees: one to revise Assembly minutes and the other to correspond with the colony's agent in London, a post created in 1731. Members of these committees were compensated, as were assemblymen. A resolution passed in 1725 that the legislature should not sit more than thirty days "upon wages" was not honored.

The Assembly also strengthened itself and built permanence into provincial government through the legislative process. Half of the bills it passed were private: appointments, compensation, hardship cases. None of these were required to follow routine legislative procedure or be signed by the governor, a procedure thereby allowing the Assembly to deal with matters usually thought to be outside its prerogative. Public bills, those of statutory nature, were usually introduced by committees, whose membership was not widely distributed but the province of a few assemblymen.

Since the deputy governor's signature was necessary on public bills, the Assembly wielded the cudgel of a withheld salary, as early as 1696, to force signing of a bill. The power of the purse also involved having all treasury drafts signed by the speaker and the treasurer, who was appointed by the Assembly. However, the deputy governor did use his veto, which might lead to negotiations between executive and legislature. The Assembly could bypass the deputy governor and go directly to the crown with remonstrances (when Governor Evans challenged this procedure, he was ignored). The proprietary sought to bolster its position by insisting on a veto over the deputy governor's signature, by calling for the provincial secretary's and Council's approval of the deputy governor's action, and by binding the executive to instructions issued at the outset of his administration. Though the Assembly successfully asserted its independence of the proprietor, the conflict between executive and legislature remained unresolved and produced considerable acrimony from the Seven Years War to the American Revolution.

Not only did the Assembly balk at proprietary interference, but it resented having to send laws to England for approval. Since there was a five-year grace period in which to submit laws to the king in Council, the procedure adopted was to face the Privy Council with a large number of laws every five years. Although the Council passed the laws to the Board of Trade, the attorney general usually made the determination; hence, the colonial agent tried to influence him. Over half the laws disallowed were so treated because they were technically defective, especially laws regarding the penal code. More laws of an economic or judicial nature were disallowed than any other. The Assembly circumvented the royal veto by enacting laws for less than five years, by reenacting laws which had been disallowed, and by not sending laws to England.

Thus the Assembly, having become the sole legislating body by the Charter of Privileges of 1701, moved into areas previously reserved to the proprietor and even outmaneuvered the crown in its quest for power. James Logan's claim concerning the Assembly—"There is no such privilege known in England, or in any other of the Plantations, as is here claimed"—though it had to be taken as the opinion of a proclaimed enemy of legislative encroachments, was not for that reason inaccurate. Among the American plantations, only the corporate colonies of Rhode Island and Connecticut and the quasi-royal province of Massachusetts, all of whose legislatures antedated Pennsylvania's by almost half a century, could boast of a lower house so powerful as the Assembly which met in Philadelphia.

The ascent of the lower house was a political phenomenon shared by all the American colonies which, in turn, viewed the seventeenth-century House of Commons as a model. There was a remarkable similarity in the pattern of acquiring power by the various lower houses: gaining control over provincial finances (raising and distributing public money, auditing official accounts, issuing paper money); establishing the salaries and fees of all public officers; setting the ground rules of the franchise, representation, elections, sessions; and, having proved legislative autonomy, moving into areas hitherto claimed by the executive. In Pennsylvania this final step was evident in the Assembly's extension of its domain to the judiciary and to local (county and municipal) government, sometimes with considerable success.

Concerning the judiciary, the Assembly's aim was to give the courts more power on the local level in the face of proprietary and royal efforts to centralize judicial authority. David Lloyd's Judiciary Act of 1701 exemplified the legislature's attitude, but it was disallowed by the crown, as were all other laws establishing courts for the next two decades. (The Charter of Privileges did not provide for a court system.) The Assembly's persistence paid off in 1722, when a Judiciary Act was allowed; apparently the Board of Trade simply did not take action on the law. This legislation, despite its resemblance to the act of 1701, was by no means a clear Assembly victory, since it allowed the proprietor, through the deputy governor, to retain his right of appointing justices of the peace, a privilege always used for political advantage, while the Assembly never obtained its desired power of removal.

These justices of the peace presided over county courts, either of quarter sessions (criminal cases, frequently concerning indentured servants) or common pleas (civil cases). County courts had both original and appellate jurisdiction. The city of Philadelphia had its own criminal court, or Mayor's Court; the mayor, recorder, and aldermen served as justices of the peace, separate from the Philadelphia County court. There were special county courts for cases involving Negroes and orphans, the former to administer justice (swift and harsh) without appeal, the latter to deal with property and guardians. Each county court had a clerk of the peace, responsible for keeping records and collecting fees. The Assembly could not control the appointment of clerks, but it did exercise some power over them through regulation of fees.

The Supreme Court, also presided over by justices appointed

by the deputy governor, was an appellate court (and could call for lower court records) with original jurisdiction clearly granted for cases of capital crimes, less clearly for civil cases. The Assembly denied that such jurisdiction derived from the Judiciary Act of 1722, but an explicit law to this effect, passed in 1727, was disallowed by the crown. The Assembly also attempted to influence appointments by withholding money for salaries, though apparently not to great effect.

In court, indictments were delivered by a grand jury, approximately twenty-four persons appointed annually by the sheriff. Except in cases of "treason or malicious murder," the deputy governor could grant reprieves pending crown review, a power the Assembly did not interfere with. The Assembly did intercede and, ultimately, abolish in 1736 a Court of Chancery established in 1720 by the proclamation of Governor William Keith. And, following the tradition of Parliament, the Assembly itself served as a court; by the Charter of Privileges it had the right to "impeach criminals and redress grievances." Unlike some other lower houses in the colonies, the Pennsylvania Assembly never heard an appeal from a lower court.

If the legislature was partially blocked regarding the judiciary, it was more successful in imposing its will on the executive in the area of county government. William Penn, empowered by his charter to divide the province into "towns, Hundreds, and Counties," decided to establish counties rather than perpetuate the towns, existing under the Duke of York's laws, as the dominant institutions of local government. In the English tradition, local affairs from the time of Penn's arrival in 1682 were conducted by justices of the peace in the court of quarter sessions. Justices were appointed on the basis of loyalty to the proprietor and, consequently, were generally drawn from the political elite of the province. Many simultaneously held other appointive offices at various levels of government, and some were also elected officials. (Twelve of twenty justices appointed in Chester County between 1730 and 1740 were assemblymen.) Justices not only sat as judges in county courts but also supervised road building and maintenance and appointed township officials as well. The chief of these was the constable, who assisted the county commissioners and assessors in levying and collecting taxes, serving court papers, presiding at elections, and, as the sheriff's deputy, enforcing laws. The long tenures of the justices gave continuity to local practice.

The Assembly encroached on the proprietary preserve of local government through its attempts to raise taxes by the agency of elected officials. As early as 1696 the legislature called for the election of six assessors by "the substantial freeholders in each respective county," thereby undercutting a function of the grand jury, which was appointed by the sheriff. County commissioners, a post unique to Pennsylvania, were first appointed by the Assembly in 1711 to levy and collect taxes so heavily in arrears; this had previously been the function of the courts of quarter sessions. Commissioners were tax collectors until, in 1718, they were empowered to determine the amount of taxes and to demand payments from the county treasurer. In 1722 the office of county commissioner was made elective, the practice becoming that of electing one of the three commissioners annually for a three-year term. Every county commissioner elected between 1725 and 1740 had previously been an assessor; often commissioners went on to the Assembly. Although succession in office was not the practice after 1732, commissioners might serve several terms. After 1723 none was appointed a justice of the peace. Together the commissioners and assessors appointed the county clerk and the county treasurer.

Thus in the early eighteenth century elected officials gradually moved into the domains of appointed officials, a situation not only consistent with the increasing power of the Assembly but brought about by that body. There were two other local officials —the sheriff, chief election and law enforcement officer of the county, and the coroner, who could act in place of the sheriff in addition to holding inquests on the dead—nominated annually by the freemen but appointed by the deputy governor. In fact, assemblymen were frequently former county officers, which probably accounted for the good relations between the two areas of government. Apart from serving as a board of appeal from the actions of county government, the Assembly did not exercise, nor did the county officials challenge, its prerogatives. Perhaps it was this good working relationship between provincial and local government which made the county in Pennsylvania a singularly important unit of government, unlike the situation in other colonies.

The county was not only unique in its strength but also was less tied to English precedent than was municipal government in Pennsylvania. The boroughs of Chester and Bristol, issued charters in 1701 and 1720 which called for the annual election of burgesses who presided over town meetings and acted within the borough with the same powers as justices of the peace, were hardly significant. The Corporation of Philadelphia was an impotent anachronism. Issued a charter in 1701 "for the more immediate and entire government of the said town, and the better regulation of trade therein," the corporation was run by a council composed of twelve men (chosen by the freemen for life), eight aldermen (chosen from the councilmen by the council), a recorder (chosen from the councilmen, serving for life), and a mayor (chosen from aldermen for a one-year term). This closed, self-perpetuating body was initially appointed by Penn, allowing him to ensconce the proprietary interest (many city officials, over the years, also served on the Provincial Council) in a corporation which could enlarge itself at its own discretion.

Despite the intent of investing Philadelphia city government with political and commercial power, a fact underlined by the presence of important provincial officials and successful merchants on the Council, it was unable to govern and suffered from bad business practices and even speculation. Service to the corporation was bothersome and expensive, but it was an honor, which meant that an institution intended to be political and commercial could become a social affair. Hastening the corporation along the road to irrelevance was the absence of specified powers in its patent, while the Charter of Privileges empowered the Assembly to regulate cities. The brash legislature convened in the midst of the genteel corporation's bailiwick, providing a conflict in style of operation, ideology and jurisdiction. A law of 1712, for example, created six city assessors independent of the corporation. Jurisdictional discords also prevailed between the city and the county of Philadelphia, with the government of the former increasingly relegated to a subordinate role. The corporation's motive energy was largely inertial.

The vigorous growth of county government created a structure which might serve to cushion the shocks of occasional outbursts threatening the province. Another stabilizing force in provincial life was the increasing stratification of society, a direct response to changing economic and demographic circumstances. Commercial expansion was evident from Pennsylvania's very beginnings, but it had been hindered by intermittent warfare from the 1690s until the second decade of the eighteenth century, when trade truly flourished. Similarly, there had been a steady stream of immigrants to Pennsylvania since the arrival of the first Quakers, but this flow became torrential in the eighteenth century. In the two decades following 1700, the population of Philadelphia doubled in size to ten thousand, a number only slightly smaller than that of Boston, the largest city on the seaboard. Many of the newcomers had been able to afford the transatlantic passage only by being indentured to masters in Pennsylvania. A wealthy merchant aristocracy and a lower class, largely composed of servants, began to emerge from a society which had been egalitarian and homogeneous.

Although Friends were noted for their dedication to equality, most of them did not fully reject the ideology of a stratified society. "The World's Respect is an empty Ceremony, no Soul or substance in it," said William Penn. "The Christian's is a solid Thing, whether by Obedience to Superiors, Love to Equals, or *Help* and *Countenance* to Inferiors." The proprietor, with his preference for the past, expected the superior men in Pennsylvania to be large landowners, and ultimately they were. But the way to wealth was commerce, a livelihood certainly sanctioned through the Puritan strain in Quakerism. God, according to John Calvin, "has appointed to all their peculiar duties in different spheres of life." Trade was not to be disdained for the life of a country gentleman, though a diligent pursuit of merchandising could lead to prosperous rural retirement and membership in the ruling class.

If commercial competition was intense, it was also controlled. Family relationships and religious connections were primary ingredients in the achievement of success and, therefore, in the growth of an aristocracy. Since a single proprietorship or a partnership was the conventional form of business organization in colonial Philadelphia—the only corporation was the ill-fated Free Society of Traders—in which an initial investment of over £2,000 appears to have been the rule, commerce was by no means open to all. In fact, many of Pennsylvania's early merchants came from other colonies where they had already been engaged in trade. Out of the West Indies came the names of Carpenter, Richardson, Norris, Dickinson, while from Boston arrived Shippen, from New York, Morrey and Frampton, from Maryland, Fishbourne, Preston, and Hill, while New Jersey supplied Morris. Still, in boom times ambitious outsiders edged into commercial ventures, causing established merchants to seek ways of limiting competitors.

One method of control was to restrict training in the field to young men who were close relatives or personal acquaintances. In other cases, apprentices usually paid to live with their tutors. During the first years on his own, the budding trader often served as a factor, making his living from commissions on the sale of another's merchandise. Again capital was a necessity, not to mention an understanding of the market, since an advance had to be made on goods to be received. The successful merchant had to have a network of relatives, friends, and agents at other ports; otherwise he would have to consign his cargo to the ship's captain or send an apprentice with the shipment as supercargo. This web of associates was partly the result of long trading experience but also the consequence of other than commercial relationships. Quakers who were constantly in touch with one another on religious matters and had a strong sense of being "a peculiar people" maintained contact regarding commercial affairs and traded whenever possible with one another. This nexus was reinforced sometimes by family connections. Quakers in Philadelphia were related to Lloyds in London, Hills and Callenders in the West Indies, Wantons in Newport, and Franklins in New York.

By the early eighteenth century the regions and cargoes of Pennsylvania's seaborne trade were fairly well defined. The greatest volume of exchange was with the West Indies, where Philadelphia merchants were the leading suppliers of flour and lumber while importing rum, sugar, molasses, and hard woods in a favorable balance of trade. Since the turn of the century there had been a growing commerce with southern Europe and the wine islands (Madeiras, Canaries, Azores), in which wheat products were sent out and salt and wines brought back, an exchange dictated by the terms of the Navigation Acts. Coastwise trade was less lucrative but featured a variety of goods: flour, salted meat, rum, and (later) bar iron were traded for a miscellaneous assortment of goods. Commerce with England, which absorbed the energy and capital of the most successful merchants, though involving fewer ships and less tonnage than the other areas, was largely a matter of importing, especially of dry goods which showed a great margin of profit in resale. For a short time in the late seventeenth and early eighteenth centuries tobacco from the Three Lower Counties was sent directly to England, but later vessels took the products of the West Indies or southern Europe and the wine islands to the mother country. Pennsylvania's economy was somewhat influenced by English officialdom, not so much through enforcement of the Navigation Acts as by policies allowing London merchants to trade effectively across the Atlantic.

Since wheat and its derivatives always comprised more than half the value of exports from Philadelphia, inland trade was of crucial importance to merchants. Natural waterways were the chief means of transportation out of the interior, with some dugout canoes carrying as much as a hundred or even a hundred and fifty bushels of wheat. The dams and weirs built by farmers to catch fish hindered this traffic, with consequent legislation in 1683 and 1700 outlawing such obstructions, testimony, no doubt, to the political influence of merchants. On land the narrow Indian trails had to be broadened for packhorse trains, while roads were a function of the density of settlement. The earliest of these, King's Highway, was begun in 1677 from New Castle toward Chester. It was continued to Philadelphia at the time of the Quaker arrival and on to Trenton in 1700, an obvious effort to bring the West New Jersey settlements into the Philadelphia market area. Road maintenance, vested in the hands of local inhabitants following the English example, was usually minimal.

Not all goods reaching the city were for export, of course. On Wednesday and Saturday of each week urban dwellers could buy farmers' products at strictly regulated markets. Other economic legislation stipulated the quality of beer and bread in the city, the rates of inland transportation, and the import and tonnage duties, which favored Pennsylvania's merchants at the expense of outsiders. A bill passed in 1700 called for the inspection of flour, beef, and pork (and, later in the century, lumber) before export in order to maintain the quality of the product and, thus, the reputation of Pennsylvania goods. This was a means of limiting the number of persons engaged in overseas trade, since well-established merchants had access to the best foodstuffs and were likely to have had a hand in determining standards.

Beyond the agricultural hinterland lay another important commercial area. Unlike the Delaware Valley, whose game resources were depleted, the Susquehanna Valley was rich in furs. The Shawnee Indians who had moved into the region during the last decade of the seventeenth century handled large quantities of pelts, but they were dominated by the Iroquois who directed the fur trade to merchants in Albany. The Pennsylvanians might have subverted this traffic by using to advantage the *coureurs du bois* who had drifted from Canada to New York, independent wilderness traders who knew no allegiance but that of the prime price. However, Penn believed that justice would be done by the Indians only if commerce with them were supervised in the open market at Philadelphia, a mode of operation highly uncongenial to the *coureurs*, whom Quakers regarded with provincial jealousy and fear. In this situation it was the Indians who seized the initiative. In 1699 the Iroquois tried to establish trade relations with Philadelphia, a move blocked by the governor of New York. By 1701 they asserted their independence of the Albany government, thus placing themselves in a position to do business elsewhere.

This change coincided with the arrival in Pennsylvania of James Logan, who did not share Penn's tender regard for the Indians nor the Quaker merchants' worries about French traders. Penn wanted the fur trade closely regulated to guard his own interests and to protect the Indians, and he signed an agreement with the aborigines to that effect as late as 1701. To Logan, however, he emphasized the selfish side of the equation, wishing aloud to his secretary in 1703 "that thou wouldst do all that is possible to master furs and skins for me." When Onondagans and Shawnees came separately to Philadelphia in 1704, Council member Logan was encouraging about a commerce in furs. At about the same time he began building covert contacts with the *coureurs*, though it was not until 1712—when the hostilities with France ended and Logan was safe from the attacks of the Assembly—that he could openly engage in this commerce, a field which he dominated almost to the exclusion of other merchants. Not only did Logan possess a sound and sometimes imaginative commercial sense matched by an aggressive self-interest, but he was in a politically privileged position: Penn was seriously ill in England, unable even to advise his steward by letter; his creditors gave Logan full responsibility to raise money necessary to release the colony from receivership; the Assembly was controlled by men sympathetic to the proprietary interest; and Logan held a number of powerful offices.

In less than a decade after 1712, Logan built a major trading organization in the Susquehanna Valley, his net worth increasing more than fivefold over eight years. He profited, of course, from the sale of skins and furs in England, as well as from commissions and storage charges for other merchants' shipments. But there was even more money in imported manufactured goods, which Logan marked up almost 150 percent. These went out on credit to traders, who resold them to Indians, also on credit. Debts were paid as the forest pelts were passed from the Indians to the *coureurs* to Logan, finally reaching the hands of London merchants who supplied more manufactured goods. As the agent of the Penn family Logan could risk proprietary money at the beginning of an uncertain mercantile adventure. As provincial secretary he could hire a trader as an official interpreter, thus giving him prestige among the Indians as well as patronage. As commissioner of property he could, though the legality was doubtful, grant land to a *coureur* as a base of operations, foreclosing on the same man's debts by taking the improved property into his own possession. In this manner, Logan the scrambling merchant became Logan the established landholder.

The pattern of Logan's movement was not extraordinary in Pennsylvania. Quaker merchants, whether engaged in seaborne commerce, inland trade, or Indian dealings, aspired to the security and prestige of a country estate, much on the order of the English gentry, the Virginia planters, or the New York patroons. Isaac Norris, who began his trading activities in Pennsylvania eight years before Logan arrived, had by 1713 gathered up a large parcel of real estate in Philadelphia, 850 acres in the "northern liberties" of the city, 6,000 acres of unallocated land, and a 7,500-acre estate on the Schuylkill. In other words, the ownership of land was becoming the token of an emerging aristocracy in the Quaker province.

In the second and third decades of the eighteenth century, however, the social structure was only beginning to change in response to new economic and demographic realities. In Chester County, for example, the distribution of wealth was extremely even in the early days of settlement. Only minor alterations took place between 1693, the year of the first provincial tax, and 1715, although the real wealth of the area was rising due to its situation as a major grain-producing region. But in the half century after 1715, when the population burgeoned from four to twenty-five thousand and the standard of living rose steadily, the distribution of wealth became notably less equal. If few people were growing poorer in an absolute sense, still a growing lower class, which included many German and Scotch-Irish immigrants, was not getting its share. In commercial Philadelphia disparities between incomes were more obvious than in agricultural Chester County, as the pretensions of newly rich merchants, expressed in fashionable clothes and house furnishings, mansions, coaches, and liveried servants, were on prominent display. Thus, even as the structure of society was only beginning to change, the new plutocrats showed a sensitivity to their altered situation which, among other manifestations, took political form.

In this process, Pennsylvania was hardly unique. A shared

characteristic of English colonies up and down the Atlantic seaboard was the growth of wealth and population, the emergence of elite groups—whether of planters in the southerly provinces or merchants and professional men in the north—and a quest for political power conducted by these economic and social leaders. At an earlier time the Provincial Council might have been the focus of their efforts, but this body had either become too small to accommodate the emergent plutocrats or it had become a vehicle of the governor's patronage. In the unusual case of Pennsylvania, it was eliminated from the legislative process altogether. Men of wealth continued to serve on the Council, but the Assembly was increasingly the seat of power. Consequently, in the early eighteenth century, leaders in the Council might also direct activities in the Assembly.

The quest for power took place on both the provincial and the imperial level. In the former case, it involved the elite's assertion of dominance within the Assembly. Men of eminence took the places once occupied by farmers and artisans, although the latter might reassert themselves if the right issues arose, such as those brought to the surface by the economic depression in 1722. On the imperial level, the battle ordinarily pitted the Assembly against the royal governor who represented the crown. In Pennsylvania, of course, this equation was complicated by the proprietary element, an obvious enemy for the Assembly in times of stress, and a friend who made claims of loyalty (at least on certain assemblymen) in times of prosperity.

Though the excesses of political life in Pennsylvania were curbed by the emergence of a governmental structure, the balance that created stability in the province was delicate. As long as the Assembly reflected the social structure and responded to economic fluctuations in a society which was dynamic, the potential for turbulence was there. Furthermore, the Assembly's gains, while real, came at a time when neither the proprietary nor the crown was able to assert its prerogatives. That situation, too, could change. In 1720 it appeared as though the province had achieved a long-sought-after calm; within five years the serenity was shattered. Political stability remained an elusive commodity in Pennsylvania.

5

TRANSPLANTS: AFRICAN AND EUROPEAN IMMIGRANTS IN THE EIGHTEENTH CENTURY

Growth was the most striking feature of the American colonies in the eighteenth century. An estimated quarter of a million inhabitants in 1700 quintupled to a million and a quarter in just half a century. Figures are indeed difficult to come by, but it may be safely stated that nowhere was the expansion of population so phenomenal as in Pennsylvania. Entering the century with something in the neighborhood of fifteen to twenty thousand people, the increase was more than tenfold over five decades. Immigration into the once-Quaker province was largely responsible for this gigantic leap, producing a society whose national and racial origins were more variegated than anywhere else on the Atlantic seaboard. Germans and some Swiss from the Palatinate region and Scots who reached America by way of northern Ireland composed the great bulk of these masses who joined English and Welsh settlers in Pennsylvania, but Africans were also part of the penetrating stream. They came as slaves, while a majority of the Europeans entered as servants.

This was hardly unusual. A majority of the people who settled in the American colonies south of New England came as servants. Next to slavery, indenture proved the easiest way to deal with labor as a commodity: it was profitable to recruiting agents, ship captains, and employers. That it was cruel to the servants themselves was not really a consideration. Rather, a legal contract binding a person to servitude was sanctioned by tradition. When servants were sent to Jamestown for employment by planters who would in turn reimburse the Virginia Company, an innovation in the English apprenticeship system foreshadowed the institution of indentured servitude. The servant was guaranteed passage to America and the necessities of life in return for seven years' labor with no wages but the promise of reward when the contract expired. Before the Virginia Company was dissolved in 1624, the labor system was in the hands of private entrepreneurs.

Many servants migrated without a written indenture, while those who did have such documents were almost always indentured to someone connected with the ship, who in turn sold them to the highest bidder. By the early eighteenth century, when immigrants were viewed less as a labor commodity and more as settlers, a variant of indentured servitude came into use. It began on the Continent, where Germans and Swiss traveling to their port of debarkation, Rotterdam, ran short of money for the American passage and, consequently, made agreements with ship captains to redeem their debts for food and passage through sale into servitude. Redemptioners, usually with families rather than individual immigrants, soon came from the British Isles as well. As to convicts, the eighteen thousand of them transported during the eighteenth century were virtually all sent to Virginia and Maryland.

The presence of servants in Quaker Pennsylvania was no anomaly. Penn's egalitarianism never led him to denounce the institution of servitude, nor did he feel compelled to explain his acceptance of it. Rather, his view was simply typical of his rank. Masters were to "mix *kindness* with authority" and servants were advised: "If thou wilt be a *good* servant, thou must be *true* . . . diligent, careful, trusty. . . . Such a servant serves God, in serving his master." Penn was forced to be more concrete when the matter of settling laborers in Pennsylvania arose, and he promised land to the immigrating servants, 50 acres at the end of his service, plus 50 acres to the master, so-called "head land." Furthermore, in the "Laws Agreed Upon in England" there was provision for a "register for all servants, where their names, time, wages, and days of payment shall be registered" as well as the stipulation that servants would be treated "justly and kindly" and "be not kept longer than their time." Further protection for servants was provided by an act of the Assembly in 1700: no servant could be sold out of Pennsylvania without his consent and that of two justices of the peace, and on his discharge he must be clothed and given tools. New York was the only other colony with such a stipulation.

However, Penn never disguised the fact that he saw servants as property. Runaways were penalized by having to serve double the time of their absence, without inquiries being made into causes of discontent. Freemen harboring other men's servants were required by law (1700) to advise the master and a justice of the peace within twenty-four hours. If the escapee were a Negro slave, the owner was to be notified and the black was to be "severely whipped."

The act of 1700 was the first formal recognition of slavery in Pennsylvania; never did the Assembly define the status of a slave. Up to 1700 the distinctions between servitude and slavery were blurred. Negroes, though held for life rather than a specified number of years, faced the same restrictions, court proceedings, and punishments as white servants. But by another law of 1700, backed by the proprietor and reenacted in 1705–6 in slightly amended form, Negroes were consigned to separate courts and faced with different punishment. In 1725–26 a law forbade miscegenation and restricted the slaves' mobility in other ways as well. After this time there was no important legislation regarding Negroes; they were already distinct from the white population.

Penn himself had set the pattern. For despite his statement that no one had the right "to inherit the sweat of the other's brow to reap the benefit of his labor but by consent," he owned slaves and did not free them at his death. (His will of 1701 provided for manumission, but not his final will of 1712.) Probably, like many other Englishmen, Penn was led to this apparent contradiction because he considered the Africans alien to his scheme of things. "No man in England is born slave to another," he wrote; the phrase "in England" was significant. Though George Fox had disapproved of slavery, the Free Society of Traders provided for manumission of Negroes after fourteen years, the citizens of

Germantown protested against slavery in 1688, and George Keith denounced the practice several years later, Penn accepted it.

And so did most English colonials by the late seventeenth century, an attitude owing not only to the exigencies of plantation life but to the peculiar reaction of Englishmen to Africans. When English sailors reached West Africa in 1550, almost a century after the Portuguese, they were suddenly face to face with one of the darkest people on earth, blacker than they would have encountered in most other regions of Africa. The very word "black" was an emotionally loaded one. It meant dirty, soiled, foul, malignant, baneful, disastrous, sinister, horrible, and wicked, while "white" represented the opposite qualities: purity, virtue, beauty, virginity, even godliness. Inevitably the question arose as to why the African was black, and a climatological explanation was rejected. Indians in the same latitude were only tawny-colored; Africans in northerly climates did not change hue.

Some observers linked black Africans to the Biblical account of Noah's son, Ham, who was cursed to be a slave, but this explanation gained only limited acceptance. Still, the Old Testament reference was pertinent, for the African was stigmatized not only by his color but by his lack of religion. He was not a Christian. While this fact made him ripe for conversion, such a transformation would eliminate one of the clear distinctions between African and Englishman. Ambivalent, the Christian Englishman did not proselytize. Heathenism remained an argument that the African was uncivilized. So much did he differ from the Englishman that he was labeled "savage." This word, like black, had special meaning. That the African was brutish or bestial meant that his character was preeminently sexual. Every man, of course, had an animal or sexual side to him, but the African was considered unusual in this regard. This thinking was confirmed by the discovery of the orangutan in West Africa; surely there was a link between the manlike beast and the beastlike man. To Englishmen, who at this time were preoccupied with the idea of controlling sexual passion, the African had to appear as a threat.

Indeed, the shock of recognition was so great that Englishmen could see no redeeming feature to African culture. But in fact, among nonliterate, preindustrial societies, the one found in the West Africa-Congo region, as defined by present-day anthropologists, should have been highly rated. Essentially agricultural, economic life featured both markets and money, permitting the production of a surplus over subsistence needs and, consequently, supporting a class structure. At the base of this society was the polygynous family, with kinship recognized through one line and guild organization usually based on that recognition. The sanction of the kinship system lay in religious tradition, based on the ancestral cult, which governed ceremonies of birth, marriage, and death. There was philosophical speculation about the world and its deities, as well as an acceptance of the operation of magic, both characteristics of which could be found in contemporaneous England. Political organization was tribal but extended over large areas. Graphic and plastic arts were practiced with competence. The similarities in the grammar of language over the entire region confirm the suggestion of cultural unity in a society which compared favorably in levels of attainment with some groups in western Europe.

It was the preconceptions of Englishmen which led to their distorted views of Africans. Yet even when colonization began in North America, there was no intention of establishing the institution of slavery for Negroes. The blacks who entered Virginia in 1619 were referred to as servants, a word commonly used at least until the middle of the century. But conditions of life in America, when combined with popular thinking about Africans, led to the establishment of chattel slavery. Of course, there was the example of the Spanish and Portuguese colonial policy of enslavement to copy, but it was more a reflection on their English past that led North American settlers down the road to slavery. Although the institution was foreign to English common law in the seventeenth century, there were certain attitudes prevalent in the mother country—slavery was captivity (certainly not the condition of servants), a slave was treated like a beast, slaves were heathens, and slavery was God's punishment for evil in men. Since the Negro was a captive, considered bestial and surely not Christian, these attitudes could be attached to him and the equation between slavery and African made. All that was needed was motive to act on these attitudes.

This was supplied by the wilderness itself: untamed, desolate, making its inhabitants feel isolated from the society they had known. The forest produced anxious longings for an England lost, and settlers responded by emphasizing their heritage, those Christian, civilized, controlled qualities which differentiated them from the savages. Indians, part of the landscape and thus symbolic of the forest, were killed or driven westward. Africans, captive newcomers to America, were enslaved and dealt with through laws which distinguished them from the English. The legislation they condoned not only served the obvious purpose of chaining the blacks but also of reassuring themselves. They were in control of the Africans and of themselves. And they were acting together to deal with an alien group. That the harsh community codes governing slavery also eased the guilt of the individual masters was a comforting by-product of the situation.

Circumstances in Pennsylvania did not reflect these generalizations in every detail. When the Quakers arrived, Negroes were already resident in the Delaware River region, having been brought in by the Swedes and the Dutch years earlier. But blacks were also shipped to the area after 1682, partly in response to specific requests. By 1700 an estimated four to five hundred Negroes lived in the province, mostly in Philadelphia. (Slavery in Pennsylvania, unlike more southerly colonies, was predominantly urban.) By this time the city's merchants could engage in slaving, the monopoly of the Royal African Company having been dissolved in 1698, but apparently it was not until after 1730 that many of them entered the trade, taking their own vessels to the West Indies and southern continental colonies where they chose the slaves who would be sold at home. Previous to this time small consignments of inferior slaves were imported, never more than fifty a year before 1715 and rarely as many as 150 a year before 1730. As early as 1705, and in several sessions thereafter, the Assembly passed acts assigning prohibitive duties to Negro importation, all of which were disallowed in England. In 1729 a compromise measure, levying a tax of only £2, was permitted by the home government to become law.

Prominent Quakers such as Isaac Norris and Jonathan Dickinson merchandised slaves, as did non-Quakers. Robert Ellis, an Anglican, was born about the time Pennsylvania was founded and lived in the colony at least as early as 1706. Fifteen years later he was a freeman in Philadelphia, trading in his own ships from his own wharf located near his Water Street house. Before he handled black slaves he was importing white servants, and his range of activities reached beyond the traffic in human beings. He might send wheat, bread, flour, and staves to Madeira where he picked up wines to be taken to Georgia, or South Carolina, Virginia, New York, Rhode Island. He also sailed into Cadiz, Lisbon, Rotterdam, and London; his London agent not only handled his buying and selling but his maritime insurance. Much of his trade was with Barbados, Jamaica, Antigua, and St. Christopher; as elsewhere, he consistently dealt with the same merchant house in each port. In the West Indies he received, in addition to rum, molasses, and sugar, the Negro slaves which he sold in and around Philadelphia and occasionally in Virginia, though his trade in blacks had begun with imports from South Carolina in about 1723. Ellis' motives appear to have been strictly commercial. He pushed slaves into a restricted market. By mid-century, ironically, he had difficulty procuring enough Negroes to meet demands; he died, deeply in debt, in 1750. Just as Africans had inhabited the Delaware Valley region before the Quaker arrival and the colonists adjusted to their presence almost willy-nilly, so the slave trade magnified the black presence thoughtlessly, leaving its consequences for later generations.

Of course, the home government, by disallowing legislation to make the importation of slaves prohibitively expensive, contributed its share to future racial conflicts. With similar disregard for English colonials, London officialdom had established a policy of shipping convicts to America, which provided the reaction in Pennsylvania that "no felons be brought into this country" (1683). Almost thirty years later the colony passed its first exclusion law, setting an import duty of £5 on every entering convict and requiring a bond of £50 from the importer for one year's good behavior; similar legislation passed in subsequent sessions. Although these acts were not allowed and became a source of conflict between the Pennsylvania and English governments, the colony was not the recipient of many convicts.

Rather, the early supply of white servants to Pennsylvania came from the British Isles of their own volition. The appeal was great. Gabriel Thomas, who had himself come to the province with the first settlers, wrote a glowing description of the place. In the *Historical and Geographical Account of the Province and Country of Pennsylvania and of West Jersey in America* (1694) he promised that "Poor People, both Men and Women, can here get three times the Wages for their Labor they can in ENGLAND or WALES." It was from these two countries that servants first came to Pennsylvania, but later Scotland and Ireland became the main source of supply.

The Scotch-Irish immigrants, Scots who had left their native land in the very early seventeenth century for northern Ireland before coming to America, emerged from a background of material insecurity and ideological certainty. Scotland in 1600 was economically and politically retarded, poor, and lawless. All towns and most of the population were in the Lowlands, which had only limited arable land farmed by tenants of various gradations; the freeholders (or lairds) and the noble landholders were but a small fraction of the population. With a hostile England on the southern border and noblemen carrying on their private feuds, life was violent, squalid, and mean. Tenants lived with their cattle in earthen-floored hovels without windows or chimneys. Disease ran rampant. Agriculture was primitive, the grain sown was of the poorest kind, no longer grown in other parts of Europe, and wheaten bread simply was not produced. Farm implements were similarly anachronistic.

A land where morals were unknown rather than unheeded and superstition was ubiquitous could not have appeared as the most fertile ground for Protestant reformers, but John Knox welcomed the challenge. His narrowness and rigidity complemented the ignorance of the Scots, while his dour countenance and relentless spirit was equal to the natural elements which ruled their lives. Once imprisoned for his faith, he was now a captive of Calvinism, a fiery preacher who depicted Catholicism as hell and a reforming, dogmatic Protestantism as salvation. The New Kirk gave Scots a sip of democracy, a swig of education, and a reservoir of religion, all-consuming and intolerant, the Spoken Word branded on the illiterate mind.

Knox had arrived in 1559, but half a century later, when James I (formerly James VI of Scotland) promoted the colonization of northern Ireland, or Ulster, by the Scots, the Calvinistic convictions were as strong as ever. Although the initial attraction of Ulster was fertile land, which Scots could acquire on easy terms just as landlords were pressing tenants off their scrubby acres at home, it was the enforced policy of episcopacy under Charles II and James II which later drove the Covenanters to the comparatively free shores of northern Ireland. There they fought off the dispossessed Irish and the ravaging wolves, raised sheep, drained swamps and bogs, and for the first time planted potatoes. The Presbyterian ministers they followed to the new land provided stability and continuity; as in New England, preachers were the purveyors of the traditional culture.

Indeed, there was practically no intermarriage with the native Irish. Ulster Presbyterianism was conservative, a pristine Calvinism characterized by an emphasis on individual discipline that was maintained by group surveillance. Yet self-discipline had not extended to acceptance of economic conditions in Scotland, and the discontent which fostered emigration could be seen in an individualism which was not responsive to community pressures. If adjustment to life in northern Ireland required adaptability, it did not produce flexibility. Rather, the character of the Ulsterman was an exaggeration of the Scottish personality.

Life was prosperous until the early eighteenth century, when the cloth industry was dealt a severe blow by the Woolens Act of 1699 while the rack-renting policy of landlords virtually thrust tenants off the land. Added to these economic burdens was an oppressive religious stance embodied in a Test Act which drove or threatened to drive Presbyterian ministers from their churches. Reports from America, especially Pennsylvania, were encouraging, the result being the migration of an estimated two hundred thousand Scotch-Irish in the sixty years before the American Revolution. Most came as indentured servants.

Some of the first immigrants went straight to Boston, anticipating the congeniality of Calvinism but receiving a frosty New England welcome. None went directly to the slave colonies, though later they would find their way south into the backcountry of Virginia and the Carolinas by way of the Shenandoah Valley. Initially, then, going to America meant migrating to Pennsylvania, the ports of Philadelphia, Chester, and New Castle being the points of entry.

Simultaneously with the beginnings of Scotch-Irish immigration was the entrance into Pennsylvania of German-speaking peoples. Even before William Penn had conceived of his "holy experiment" he had preached in the Rhine country. His *Some Account of the Province of Pennsilvania* (1681) was quickly translated into German at Amsterdam and Dutch at Rotterdam, the latter being the home of Penn's friend Benjamin Furley, the Quaker merchant who saw that word of Pennsylvania was broadcast into Germany. Thus, Francis Daniel Pastorius' *Umstandige geographische Beschreibung* (1700) and Daniel Falckner's *Curieuse Nachricht von Pennsylvania* (1702), among other works, were well circulated. In his role as colonizer, Penn had been a strong exponent of mercantilist theory, emphasizing the increased value of labor in the plantations. For those Englishmen who in the early eighteenth century worried that the exodus of their fellow countrymen to America could weaken the homeland, there was great appeal in the thought of German Protestants populating the New World.

Penn authored a general naturalization bill for the colonies in 1708, arguing that it was in "the interest of England to improve and thicken her colonys with people not her own." Although the act became law in March 1709, the British government was not prepared for the more than eleven thousand Palatines, émigrés from the war-torn Rhine Valley in Germany, who gathered in London in an almost totally dependent situation. At first intrigued with the novelty, Londoners were initially generous in their judgment: "On the whole, they appear to be an innocent, laborious, peacable, healthy and ingenuous people, and may be reckoned a blessing than a burden to any nation where they shall be settled." Soon, however, they were being attacked by the mob without and by disease within. Yet Penn was not financially able to send them to the Quaker province. It was an inauspicious but symptomatic beginning for German immigration. A few of these Palatines were sent to Ireland and Carolina, but most went to New York to manufacture naval stores for the British government in return for their passage, a sort of government redemptioner system. In 1723 fifteen of these families, including that of Conrad Weiser, pushed on to the Tulpehocken region of Pennsylvania, now in Berks County.

Despite Penn's widespread advertising and his explication of the "holy experiment" as a laboratory for all peoples, the settlement at Germantown marked the boundaries of non-British immigration until 1710, when a group of Swiss Mennonites settled at Pequea Creek, south of Tulpehocken, in what became Lancaster County two decades later. These sectarians, persecuted by Reformed Protestants in their home country, had sought refuge in the Palatinate, where their pacifism and other peculiarities found no more favor. Mennonites were already settled in Germantown, and in 1710 hundreds, possibly thousands, of the brethren settled farther west, to be followed later by other like-minded sectarians, such as Dunkards (1719), Schwenkfelders (1733), and Moravians (1741). More important, at least in sheer numbers, were the church groups, the Lutherans and the Reformed Germans.

It was in 1717 that the influx of Germans to Philadelphia created concern, Governor Keith giving his opinion that immigration could prove dangerous. A decade later, when the stream again swelled notably, the Council adopted a resolution that all Germans entering Pennsylvania should be listed by name, occupation, and place of origin, in addition to which a pledge of loyalty to the crown must be taken. At this time an estimated 15,000 to 20,000 Germans lived in the province; close to 70,000 more arrived before the Revolution, making a total population, with allowance for natural increase, of 110,000.

The fundamental cause of this immense migration was to be

found in European rather than American conditions. Unlike Scotland, Germany in the sixteenth century was making giant strides toward the modern age, as the foundations of large-scale commerce were laid, cities grew, and agricultural production kept pace. But the Thirty Years War (1618–1648) wiped out these gains and more. Population plummeted, some cities actually being decimated, and farming suffered proportionately, both in terms of cultivated land and livestock. Indeed, not until the end of the eighteenth century were the earlier agricultural conditions reestablished. Under these conditions, peasants lived on a marginal level at best. Though the state intervened in the economy—this, after all, was the assumption of mercantilism— its policies were intent on ensuring stability, which meant keeping the peasants in their place. Mobility was temporarily arrested socially, only to take place later geographically.

Thus, the German peasant at 1700 was personally subject to his lord, most often in a servile relationship which demanded of him and his family services and payments. However, most tenants could bequeath land to members of their own families. Their lot remained difficult, not least of all due to the contempt with which they were held by their superiors. The sixteenth-century rhyme, "The peasant could take the ox's place / Had he but horns above his face," recurred in the eighteenth-century lawyer's observation that "the peasants stand between the unreasoning beast and man." And in Württemberg in the Palatinate, where the Pennsylvania Germans originated, it was said that many peasants lived "in a kind of slavery. . . . Often they are not as well off as cattle elsewhere."

Indeed, it was not until the late eighteenth century that methods of animal husbandry began to improve, largely as a result of the increased production of fodder (clover and turnips). The introduction of these crops was intended to replace the three-field system with scientific rotation. The result, more and fatter animals yielding more manure, in turn enriching the soil, was clearly beneficial to the German peasant as it had been to the English farmer a century earlier. But these reforms largely came after the exodus to America, and it is by no means certain that agricultural improvements would have stemmed the tide of migration.

After the devastation of the Thirty Years War, the armies of Louis XIV marched through and raided the Palatinate with impunity. Even Louis' style of life invaded the Rhine Valley, as minor princes and despots sought to emulate the sumptuousness of Versailles in their own castles, efforts that sent taxes soaring. The coincidence of a few events was enough to precipitate the westward flow. In May and September of 1707 the French plundered southwestern Germany. The winter of 1708/9 was the cruelest in a century, killing fruit trees and vines. In the spring of 1709 the first group of Palatines left for England and, later, New York. A much larger company followed on their heels the next year. After that, the tide ebbed and flowed, but was always substantial.

The stream of immigration, once begun, was pumped up by men who saw an opportunity for profit in it. Immigrant agents, often referred to as *Nueländer* (newlanders), were employed by ship companies in England or Holland to recruit passengers to America. Often dressing to affect wealth supposedly gotten in the New World, carrying advertisements and skillfully forged letters from successful immigrants known to the prospective recruits, the newlanders traveled from house to house proselytizing. Although a German newspaper in Pennsylvania reported in 1751 that the Elector Palatine had threatened these agents with prison, their activities continued.

By this time, however, another sort of literature had begun to emerge, the most famous piece of which was *Reise nach Pennsylvanie* (*Journey to Pennsylvania*), published in 1756 by Gottlieb Mittelberger, a native of Württemberg who came on invitation to Philadelphia in 1750 to serve New Providence township as organist and schoolmaster. He returned four years later, at which time "numerous Würtembeyer, Durlacher, and Palatines (a great many of whom live there and spend their days moaning about ever having left their native country) begged me with tears and uplifted hands, and even in the name of God, to publish their misery and sorrow in Germany." Mittelberger promised to reveal both good and bad aspects of immigration, but he inclined to the latter, asserting that for most immigrants the journey would involve "the loss of all they possess, of freedom and peace," and for some the loss of their lives and even their souls.

It was a long and trying trip, lasting from the beginning of May until the end of October: four to six weeks on the Rhine, another month and a half in Holland, an uncertain voyage of a week to a month reaching England, and two to three months from weighing anchor to landing in Philadelphia. The cost of getting to Rotterdam, barring emergencies, could not be less than forty florins, and the passage to Pennsylvania, including board, was sixty florins for anyone over ten. But Mittelberger assured his readers that many travelers spent 200 florins (about £34) from home to Philadelphia. And the cost was not the worst part!

The "pitiful signs of distress" on the journey should have given any traveler pause: "smells, fumes, horrors, vomiting, various kinds of sea sickness, fever, dysentery, headaches, heat, constipation, boils, scurvy, cancer, mouth-rot. . . . caused by the age and the highly-salted state of the food, especially of the meat, as well as by the very bad and filthy water. . . . hunger, thirst, frost, heat, dampness, fear, misery, vexation, and lamentation. . . . so many lice, especially on the sick people, that they have to be scraped off the body." All of these miseries were compounded in a storm, but even in good weather the conditions turned people against one another, and finally most passengers wished they had never left home.

And, said Mittelberger, many never saw land again. Children under seven seldom survived; "parents must often watch their offspring suffer miserably, die, and be thrown into the ocean." But reaching Philadelphia was not inevitable good fortune. Those who lacked funds or security for the sea freight had to be purchased; adults bound themselves from three to six years, while children had to serve until twenty-one. "Many parents in order to pay their fares in this way and get off the ship must barter and sell their children as if they were cattle." Thus were whole families separated under the so-called redemptioner system. Work in America was as strenuous as in Germany, with no chance of running away from a harsh master. Worse still, servants were exposed to a variety of religious, or irreligious, ideas. Mittelberger could understand the exodus to Pennsylvania only by blaming "the swindles and perversions practiced by the so-called Newlanders."

Other narratives besides Mittelberger's testified to the veracity of his recollections. Johannas Naas remembered the crossing with horror: "I do not think that with all the unclean spirits of Hell there could be worse going on with cursing, swearing, and drinking, quarreling day and night. . . . Husband, wife and children fought bitterly." Johann Carl Buettner recalled the humiliation, after a storm had torn away the private chambers on the deck, of passengers having to relieve themselves publicly while holding onto the ship's rope for dear life. Surely such extraordinary personal encounters must have left a deep imprint on family and social relationships in the New World.

But memories of the journey to Pennsylvania were often short, while conditions in the province were compensatory. The German newspaper editor Christopher Sauer recalled at mid-century: "When I came into this province and found everything to the contrary where I came from, I wrote largely to all my friends and acquaintances of the civil and religious liberties [and] privileges, and of all the goodness I have heard and seen. My letters were printed and reprinted, and provoked many a thousand people to come to this province. Many thanked the Lord for it, and desired their friends also again to come here."

The "goodness" referred to by Sauer and others was the economic opportunity: high wages, plenty of food, lots of land. By the 1720s, at least, the reputation of Pennsylvania for tolerance of diversity and encouragement to the industrious was established. Mittelberger himself described the physical attributes of Pennsylvania in terms as glowing as any used by the proprietor. And though he noted that constant hard work was the lot of the immigrant, he also pointed out that "all trades and professions bring in good money. No beggars are to be seen; for every township feeds and takes care of its poor." The servant woman in Pennsylvania dressed as well as the aristocratic lady in Germany!

Still, a servant was considered the chattel of the master.

Pennsylvania and New York were the only two colonies where his indenture could not be bought and sold freely; court consent was necessary in these two colonies in order to assign a servant for over a year. The servant could not marry without his master's approval, or vote, or engage in trade. Though he could hold property, money earned in his spare time could be taken by his master. But because of his color and his religion, he was afforded protections not available to the slave. The terms of his indenture were generally honored in court, where he could sue and expect to find justice. And when he was freed, he got his "dues." At first, Penn had promised 50 acres; later, the dues amounted to two suits of clothes (one new), an axe, and two hoes.

The conditions under which the white servant and the black slave labored were otherwise identical. Provisions for food and clothing were the same. Both were employed in agriculture but were also trained in the various trades. Neither was entirely welcome, as Alexander Mackraby made clear in writing to his brother: "You can have no idea of the plague we have with servants on this side of the water. If you bring over a good one he is spoilt in a month. Those born in the country are insolent and extravagent. The imported Dutch are to the last degree ignorant and awkward. The Irish (upon which establishment my gentleman is) are generally thieves, and particularly drunkards; and the negroes stupid and sulky, and stink damnably. We have tried them all around, and this is the sum total of my observations, ' 'tis the devil take the hindmost.' "

But to focus on servile conditions and aristocratic contempt was to miss the point of the psychological effect of immigrating to Pennsylvania. Mittelberger did not overlook this meaning. The province "offers people more freedom than the other English colonies, since all religious sects are tolerated there. . . . Freedom in Pennsylvania extends so far that everyone's property . . . is exempt from any interference or taxation. . . . Liberty in Pennsylvania does more harm than good to many people, both in soul and body. They have a saying here: Pennsylvania is heaven for farmers, paradise for artisans, and hell for officials and preachers." This atmosphere both intrigued and repelled the German visitor. He described court cases of impregnated females, whose condition he attributed to the fact that "women possess considerable privileges and liberties," an observation probably influenced by his own wife's absence. He enjoyed telling the story of a charlatan preacher who exposed his bare behind in public, compensating for his unseemly relish by labeling the tale "a disgusting incident." Obviously, Mittelberger was made uncomfortable by what he perceived to be the consequences of liberty. He returned to Germany, but thousands of other immigrants remained, content or even happy with the change in conditions.

Migration was a selective process, drawing off the more discontent members of a society. It was by no means clear, however, that migrants rejected the values of the society they left, despite the fact that they probably were, as a group, antisocial. In Massachusetts Bay the immigrants were more traditional in their thinking than their peers left behind. But in Pennsylvania the newcomers, not only in the eighteenth century but from the time of the colony's founding, seemed to embrace the liberties of the New World.

At least William Penn thought so. He had put forward plans for the government of the place and for its orderly settlement and development. In the sphere of politics his blueprints were altered until, in 1701, the structure suited not him but the colonists, who built the new political edifice in a spirit Penn considered unbecoming when not incomprehensible. Similar changes took place in social life and institutions: the patterns envisioned by Penn were notably altered by the settlers. The proprietor's penchant for order, for the straight line and the right angle as the guiding principle of human organization, was somewhat in character with the triumph of discipline over spontaneity in Quakerism. He was a proponent of religious toleration but not social anarchy. Even the natural bounty of Pennsylvania was appreciated for its usefulness to society; man was superior to nature.

Indeed, Penn left no doubt as to his thinking on this matter when he imposed a gridiron plan on the forest to create Philadelphia. And when the initial settlers appeared to succumb to the lures of the frontier, Penn warned the city magistrates: "There is a cry comes over into thes parts agst the number of the

drinking houses & Loosness that is committed in the caves."
Provincial laws were aimed at preventing "clandestine Loose,
and Unseemly proceedings," a statutory response which was not
heeded, judging by the excesses of Pennsylvania politics.

For country living, Penn's thinking was similarly pervaded by
orderliness. He proposed a five-thousand-acre township, square,
with the village in the center and a symmetric layout of the
houses. In *A Further Account of Pennsylvania* (1685) he wrote:
"Many that had right to more Land were at first covetous to
have their whole quantity without regard to this way of
settlement, tho' by such Wilderness vacancies they had ruined
the Country, and then our interest of course. I had in my view
Society, Assistance, Busy Commerce, Instruction of Youth,
Government of Peoples manners, Conveniency of Religions
Assembling, Encouragement of Mechanicks, distinct and beaten
Roads, and it has answered in all those respects, I think, to an
Universall Content." Though the judgment was premature,
Penn was attempting to execute his plan.

Through the agency of a land office staffed by the provincial
secretary, a surveyor general, and three to five commissioners of
property, all proprietary appointees, the matters of field surveys,
land grants, and titles would be handled. For about two decades
the land office operated with partial success, although Penn's
plan in 1690 for a major settlement (100,000 acres and a city on
the east side of the Susquehanna River) was never realized.
Again, the proprietor's financial condition dictated behavior
which diverged from his original intentions. He sold land to
speculators, and he did not enforce the proviso that settlers be on
the land within three years or ownership rights must be forfeited.
Contrary to his statement about "Wilderness vacancies," he
allowed "townships" to be laid out beyond the line of settlement.
And proprietary manors were designated: one-tenth of the land
in all townships, according to the royal charter, but the figure
might be as high as one-fifth, the case in Chester County.
Pennsylvanians viewed these practices as speculative operations,
another irritating feature of Penn's land policy. That land
policies in the neighboring colonies of New York and Maryland
were truly aristocratic, involving the creation of great private

.

estates with special privileges for their owners, did not soften the judgment made on Penn. And this antiproprietary feeling spilled over into politics, making the task of the underpaid land office staff even more difficult.

By the turn of the century a new ingredient further diluted Penn's concept of orderly settlement. People were settling on the land before getting survey warrants; though, in the interest of their own security, they usually applied for them later. The proprietor, apparently unwilling to accept this pragmatic approach to occupation, bemoaned "land enter'd upon without any regular Method." He worried about the difficulties of administration and the loss of revenue. But after his death in 1718 the land office became almost inoperative for a decade and a half, encouraging even more squatting and its consequent problems.

Related to regularity in land occupation was Penn's expectation that the settlers would gather in agricultural villages. Commerce and transportation, education and religion, even the proper observation of social convention would be facilitated by such clusters of people. Farmers, like artisans, would have town houses, though each farm, extending outward from the village, would be one lot rather than a congeries of scattered fields in the European tradition. Farm size would vary from 100 to 500 acres; farm locations along a road bisecting the township were planned; future generations would be provided for by setting aside land for children. The centripetal force of village life would be accentuated by the central location of the meetinghouse, local (or township) administration of affairs, and proprietary control of land tenure by land disposition, rent, and even the placement of mills and ferries. Penn, whose paternalism was evident in these plans, went so far as to calculate that ten families would live in each township. He encouraged the first purchasers of land in the province, who bought township-sized chunks, to follow his concept of settlement.

Thomas Holme, Penn's faithful surveyor general, laid out regular townships and published maps of his work until his death in 1696. But, despite Penn's early assertion to the contrary, the colonists were not settling in agricultural villages. Farms were widely dispersed. Townships were administratively unimportant.

Penn's idea of regular local communities was not effected. The fault was partly his own. Rather than granting land, he sold it, forsaking control in favor of underwriting his venture. The people accentuated this. In the Charter of Property of 1701, the Assembly-initiated document which Penn accepted, then rejected, the individual landholder was given powers which the proprietor had initially denied him regarding land disposal. Land grants without proprietary strings became the practice in Pennsylvania, despite Penn's retraction of the Charter of Property.

As to the faltering role of the township as a unit of local government, Penn did not endow it with sufficient power. The county was created stronger and overshadowed the township. Nor did the township define ecclesiastical boundaries; meeting-houses were neither centrally located nor coincident with political lines. Schools, though initially attached to religious groups, largely Quaker at this time, were haphazardly located when they existed at all. Economic institutions in this preindustrial era were located alongside the individuals who operated them—blacksmiths or shopkeepers, ferry operators or millers—and might serve as the beginnings of a community. There were also the itinerant entrepreneurs, butchers, tailors, and shoemakers, as well as cottage industries, especially weaving. Transportation in the early eighteenth century was hardly developed. Institutional life in Pennsylvania encouraged dispersal.

In Massachusetts, by way of contrast, a town-centered society grew up in response to a variant manner of granting land, different powers of local government, and a topography that favored the gathering of people. At the other extreme was Virginia, where extensive waterways, large land grants, and county/vestry organization produced greater dispersal than in Pennsylvania. Rural communities existed in Pennsylvania, but they were not so precise, so easily comprehended on a map as in New England. The divergence in settlement patterns might be viewed in terms of the contrast between Puritanism and Quakerism, the former being a more structured religion, with its emphasis on pastor, Bible, strict membership requirements, than the latter. And as other denominations reached the Pennsylvania backcountry, the theological aspect of dispersal was accentuated. Religious distinctions were of real significance.

From the founding of the colony, segregation of national groups had taken place, the Germans and the Welsh living apart from the English Quakers. These divisions continued into the eighteenth century. The English were dominant in the east, the Germans in the north, the Scotch-Irish in the west, though there were overlapping areas, as in the south, where Scotch-Irish settled among the English and between the English and the Germans. Furthermore, it was important that the immigrants (Africans, of course, excepted) were virtually all Protestant, drawn from the large middle stratum of western European society and sharing a belief in bourgeois liberal individualism (rather than communitarianism) and the psychic disposition that made immigration possible. Coming from and moving into agricultural societies, their farming techniques and dietary preferences were largely the same. The ways in which they occupied, organized, and used the land were hardly at odds. Despite differences in language and customs stemming from divergent Old World backgrounds, variation in economic status or even social practice among immigrants was not notable in Pennsylvania. It was fairly common for national groups to mix.

Religious distinctions, however, persisted. The sectarian nature of Quakerism was reproduced among the Mennonites, most important of the German sects, as well as Dunkards, Schwenkfelders, and Moravians. Perfectionist and sometimes otherworldly, exclusive and self-righteous, individually hard working yet advocates of mutual help, these groups attained a higher economic status than the members of traditional church denominations. Among the latter type, the Presbyterians were the largest, including many of the English and most of the Scotch-Irish, while the Germans were divided between the Lutheran and Reformed denominations. Anglicans were mainly located in Philadelphia.

But it was not religion nor, for that matter, the whole range of attitudes composing an ideology which alone determined a settler's behavior. He had also to consider the social and natural environment of his new home. Obviously, if he began life in

Pennsylvania as a servant he had little or no choice as to placement, except insofar as his demeanor might appeal to a prospective master. But assuming that the immigrant would, on arrival, begin farming in the hinterlands of the Delaware River, what would determine his choice of place?

The natural environment of Pennsylvania corresponded to that of western Europe, so that adaptation was relatively easy (again, Africans excluded). The climate, with a growing season ranging from 165 to 200 days, was favorable to raising a wide variety of crops and livestock. The gently sloping quality of the land and the fertility of the soil were also friendly to prosperous farming. The drainage system was less important for navigation than as a source of energy. No single national group excelled any other in locating farms that benefited from all these qualities: good soil, level land, and accessible water, not to mention proximity to markets and courts. Choices were dictated in part by the availability of unoccupied or unsurveyed land. Germans had to come into the province through Philadelphia after 1725, where they took the required loyalty oath, whereas the Scotch-Irish could debark at New Castle, and thus were prone to settle farther south. To this extent, and by the fact of earlier settlement exerting some pull on later arrivals of fellow countrymen, national background did influence placement.

It apparently had no effect on crops grown or livestock raised. The shared European background was determinative; maize was the only local addition. Wheat, of course, was far and away the major crop. Rye was sown to the amount of one-fifth to one-third the acreage of wheat, with spring grains, oats, barley, buckwheat, hemp, and flax also in cultivation. Fruit orchards and vegetable gardens were common. Forage crops included clover, bluegrass, and timothy. Horses, cattle, pigs, and some sheep were raised, but by no particular national group. Farming was extensive, although the techniques of intensive use of the land already adopted in England and to a lesser degree in Germany—crop rotation and manuring—were recognized if hardly utilized in Pennsylvania. Neither of these practices, nor such other departures as meadow draining or stall-feeding of cattle, could be attributed to any one group. Indebtedness, farm ownership, as opposed to tenancy, mobility, wealth—none of these qualities could be assigned by national background. It is safe to say the American melting pot was working in early eighteenth-century rural Pennsylvania.

American ingenuity was not. Contemporary observers frequently noted the absence of innovation on farms, which probably meant that the tillers and husbandmen were satisfied with the results of their mixed agricultural methods. Wheat yields were low, twenty to forty bushels per acre on new land but only five to twelve on old. The meat and dairy products derived from cattle were seen as scanty, at least by Europeans. Live weight probably varied from six hundred to a thousand pounds, while a cow commonly produced but a quart of milk a day; two gallons were necessary for a pound of butter. The care and quality of feed for cattle was simply not a matter of concern; there was no selective breeding. Sheep were generally small and the quality of wool poor. Perhaps 50 acres of the average farm of 125 acres was uncleared; almost half of the remainder would be devoted to crops, the rest for meadow, pasture, and homestead. Crop rotation was haphazard, with six-field rotation most often used, a year each for wheat, barley, and corn, followed by three fallow years, or some variant of this system; and clover and grasses were not introduced until about 1750, a full century behind English practice. The importance of using fertilizer—manure, lime, or gypsum—was unrecognized, at least before mid-century. Plows were primitive, and there was small interest in labor-saving devices; few were invented.

Still, the average farmer not only produced enough for his family but had a surplus to sell as well. And the profitability of wheat discouraged interest in alternate uses of the land or in livestock. Rather, conditions promoted the continuation of extensive rather than intensive farming. A farmer alone could probably not cultivate more than twelve acres in one year, and until population pressures caused the subdivision of farm lands to the point where livestock could not be maintained on fallow land, there was no apparent need to raise fodder, rotate crops, use fertilizer, or turn to technology and a more scientific approach to the land.

The settlers in Pennsylvania adapted to their environment. If in agriculture this allowed them to remain tied to old ways while Europeans were at the same time being forced to find new methods of dealing with the land, in social intercourse the novelty of the New World was apparent. William Penn's attempts to impose order on the wilderness were jettisoned not only by the extraordinary growth and diversity of population and its uncontrolled dispersal westward from Philadelphia but also by a spirit inimical to restraint. Indentured servitude, an Old World institution adapted to America, could not survive in these conditions. Slavery, a New World creation, was more durable, because it was an answer to the anxieties generated by freedom. The "holy experiment" was producing results which the proprietor had never envisioned.

6

A GRAFTING: BENJAMIN FRANKLIN, AGENT OF CHANGE

Early on a Sunday morning in October 1723 a tired young man stepped off the boat from Burlington onto the Market Street wharf in Philadelphia. "I was in my working dress, my best clothes being to come round by sea. I was dirty from my journey; my pockets were stuffed out with shirts and stockings; and I knew no soul nor where to look for lodging. I was fatigued with travelling, rowing, and want of rest; I was very hungry; and my whole stock of cash consisted of a Dutch dollar and about a shilling in copper." For breakfast he bought "three great puffy rolls . . . and, having no room in my pockets, walked off with a roll under each arm, and eating the other . . . I made . . . a most awkward, ridiculous appearance." Other immigrants to Pennsylvania entered inauspiciously but none were to rise to such heights as Benjamin Franklin. The story of his achievement would become the metaphor of success in America—as, indeed, he wanted it to be when he recreated it in his *Autobiography*.

For a man whose name is synonymous with mobility, Franklin had a surprisingly strong sense of family roots. He learned from an uncle that the Franklins had lived in Ecton, Northampton-shire, for at least three hundred years and, on searching the parish register, discovered that he "was the youngest son of the youngest son for five generations"; the records went back no further. More to the point of his own career, his Uncle Thomas was a "scrivener; became a considerable man in the country; was a chief mover of all public-spirited undertakings for the county or

Portrait of Benjamin Franklin by Robert Feke. *Harvard University Portrait Collection, bequest to Harvard College by Dr. John C. Warren, 1856.*

town of Northampton, and his own village." (There was some speculation within the family of transmigration of souls from uncle to nephew.) Another uncle, Benjamin, left some poetry and was "much of a politician." But he was also "very pious," something the younger Benjamin was not. This uncle, who lived in the Franklin household in Boston for several years, retailed anecdotes of the family's Protestant nonconformity in England.

It was religious conflict which drove Josiah Franklin to America in 1683 with his wife and three children. Four more youngsters came before her death. His remarriage produced an additional ten, Benjamin being the youngest son and third-youngest child. Josiah was a man of "excellent constitution of body," was skilled in drawing and music, "had a mechanical genius, too . . . but his great excellence lay in a sound understanding and solid judgement in prudential matters, both in public and private affairs." He was a fine model, even if there had been no others; he "convinced me that nothing was useful which was not honest."

Franklin had less to say about his mother, Abiah Folger, though her roots and family were not unimportant. She was the daughter of Peter Folger, "one of the first settlers of New England. . . . he wrote sundry small occasional pieces, but only one of them was printed. . . . It was in favor of liberty of conscience." Abiah breast-fed all ten of her children, an act which her youngest son interpreted as an indication of her "excellent constitution," though it also demonstrated the healthy mothering he received.

Benjamin's elder brothers were tradesmen, but Josiah, a grandfatherly fifty years at his youngest son's birth, decided to send the bookish boy to grammar school at age eight, though a year was as much as he could afford. Benjamin did spend a second year studying writing and arithmetic before he was apprenticed, thus forsaking his "strong inclination for the sea." Two years of tallow chandling convinced the boy that he was in the wrong line of work and, after Josiah allowed him to observe different tradesmen at work, he settled into printing as the apprentice to his half-brother James.

That he managed a great amount of reading over the next

several years was testimony to self-discipline as well as curiosity. When one of his books led him to vegetarianism, he ate alone and utilized for study the time others took for meals outside. His choice of books forecast his future development: *Pilgrim's Progress* (and, later, the rest of Bunyan) and Plutarch's *Lives* contributed to a sense of personal destiny, while Defoe's *Essay on Projects* and Cotton Mather's *Essays to Do Good* provided a means to greatness through public achievement. His omnivorous appetite for reading, later paralleled in his joy of life, was reflected in Burton's *Historical Reflections* (an omnibus of literature), books on arithmetic, navigation, grammar, politics, and—not least important—Locke's *Essay Concerning Human Understanding.* Stumbling by chance across a volume of the *Spectator,* he used it as a model for his own prose, paying close attention to the "stock of words . . . measure . . . rhyme . . . variety . . . order . . . arrangement of thoughts. . . . I sometimes had the pleasure of fancying that, in certain particulars of small import, I had been lucky enough to improve the method or the language, and this encouraged me to think I might possibly in time come to be a tolerable English writer, of which I was extremely ambitious."

Indeed, he was so bent on publication that at age sixteen he submitted an essay to his brother's paper, the *New England Courant,* under the pseudonym Silence Dogood, the first of a number of literary roles he would play. In opening her second of fourteen letters, Silence announced: "Histories of Lives are seldom entertaining, unless they contain something either admirable or exemplar." Franklin set out at an early age to shape his own life in this fashion. Quarreling with James (the younger brother resented "the blows his passion too often urged him to bestow upon me, though he was otherwise not an ill-natured man. Perhaps I was too saucy and provoking"), he escaped his apprenticeship for the freedom of the world beyond Boston; he was to see his father only three more times.

The Philadelphia which Franklin entered was particularly receptive to an ambitious young man. Where Boston was a long-established place, with mature social institutions which reflected religious and economic distinctions, Philadelphia was in its adolescence, as unformed as the seventeen-year-old who straggled in that Sunday morning. But Market Street wharf where Franklin landed, one of the many that distinguished the city's waterfront, testified to a thriving commerce that was fostering the growth of class divisions. The plain brick houses that lined the unpaved streets also bespoke prosperity. From these domiciles emerged the "clean-dressed people" whom Franklin followed to a Quaker meetinghouse where, in the silence, he promptly fell asleep.

Though Franklin sometimes pretended indifference to the spiritual qualities of the Quakers, he was impressed by their material achievements. The ships of Quaker merchants sailed to the West Indies, still the major trading area for Pennsylvanians, although by the mid-1730s the British Isles would be equally important. Southern European and coastal North American commerce also gained notably. Cargoes containing books and immigrants raised Philadelphia from mere provinciality to some semblance of urbanity. The mainstay of exports was the grain gathered from the city's hinterland, which stretched forty miles west from the Delaware at the time of Franklin's arrival. As the population of the province mounted from thirty-one thousand to eighty-five thousand in the years between 1720 and 1740, attention had to be paid to the development of highways, ensuring that Philadelphia would remain the focus of provincial life.

In the city itself, which had grown in barely four decades to some ten thousand inhabitants (only two thousand short of Boston and three thousand ahead of New York) there were increasing signs of heterogeneity as some of the German and Scotch-Irish immigrants remained at the point of debarkation. Even before this influx, Anglicans and Swedish Lutherans had made their presence known through the erection of churches whose architecture stood in notable contrast to the plain Quaker meetinghouse where Franklin fell asleep. In addition to the cultural stimulation and social antagonisms produced by the mixture of peoples, there was a real threat to the Society of Friends which young Benjamin's behavior clearly, if somnolently, portended.

Prosperity was general in Philadelphia, but the wealth was not equally distributed. The merchant group, acting in the manner of the upper strata elsewhere in America, distinguished itself from the lower orders in matters of dress and housing as well as through largely successful efforts at political control. Indeed, this power was used to forestall the sort of competition that would have enabled those in lower positions to grasp a larger portion of business profits. Money, after all, was the real barrier to success and status. The pervasive values of this society were bourgeois, and no one would be able to articulate them and, to outward appearances, live them better than Benjamin Franklin.

Arriving in Philadelphia with no financial resources, he quickly found employment in the printing shop of Samuel Keimer, though he respected neither Keimer, "a mere compositor," nor the rival printer in town, Andrew Bradford, "very illiterate." With an income and a room of his own in the home of his future wife, Deborah Read, Franklin enjoyed a freedom he had not known in Boston. Where formerly his existence had often been solitary—his closest companions were books—now he visited among "the young people of the town, that were lovers of reading, with whom I spent my evenings very pleasantly." When he returned to Boston for a visit in April, he offended his brother James by appearing in his printing shop in fine clothes, pockets ostentatiously filled with silver. He also called on Cotton Mather who, when the young man inadvertently walked into a low beam, advised him: "You are young, and have the world before you; stoop as you go through it, and you will miss many hard bumps."

Franklin did not take this advice. He had come to Boston to borrow money from his father so that he could set up a business of his own, having been encouraged to do so by the eccentric governor of Pennsylvania, Sir William Keith. (The young man was understandably impressed to have met the governors of Pennsylvania and New York shortly after leaving Massachusetts.) Josiah Franklin thought his son not sufficiently mature for the responsibility of a printing shop and refused the request. Governor Keith then promised to provide the capital and easily persuaded Benjamin to go to London to purchase stock and meet some booksellers as well. When Keith reneged on his pledge, the budding capitalist was stranded in London, barely a year after he reached Philadelphia, with some £12 to his name.

But if Franklin would not stoop, neither did he bump his head. As always, he turned a mistake into a lesson and an ultimate triumph. He immediately secured a printer's job, on the advice of a Quaker merchant, Thomas Denham, who assured him that "when you return to America, you will set up to greater advantage." He read more and took up writing again, producing *A Dissertation on Liberty and Necessity, Pleasure and Pain* which gained Franklin a small reputation, more friends, some of them eminent, and a few detractors who found his denial of natural virtue and vice, not to mention a hereafter, offensive. His success as a printer was partly due to his physical stamina; he reformed the dietary habits of his coworkers, taught swimming, and learned something about women during his eighteen-month stay.

Denham coaxed him back to Philadelphia with the promise of employment as clerk and bookkeeper, a task that added to Franklin's business acumen. But it ended several months later with Denham's untimely death, and the young man, barely twenty-one, reluctantly went back to work for Keimer, who now had five other men working in his shop. These included a Scotch-Irish indentured servant, an apprentice from the country, two other rural émigrés (one Welsh), and an Oxford scholar (also an indentured servant)—an index to the city's drawing power and an ingredient in its prosperity. A fluid though always short supply of labor was complemented by a relative dearth of craft guilds which would have controlled the trades; only cordwainers and tailors held corporate privileges. Although Franklin knew that Keimer had taken him on at high wages with the expectation that the young printer would train the others and could then be let go, Benjamin acquiesced because he realized he could set up for himself when he had the necessary equipment.

At this juncture capital was necessary for a new venture, and given Philadelphia's position as a commercial entrepôt, it was available. One of the men in Keimer's shop, Hugh Meredith, proposed that his father supply the money for a partnership, telling Franklin, "Your skill in the business shall be set against the stock I furnish, and we will share the profits equally."

Meredith's father came up with only half the promised sum, but Franklin found it easy to borrow from friends, buying his partner out in the summer of 1730, a little more than two years after they had joined. At the age of twenty-four he thus was the independent proprietor of a printing business which, among its regular chores, published weekly the *Pennsylvania Gazette*. His only rival in Philadelphia was Andrew Bradford, who had originally introduced him to Keimer.

Franklin owed his business achievement not only to the openness, prosperity, and friendliness to individual entrepreneurship of Philadelphia but also to his own special talents, not least of which was a mastery of technical problems. While working for Keimer, he recalled, "there was no letter-founder in America; I had seen types cast at James's in London, but without much attention to the manner; however, I now contrived a mould, made use of the letters we had as puncheons, struck the matrices in lead, and thus suppl'd in a pretty tolerable way all deficiencies. I also engrav'd several things on occasion; I made the ink, I was warehouseman, and everything, and, in short, quite a factotum." When Keimer was given the opportunity to print paper money for the colony of New Jersey, Franklin designed the first copperplate press to be used there and cut the ornaments for the bills. Furthermore, when he and Keimer journeyed to Burlington, Franklin "made an acquaintance with many principal people of the province." He was a charming companion, and he never failed to see the usefulness of friends.

Arguments as well as acquaintances had their utility. When the matter of paper money became an issue in Pennsylvania politics in 1729, Franklin, recalling that "the first small sum struck in 1723 had done much good by increasing the trade, employment and number of inhabitants in the province," anonymously published *A Modest Enquiry into the Nature and Necessity of a Paper Currency*, arguing not only from the viewpoint of the commercial interests but also for a labor theory of value. And, needless to say, he had not forgotten his own situation as a borrower. Franklin claimed that the common people applauded paper money while the rich did not, but by securing the printing contract when the measure passed the Assembly from "friends there, who conceiv'd I had been of some service," he took a step toward the ranks of the wealthy. For the achievement of such worldly success anonymity had its disguised purposes, but Franklin openly advocated self-advertisement: "In order to secure my credit and character as a tradesman, I took care not only to be in *reality* industrious and frugal, but to avoid all appearances to the contrary. I drest plainly; I was seen at no places of idle diversion . . . to show that I was not above my business, I sometimes brought home the paper I purchas'd at the stores thro' the streets on a wheelbarrow."

It was fitting that Franklin, whose success so exceeded the general parameters of upward mobility even in Philadelphia, should have been viewed as a typical example of the ability of an American workman to rise. He never tired of representing himself as a leather apron man; he made his achievements appear easy; he was an advertisement for himself, and also for a regimen that was probably not characteristic of the urban laborer. Storekeepers and craftsmen usually worked alone or with a helper and could be interrupted easily. Although the day stretched from sunrise to sunset, the pace was often slow and varied with the seasons. Franklin advocated greater regularity in work habits.

Respectably established in business and disturbed by the health hazards attendant on "intrigues with low women," Franklin took as his common-law wife Deborah Read who, though illiterate, "proved a good and faithful helpmate" and the mother of two of his four acknowledged children. His concern, however, was not his domestic but his public life, where he put into practice the virtues of sociability and utility through "a club of mutual improvement, which we called the JUNTO." Most of the members were, like Franklin, tradesmen. They discussed the usefulness of their reading, the behavior of their fellow citizens, and the actions of the state. Franklin himself queried the group about perfection and personal happiness, justice and honesty, even diet, the very questions he asked himself.

He also proposed the pooling of literary resources for common use, an enterprise which lasted only a year but served as a basis for his recommendation in 1731 that the Junto organize a

subscription library—"my first project of a public nature"—
which became the Library Company. The immediate result was
a new influence in Philadelphia. Quakers, despite the scholarly
attainments of men like Penn and Logan, did not favor
education beyond the elementary level. Aside from the parochial
library established in Christ Church in 1710, Philadelphians who
wanted books had to turn either to Andrew Bradford's bookstore
or to the several merchants who retailed books. "At the time I
establish'd myself in Pennsylvania," Franklin recalled, "there
was not a good bookseller's shop in any of the colonies to the
southward of Boston." Franklin put reading in closer reach of the
leather apron men. Any "civil gentleman" was allowed to read
the books, but only subscribers could take them from the
premises.

Sunday was Franklin's time for reading, an activity he judged
more important than church services. He claimed never to have
doubted the existence of God nor His creation and governing of
the world. Nor did he doubt the immortality of the soul and the
punishment of vice and reward of virtue. (In his autobiography
he conveniently forgot some of his earliest writings.) But his own
emphasis was distinctly this-worldly: "The most acceptable
service of God was the doing good to man." It was a useful adage
in Philadelphia, where government provided no social services
whatsoever. Quaker benevolence was restricted to members of
the sect; only in the latter part of the century would it be
extended to outsiders. Nor did other religious groups see charity
as incumbent on them. Franklin's final exasperation with the
local Presbyterian parson came when the latter passed up an
opportunity to lecture on morality and, instead, preached on
piety. Franklin would play the major role in filling this void in
public services.

Meanwhile, he decided that he would worship privately. "It
was about this time," he remembered, "that I conceiv'd the bold
and arduous project of arriving at moral perfection." He found
himself so riddled with faults that he decided to root them out
one by one "like him who, having a garden to weed, does not
attempt to eradicate all the bad herbs at once." He drew up a list
of twelve virtues in logical order and, prompted by a Quaker

acquaintance who thought him proud, added Humility as an afterthought, if "Imitate Jesus and Socrates" can be considered a humble aspiration. Perhaps the addition was made tongue in cheek. Indeed, the whole project may have been a humorous invention of Franklin's; he was never above such a joke.

A much more sober-sided attempt at defining thirteen virtues in order of importance was made in *Fruits of a Father's Love* (1699), the work of Franklin's famous predecessor in Philadelphia, William Penn. Ironically, one of the last essays Franklin wrote for the *New England Courant* was a parody on Penn's *No Cross, No Crown* (1669), irreverently ridiculing Quaker practice: "*Honour, Friend, says he,* properly ascends, and not descends; yet the Hat, when the Head is uncover'd, *descends,* and therefore there can be no Honour in it." The two men shared no sense of humor, nor many other qualities. They were separated in time and place, one born in London in 1644, the other in Boston in 1706, and they grew up in different worlds. Penn, the product of English society's upper stratum and the cultural benefits it bestowed, descended to the level of bourgeois and lower-class Quakers, embraced their belief, and delivered them to the New World, never, for all his trials, forsaking his faith in God but occasionally losing patience with fellow Friends. Franklin, up from a New England tradesman's family and always disdainful of aristocratic values, was concerned to improve himself and the rest of society along with him.

Their respective inventories of virtue demonstrated the consequences of such divergent origins:

Penn	Franklin
1. Be Humble	1. Temperance
2. Meekness	2. Silence
3. Patience	3. Order
4. Mercy	4. Resolution
5. Charity	5. Frugality
6. Liberality	6. Industry
7. Justice	7. Sincerity
8. Integrity	8. Justice
9. Gratitude	9. Moderation
10. Diligence	10. Cleanliness
11. Frugality	11. Tranquility

12. Temperance   12. Chastity
13. The External Word   13. Humility

The most obvious difference between the two lists was the value assigned to humility. To Penn, humility was the natural product of a Calvinistic view of the world: "if you dwell in the holy fear of the omnipresent and all-seeing God: for that will shew you your vileness, and his excellency." The alternative was damnation: "avoid pride as you would avoid the devil." Penn was dead serious about the matter. But Franklin, who candidly admitted that his autobiography itself was an exercise in vanity, regarded his own efforts as humorous: "There is, perhaps, no one of our natural passions so hard to subdue as *pride*. . . . even if I could conceive that I had compleatly overcome it, I should probably be proud of my humility." The best he could do, Franklin concluded, was achieve the appearance rather than the reality of humility. To be a paragon of social virtue was, in the judgment of the seventeenth-century Puritan, equivalent to admitting damnation. But Franklin was an eighteenth-century man, who valued good citizenship over salvation.

Religious zeal was unappealing to Franklin; he would have found the early Quakers objectionable. His list of virtues was headed by an altogether different quality: "Temperance first, as it tends to procure that coolness and clearness of head, which is so necessary where constant vigilance was to be kept up, and guard maintained against the unremitting attraction of ancient habits, and the force of perpetual attractions." Franklin's humanistic tribute to man's ability to win against the odds of human nature stood in contrast to Penn's theistic approach: "Therefore bound your desires, teach your wills subjection, take Christ for your example, as well as guide. . . . His sermon upon the Mount is one confirmed divine authority in favor of an universal temperance. . . . O may this virtue be yours! you have grace from God for that end." The Sermon on the Mount eulogized the virtues of meekness, mercy, and charity which Quakers prized most highly. Franklin did not mention them.

Rather, second on Franklin's list was Silence, not meek acquiescence but the hush of utilitarianism: "Speak not but what may benefit others or yourself; avoid trifling conversation." It was to be achieved only at personal sacrifice, as he made clear in depicting his struggle for Humility: "When another asserted something I thought an error, I deny'd myself the pleasure of contradicting him abruptly, and of showing immediately some absurdity in his proposition." Indeed, Franklin attributed his influence in the community not to eloquence—"I was but a bad speaker"—but to flexibility, "Perhaps for the past fifty years no one has ever heard a dogmatical expression escape me."

Although Penn did not include Silence among his virtues, he firmly endorsed the tight lip: "In conversation, mark well what others say or do, and hide your own mind, at least till last; and then open it as sparingly as the matter will let you." In contrast to Franklin's repressed sociability was Penn's typically seventeenth-century caution, amounting almost to fear, of the outside world: "Be always on your watch, but chiefly in company; then be sure to have your wits about you, and your armour on." Ultimately, the virtue was religious: "True silence is the rest of the mind; and is to the spirit, what sleep is to the body, nourishment and refreshment." The contrast between Penn's theistic solitude and Franklin's humanistic sociability was striking.

It would be misleading to locate Penn and Franklin at opposite poles in their respective views of the world. Penn, after all, had a goodly share of bourgeois wisdom to offer his readers, even to the point of anticipating Franklin's influence: "The wisdom of nations lies in their proverbs, which are brief and pithy: collect them and lern them, they are notable measures and directions in human life." Yet Penn could not have conceived of issuing his social philosophy in almanac form or assigning himself a role such as Poor Richard (not, of course, Franklin's first anonymous performance). When Penn discussed "your religious and civil direction in your pilgrimage upon earth," he, like Bunyan before him but not Franklin after him, had in mind the omnipresence of God in Whom all was lodged. Penn would not have thought to distinguish between the appearance and the reality of industry. His religion buttressed his social conservatism: "Choose *God's* trades before *men's.* Adam was a gardener, Cain a plowman, and Abel a grazier or shepherd: these began with the world, and have least of snare, and most of use. When Cain became *murderer*, as a witty man said, he turned a builder of *cities*, and quitted his *husbandry*. Mechanicks, as handicrafts, are also commendable; but them are but a second brood, and younger brothers."

Franklin's thinking ran directly opposite to Penn's on this important matter. Franklin prized Order, Resolution, and Industry (these virtues occupied the places on his list that were filled by Patience, Mercy, and Liberality on Penn's), the values of work-oriented society, where job schedules would replace a more casual, even seasonal, approach to daily chores. Not surprisingly, Franklin was more interested in explaining the process by which he tried to adhere to his thirteen virtues than in defining the virtues themselves. And he clearly believed that the incorporation of these qualities into one's life would come as a result of self-discipline. Penn as a Quaker saw inspiration as coming from within but, as an aristocrat, viewed control as externally imposed.

It was significant that both *Fruits of a Father's Love* and the *Autobiography*, the former a book of advice, the latter a model for behavior, were written for their respective authors' offspring, since the contrast between Penn's and Franklin's perspectives testified to an alteration that had taken place in Anglo-American patterns of child rearing. In the seventeenth-century England of Penn's birth, parents attempted to mold their children through external devices such as swaddling and beating; when Penn wrote "never strike in passion," he was cautioning against a loss of temper, not the use of force. In early eighteenth-century New England, the efforts of parents were directed toward shaping their children mentally rather than physically, swaddling them in ideology rather than cloth bands. If controls were to be self-imposed, the seventeenth-century notion of man being responsible only to God would be eroded. Rather, repression was for the benefit of society, and the work ethic was directly related to such restraint. Franklin's notion of giving the appearance of industry was also novel, since society rather than the Deity was now the judge. Among the self-imposed controls was the

introduction of toilet training for children—Penn's friend John
Locke was probably the first Englishman to write of "going
to stool" regularly—with its important implications for the
work day.

The differences between the worlds of Penn and Franklin
delineated a watershed in the history of colonial Pennsylvania.
During the first four or five decades of the colony's existence,
Penn's English Quaker ideas were adapted to the conditions of
America. The second forty or fifty years of provincial life
witnessed the emergence of an indigenous citizen, whom contemporaries and historians alike epitomized in Franklin. He reflected
the age, and he played a mighty part in shaping it. His projects
in Philadelphia were a further demonstration of his unity with
his time, so frequently did they reflect his personal preferences.
Clearly the idea for a public library stemmed from an avaricious
appetite for books that his pocketbook could not sate. His
penchant for organization and sense of economic justice were
offended by a badly run city watch, for which rich and poor were
taxed alike; Franklin's program, later to become law, called for
regular policing supported by equitable taxation. An enemy of
waste, he designed a stove to conserve fuel as well as warm the
air, and he proposed to protect property from fire not only by
broadcasting precautionary measures—"An Ounce of Prevention is worth a Pound of Cure"—but by licensing chimney
sweeps, checking public pumps (Philadelphia was noted for its
large number of these), and forming a volunteer fire company on
the model of Boston's. Scorning sectarianism, Franklin favored
the building of a hall "for the use of any preacher of any religious
persuasion who might desire to day something to the people at
Philadelphia . . . so that even if the Mufti of Constantinople
were to send a missionary to preach Mohammedanism to us, he
would find a pulpit at his service."

Having established both his personal and public life on sound
footings, thus releasing his full energies to follow his natural
curiosity, Franklin wrote in 1743: "The first Drudgery of Settling
new Colonies, which confines the Attention of People to mere
Necessaries, is now pretty well over; and there are many in every
Province in Circumstances that set them at Ease, and afford

Poor Richard, 1733.

AN

Almanack

For the Year of Chrift

1733,

Being the Firft after LEAP YEAR:

	Years
And makes fince the Creation By the Account of the Eaftern *Greeks*	7241
By the Latiñ Church, when ☉ ent. ♈	6932
By the Computation of *W.W.*	5742
By the *Roman* Chronology	5682
By the *Jewifh* Rabbies	5494

Wherein is contained

The Lunations, Eclipfes, Judgment of the Weather, Spring Tides, Planets Motions & mutual Afpects, Sun and Moon's Rifing and Setting, Length of Days, Time of High Water, Fairs, Courts, and obfervable Days. Fitted to the Latitude of Forty Degrees, and a Meridian of Five Hours Weft from *London*, but may without fenfible Error, ferve all the adjacent Places, even from *Newfoundland* to *South-Carolina*.

By *RICHARD SAUNDERS*, Philom.

PHILADELPHIA:
Printed and fold by *B. FRANKLIN*, at the New Printing-Office near the Market.

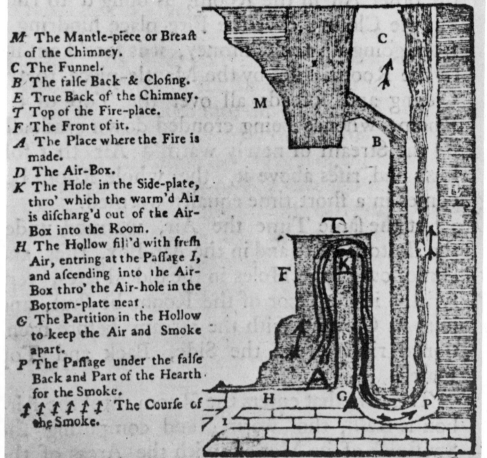

PROFILE of the Chimney and FIRE-PLACE.

M The Mantle-piece or Breast of the Chimney.
C The Funnel.
B The false Back & Closing.
E True Back of the Chimney.
T Top of the Fire-place.
F The Front of it.
A The Place where the Fire is made.
D The Air-Box.
K The Hole in the Side-plate, thro' which the warm'd Air is discharg'd out of the Air-Box into the Room.
H The Hollow fill'd with fresh Air, entring at the Passage *I*, and ascending into the Air-Box thro' the Air-hole in the Bottom-plate near.
G The Partition in the Hollow to keep the Air and Smoke apart.
P The Passage under the false Back and Part of the Hearth for the Smoke.
↑↑↑↑↑↑ The Course of the Smoke.

The practical interests of Benjamin Franklin. (right) Franklin fireplace by Lewis Evans. *From the collections of the Library Company of Philadelphia.*

Leisure to cultivate the finer Arts, and improve the common Stock of Knowledge. To such of these who are Men of Speculation, many Hints must from time to time arise, many Observations occur, which if well-examined, pursued and improved, might produce Discoveries to some or all of the British Plantations, or to the Benefit of Mankind in general." But, because such persons were dispersed along the length of the Atlantic seaboard and not in communication with one another, Franklin proposed founding the American Philosophical Society. The treasurer would be located in Philadelphia, as well as the corresponding secretary, which post Franklin volunteered to fill "till they shall be provided with one more capable."

Franklin was self-educated and continually thirsty for knowledge, but he sired a son who did not share his drive for solitary enlightenment. When William Franklin was twelve or thirteen, the father drew up a proposal for an academy, a scheme he revived six years later in 1749. Again he noted that the energies of the first planters could not be focused on education (forgetting the founding of Harvard six years after the establishment of Massachusetts and overlooking the Quakers' hostility toward advanced learning), that "the *culture* of *minds* by the *finer arts* and *sciences,* was necessarily postpon'd to times of more wealth and leisure." But now "numbers of our inhabitants are both able and willing to give their sons a good education, if it might be had at home, free from the extraordinary expense and hazard in sending them abroad for that purpose." As the province itself emerged from adolescence, the autonomy afforded by knowledge was necessary. "The good Education of Youth has been esteemed by wise men in all Ages, as the surest Foundation of the Happiness both of private Families and of Common-wealths."

The depiction of the family as a little commonwealth was not an invention of Franklin's; it was accepted by William Penn and other seventeenth-century Americans as well as by their English forebears. The novelty of the eighteenth century, in both domestic and public life, was reflected in the change from a patriarchal family and an authoritarian state to a family whose relations were mutual and contractual and a state whose forms were increasingly republican. This alteration in the nature of authority was evident in Franklin's *Proposals Relating to the Education of Youth in Pennsylvania*, 1749: "To form their [the students'] Stile, they should be put on Writing Letters to each other, making Abstracts of what they read; or writing the same Things in their own Words; telling or writing Stories lately read, in their own Expressions. All to be revis'd and corrected by the Tutor, who should give his Reasons, explain the Force and Import of Words, & c."

The seventeenth-century schoolmaster was never pictured without birch rods in hand, but Franklin expected him to wield rational explanations. Surely this was an expression of the indulgence Franklin received as a boy, as the emphasis on self-expression, rather than rote learning, reflected his own educational experience.

In this, as in so many of his projects, Franklin recognized the resistance he was likely to encounter. He turned to the authority of Locke, Milton, and others because "some things here proposed may be found to differ a little from the Forms of Education in Common Use." Indeed, the emphasis on diet, exercise, utility of subject matter ("History will also afford frequent Opportunities of showing the Necessity of a *Publick Religion* . . . the Mischiefs of Superstition, & c.") could hardly be construed otherwise. With characteristic optimism, economy of language, and graceful turn of phrase, Franklin concluded: "Long settled Forms are not easily changed. For us, who are now to make a Beginning, 'tis, at least, as easy to set out right as wrong." An uncharacteristic note of pessimism in the *Proposals*—"Something seems to be wanting in America to incite and stimulate Youth to Study"—displayed, no doubt, discouragement with his own son.

Although the plan for an academy was distinctly Franklin's, he distributed *Proposals* as the work of "some publick-spirited Gentlemen" and gathered together a subscription of about £5,000 in 1749. He was not among the original trustees, whose total composition was to be nonsectarian, but when one died, Franklin was chosen to take his place as "merely an honest man, and of no sect at all." Meanwhile, the academy had outgrown its original building and Franklin, who also served as a trustee for the group which had erected a hall for preachers of any religious persuasion, negotiated an agreement for this hall to house the academy. The University of Pennsylvania was thus launched.

Although the academy was nonsectarian from the outset, three-quarters of the original twenty-four trustees were Anglican. Even more significant was the absence of the Society of Friends; Quakers were involved neither in the founding, the funding, nor the governing of the new institution. They had never been sympathetic to higher education, but their aloofness from this project was probably more a consequence of the threat posed by the increasing power of the Anglicans, not to mention the Presbyterians and Lutherans, who by mid-century already outnumbered Friends. Finally, however often Franklin was later identified as a Quaker in Europe (an illusion which he fostered), however many Quaker friends he had, however much he praised economic virtues which Quaker merchants embodied, the fact was that Franklin symbolized a challenge to Quaker authority in Pennsylvania.

He represented a challenge not only through activities in Philadelphia that threatened or actually usurped the leadership of prominent Friends but also by his participation in provincial politics. He later explained his entry into the public arena in terms of private gain. "My first promotion was my being chosen, in 1736, clerk of the General Assembly . . . which secur'd to me the business of printing the votes, laws, paper money, and other occasional jobbs for the public, that, on the whole, were very profitable." He had six years earlier been chosen to print money for Pennsylvania as a reward for his pamphlet advocating paper. And, Franklin recalled, "I soon after obtain'd, thro' my friend Hamilton, the printing of the Newcastle paper money. . . . He procured for me, also, the printing of the laws and votes of that government [the Three Lower Counties]." Andrew Hamilton, speaker of both the Pennsylvania and Delaware legislatures, could recognize in Franklin's social ascent success similar to his own.

Hamilton (not to be confused with an earlier Andrew Hamilton, who served as deputy governor of Pennsylvania and the Three Lower Counties at the turn of the century) was apparently of Scotch background. He appeared in Virginia about 1700, where he later inherited land from a childless family that had befriended him. He practiced law on the Eastern Shore, married the widowed daughter of a prominent Quaker merchant, moved to Maryland where his practice broadened, and, in January 1712/13, visited Philadelphia where he met James Logan. Soon afterward he successfully handled a legal case for the Penns in the Three Lower Counties. A year later he was briefly in London, where he may have met Hannah Penn; Logan had written him a letter of introduction. He registered at Gray's Inn and was called to the English bar, thereby continuing his professional advancement. He was elected to the Maryland House of Delegates in 1714 but had already planned his move to Philadelphia, which occurred a year or two later. When David Lloyd became chief justice in 1717, Hamilton succeeded him as attorney general and four years later became a member of the Council. He resigned both posts in early 1724 and left for London on the same ship as Franklin, giving the two new Philadelphians an opportunity to build a friendship.

Logan recommended Hamilton to John Penn and one of the trustees of the province as a man who in recent years "appeared very hearty in ye Proprietor's interest here . . . but of late he has somewhat recoiled," a man to be cultivated for his legal experience, integrity, and influence. The Penns did draw on Hamilton's talents, rewarding him with Bush Hill, a 153-acre estate adjacent to Philadelphia, where the now-eminent lawyer was to settle with his wife and three children. Within a week of his return in June 1727, he was chosen recorder of the city and in the October election he was seated in the Assembly from Bucks County.

During Hamilton's London sojourn, the proprietary family decided that Major Patrick Gordon should replace the charismatic Sir William Keith as deputy governor of Pennsylvania, a choice which Hamilton influenced. Gordon arrived in Pennsylvania to find that Keith had created an uproar in the wake of his departure, and he quickly perceived the advantage in backing David Lloyd's partisans against the less numerous Keithians. He also conceded Lloyd's lifelong contention about the power of the Assembly, observing that "a Legislative Assembly, in Conformity

The career of Andrew Hamilton (right), like Franklin's, was testimony to versatility and mobility among Pennsylvania's leaders. Hamilton is thought to have been the architect of the State House, 1732 (below). *Historical Society of Pennsylvania.*

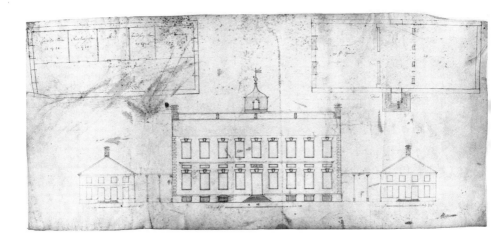

to a British House of Commons, is invested with a very great Authority. . . . You . . . are one part of the Legislature which in every Government is the Supreme, & are the Grand Inquisitors of the whole Province."

This was David Lloyd's last Assembly; his retirement from public affairs was followed by his death two years later. His successor as speaker was Andrew Hamilton, the first man in the chair who was not a Friend. Despite his Bucks County constituency, he did not represent the farmers who voted for Lloyd and certainly not the artisans who stood behind Keith, but rather the merchant-proprietary group. It was certainly significant that he farmed the legislature's printing out to Franklin, the aspiring capitalist, whose initial venture was fostered by Keith's capriciousness.

Hamilton and Franklin shared a belief in continued business prosperity and a friendship with its most visible Quaker exponent, James Logan. But the speaker, while he presided over a body which had waged and largely won its quest for political power in the province, was allied to the Penns and represented the continuing sway of the elitist Council. Franklin, despite his own increasingly prominent role in provincial affairs, ultimately found friendship with the proprietary family impossible and used the Assembly as a base to wage his fight against the Penns.

The emergence of Franklin and Hamilton, as well as the tranquillity of the late 1720s and early 1730s, was testimony to certain basic changes in Pennsylvania which were reflected in its political life. Age had brought maturity to government. A structure, including the importance assigned to the speakership, had grown to the point where it could absorb the shocks of ephemeral battles, such as the one which broke out around Keith. Migration had brought new men to the province, changing the political personnel. Up to the 1720s, when conflict had existed in Pennsylvania, it was warfare among the people of peace, with factional leaders David Lloyd and James Logan representing not only different concepts of government and divergent economic interests, but also variant brands of Quakerism. Sir William Keith finally succeeded in bringing the two opponents together, soon after which Lloyd retired from political life. This fact hastened harmony on public matters within the Society of Friends, but conciliation was highly probable in any event, since Quakers were being rapidly outnumbered in the province. Unity was imperative for continued rule, notwithstanding Friends' tradition of leadership in Pennsylvania (which included Assembly apportionment that favored Quaker areas), their commanding economic and social positions, and political support from German sectarians who felt a kinship to the Society of Friends. Yet Franklin posed a threat to Quaker leadership in all areas of provincial life.

Contributing to the complexity of the situation was the reemergence of the proprietary family as a force in the colony. In December 1726 the Court of Exchequer upheld the will of the founder, now dead eight years, thus finally establishing ownership of Pennsylvania in the younger branch of the Penn family. Hannah died a week later, but agreement had already been reached that her eldest son, John, would inherit half the province, while sons Thomas and Richard were left the other half. Although the family had abandoned the idea of selling the government to the crown, the court's failure to comment on that matter (its decision concerning only the disposal of the land) left the question unresolved until Springett Penn (son of William, Jr.) died and his brother William agreed to relinquish all claims to the soil and government, for a sum, in 1731. Thomas Penn went to Pennsylvania the following year, and his older brother John arrived in 1734 with their sister Margaret and her husband. John stayed only a year, but Thomas remained until 1741 in a residence between Hamilton's Bush Hill and the Schuylkill River.

Living on a country estate was Thomas Penn's single concession to gentility. His visit to Pennsylvania was not motivated by a desire to view his acres but to exploit them. He had been well schooled in business. When he was barely fourteen Hannah, whose acumen he inherited, sent him to London where he was apprenticed to a mercer. Her letters to him conveyed the anxiety she felt as she conducted the affairs of the province for her ailing husband. Thomas remained in the commercial world of the capital until he sailed for America, his thoughts of Pennsylvania

Thomas Penn Esqr.
*Yale University Art
Gallery. The Mabel Brady
Garvan Collection.
(Inventor—Martin;
Artist—Davis)*

James Logan.
*Historical Society
of Pennsylvania.*

necessarily occurring in the context of the marketplace. He had no large vision for the place, certainly no concept of a "holy experiment." Indeed, he was not even a Quaker, though it would be several decades before he joined the Church of England. Rather, he viewed the province as a source of income which, however meager the returns thus far, must be made to yield a handsome profit. Yet if he did not share his father's imagination, neither did he partake of the founder's paternalism. Thomas Penn would participate in Pennsylvania politics without illusions. Several years after his arrival he wrote: "I never desire to have views so noble, extensive, and benevolent as my father, unless he had left a much larger fortune; because these views, though good in themselves, yet by possessing him too much, led him into inconveniences which I hope to avoid." This sentiment was an echo of the hardheaded wisdom of James Logan, who had been handling proprietary affairs since William Penn's departure in 1701 and whose letters to the Penn family were its main source of information on the province. Now the founder's son was coming to put Pennsylvania on a sound financial footing.

Even before Thomas Penn's arrival, Andrew Hamilton had been appointed a trustee of the Loan Office; in addition, he had worked through the Assembly to reorganize the colony's finances. When, in 1733, Hamilton was attacked for sinister behavior and dictatorial power, Franklin rushed to his defense in the *Gazette*, ridiculing the charges of Hamilton's enemies. The printer eulogized the former speaker at the time of his death in 1741, recalling his public service: "He steadily maintained the Cause of Liberty; and the Laws made, during the time he was Speaker of the Assembly, which was many Years, will be a lasting Monument of his Affection to the People, and of his Concern for the welfare of the Province."

Franklin could respect a man of Hamilton's stature, whose greatest moment in "the Cause of Liberty" was the defense of John Peter Zenger; freedom of the press had more than academic meaning to the publisher of the *Gazette*. But Thomas Penn's housekeeping approach to provincial life was simply uninteresting until it stood in the path of Franklin's own designs, thus providing the major source of political controversy at mid-century. Franklin's was by far the larger vision (however petty his feelings of revenge toward Thomas Penn might become), a view of Pennsylvania's future which corresponded in breadth, though not in substance, to the plans of the founder.

7

NEW SPROUTS:
WESTERN SETTLEMENT,
IMPERIAL WAR,
AND THE GREAT AWAKENING

"He that hath a Trade hath an Estate," observed Poor Richard, summarizing in one pithy statement the ways to wealth in Pennsylvania: commerce and land. Their relative importance varied through time. The two activities were closely related and sometimes collided; Europeans and Indians traded with each other, but they could not share the soil. At the outset of colonization, William Penn established the policy of buying land from the aborigines. In order to underwrite the founding of the colony, he had to sell large chunks of property to wealthy Englishmen. Speculation in real estate was made difficult by the requirement that land had to be settled within three years of the purchase date. The land office, staffed by the secretary of the province, the surveyor general, and three to five commissioners of property, handled the sales of common lands. Usually the secretary issued a warrant of survey to the surveyor general, who would have the land laid out, after which both the warrant and the certificate of survey were registered in the secretary's office; then the purchase money would be paid and the patent, or land grant, would be issued, giving legal title to the settler and reserving the quitrent to the proprietor. (£5 per 100 acres, with one shilling annual quitrent, was the usual rate to 1713, after which it climbed to £10 and two shillings quitrent until 1732, then moved up to £15 10s. with a quitrent of a halfpenny sterling.)

The system was logical, but its dependence on orderly procedure and disregard for human frailty, not to say avarice, created problems. The money for purchase might be promised or paid only in part. Quitrents were difficult to gather; collectors were ridiculed, refused, even assaulted. Rent rolls were irregularly kept. Settlers who toiled day after day to clear and cultivate the land were unsympathetic to Penn's policy of reserving one-tenth of all land to the proprietary estate for speculative purposes, and their discontent was expressed through the Assembly's attempts, during the first two decades of the eighteenth century, to control the land office. Penn's perspective was entirely different for, despite the settlers' wild imaginings of proprietary wealth, he was always in a precarious financial condition and became increasingly bitter toward colonists so ungrateful as to deny him his rightful dues from the land.

After Penn's departure from the colony in 1701, no more real estate was purchased from the Indians during his lifetime. But trade with the natives was another matter. The economic development of Pennsylvania depended on commerce, and the Indians possessed a commodity which would foster exchange abroad: the peltry of the forest. It was axiomatic that merchandising in furs was a function not only of the available game in the province but of the number of Indians who would hunt it, the natives being bound to their white neighbors by a progressive dependence on European supplies. They could pay only in furs or land, and their homes were secure only so long as real estate values remained secondary to commercial prospects. It was in the proprietary interest to maintain an orderly occupation of the land by European settlers, properly surveying, recording, and collecting, while sustaining prosperous trade relations with the natives. This proved virtually impossible as hordes of immigrants arrived after 1720.

The career of James Logan, proprietary agent and private merchant, illustrated the working methods and emergent problems on the way to wealth. As secretary of the province and commissioner of property after Penn's exit, Logan was involved in all land transactions, and by securing the surveyor general's post for a friend, he virtually controlled the business. At the same time he was deeply entangled in the Indian trade; it appears as though he discouraged the proprietor from intervening in this activity so that he could pursue his own private gain unhindered. He was first clerk, and later a member of the Provincial Council, and his political power was augmented by Penn's stroke in 1712, which almost removed any checks on his action as proprietary agent. Deputy governors were dependent on him and followed his advice regarding political appointments. Settlers needed his confirmation of land titles. Indians saw him as a merchant engaged in the fur trade and, in his role of provincial secretary, as a diplomat.

The natives did not recognize, because Logan took pains to hide, his speculative concern with real estate. But when, in 1702, a settler applied to the land office for a parcel of ground which the Lenapes along Brandywine Creek in Chester County thought they owned, Logan and the commissioners of property approved the grant. Enough Indians protested this violation of their territory to make Logan cautious in his land dealings. Besides, with the Iroquois directing the fur trade away from Albany to Philadelphia through the local Shawnees, much of Logan's energy was invested in merchandising pelts. Here he found he could pay off his employees in real estate which the surveyor general generously laid out, often uncomfortably close to Indian settlements. Indeed, the commercial operation itself became a means of preempting valuable land. With Logan seizing the sites cleared by Indians engaged in hunting and trapping, the fur trade served to accelerate rather than retard settlement.

In addition to taking advantage of his positions as fur trader and diplomat, Logan capitalized on his status as proprietary agent. In 1717 a group of Palatines applied to the commissioners of property for a place to settle. Logan handled the transaction personally, assigning some of the Germans land he had secretly bought as well as plots within the recently surveyed Conestoga Manor, without informing the proprietors. Two years later he had proprietary land surveyed at Paxtang (near present-day

Harrisburg), purchased a parcel for himself, and directed Scotch-Irish settlers into the region.

But Logan's real estate activities were rudely interrupted at about this time by Governor Keith. Unlike previous deputy governors, Keith refused to be dominated by Logan, especially when he realized that his salary was dependent not on the Council but the Assembly. At William Penn's death, Keith asked for and received royal endorsement as governor until the conflict within the proprietary family was resolved, thus strengthening his position. Realizing that he needed more money than the Assembly would provide, he saw his chance in real estate speculation and took control of the patenting of land from Logan. The Indians along the Susquehanna turned to Keith when several of their number were killed by a Logan employee, who was protected against prosecution by his master. Suddenly Logan was on the defensive, using what delaying tactics he could to keep Keith from seizing land in the west.

For Keith himself was hardly a champion of the Indians. He invited Palatines from New York to travel south and settle on Tulpehocken Creek, forcing the Lenape out. Logan's traders worked this area, and the provincial secretary attacked the deputy governor's actions, complaining to Hannah Penn of the "unruly Palatines" and "disorderly" Irish invading her land. Keith, in turn, pointed to Logan's dealings with the Brandywine Lenape, causing the Assembly to question Logan. The real losers were the Indians, who between 1723 and 1729 were forced out of both the Brandywine and Tulpehocken areas. Keith also lost, ultimately, and Logan picked up the pieces along the Susquehanna as the deputy governor exited.

Logan settled on tracts two men who were to supervise the new settlement of Hempfield (now Columbia), though the Conestoga Indians there protested as they moved across the river, where the indefatigable Logan was soon surveying their settlement again. Meanwhile, the Iroquois had warned their tributaries, the Lenape and Shawnee, that the Europeans were determined to take all Indian land and should be forcibly opposed. When this alarm went unheeded, the Iroquois in the late 1720s withdrew support from the Shawnee on the lower Susquehanna and told them to relocate their villages on a line drawn from the upper branches of the river to the Ohio, where the Six Nations were now focusing attention. The remaining Shawnee in eastern Pennsylvania were put under the guidance of an Oneida named Schickellamy, who was stationed at Shamokin.

Of all Pennsylvanians, Logan played the major role in pushing the Indians from the east into the Ohio Valley where, ironically, they proved to be less subject to his control of the fur trade. Lenape from the Brandywine and Tulpehocken regions joined Shawnee from the lower Susquehanna and some dissident Iroquois from New York in the west. Logan and Schickellamy reached a formal agreement based on the former's willingness to pay the latter to discipline Indians obstructing the advancing line of European settlement. Logan was selling lots to Palatines in Tulpehocken, despite the fact that the Indian claim on the region still existed and the resident leader, Sassoonan, was proving intractable.

Surely Tulpehocken was one of Logan's most complex embroilments. While selling lots he was attempting to alter, for his own advantage, the boundaries of a 10,000-acre proprietary manor surveyed in Tulpehocken for Letitia Penn Aubrey in 1722 and sold by her husband soon afterward to one John Page who, getting wind of Logan's mode of operation, demanded a reliable survey of his tract. Meanwhile, Logan had reacted to Sassoonan's stubbornness by having his brother in England buy the original rights to 2,000 unlocated acres, since land purchased in this manner was to be free of Indian claims no matter where situated. But the Penns had begun to suspect their agent and ruled that no more original rights were to be surveyed.

Despite the tide of white westward movement, there were still islands of Indians in the east. In the Wyoming Valley, where there was little or no settlement pressure, lived the Minisinks, a mixture of Lenape and Shawnee. More troublesome was the presence of Lenape and Shawnee Indians in the Lehigh Valley, or Forks of Delaware, north of Tohickon Creek along the Delaware River. They would not negotiate with Logan but insisted on meeting with a member of the Penn family, a request they would later rue. Because Logan saw the removal of these natives as imperative, he put as much pressure as he could on the Penn family to send a delegate; Logan, too, would regret his request. For when Thomas Penn came to the province in 1732 he proved to be more perceptive than Logan would have guessed and more avaricious than the Indians could have imagined.

Penn arrived as Logan was about to negotiate with Sassoonan on Tulpehocken. When that payment was settled, the only Indian land in the region of Pennsylvania bounded by the Delaware to the east, South Mountain to the north, the Susquehanna to the west, and the disputed Maryland boundary to the south, was in the Lehigh Valley, or Forks of Delaware. Title to the area was unclear, but since agents of William Penn had in 1686 bought a parcel of land west of the Delaware and north of previous purchases, Tohickon Creek, which flows into the Delaware north of present-day New Hope, had been recognized as the boundary between Indian and white settlement.

Not surprisingly, Logan tried to intrude on this arrangement. A parcel of land sold in 1682 but not surveyed until 1702—and then in the face of Indian protest, because the commissioners of property survey was conducted immediately north of Tohickon Creek—was bought in 1725 by Logan, who turned the parcel back to the proprietary estate. In return he was compensated with a grant at Durham, twelve miles north of Tohickon, where he built an iron furnace and further extinguished the Indian claim by private purchase, although citizens of Pennsylvania were prohibited by law from buying Indian land. In addition to Logan, a budding provincial capitalist named William Allen, whose financial assistance to the Penns threatened to make them less dependent on Logan, was pushing into the region through his proprietary connections.

John Penn arrived in Philadelphia rather unexpectedly in 1734, so in debt that he had earlier favored selling the province. He and his brother Thomas agreed on the importance of a revenue from land sales north of the Tohickon, and together they journeyed to the area to buy the Indian claim from Nutimus, chief of the Forks of Delaware tribes, who asked too high a price. Consequently, the Penns produced the 1686 deed to the region which, they said, made it clear that the proprietors still had land coming to them from the resident Indians to the extent of the distance a man could walk in a day and a half. While trial walks were conducted to locate the most advantageous route northwest, pressure was put on the local Lenape and Shawnee through the Six Nations (formerly the Five Nations, now enlarged with the adoption of the Tuscaroras in the early eighteenth century). Logan interpreted the Iroquois refusal to claim Nutimus' land as a release of the Indian claim. The Iroquois, vying for the good offices of the Pennsylvania government out of fear of the French in Canada and the English in New York, willingly perpetuated this fraud by sacrificing their tributaries.

Even after they signed the Pennsbury Treaty which gave legal sanction to the land seizure, the Indians were unprepared for the extent of the confiscation. On September 19, 1737, the "walk" began. Three speedy athletes prepared to travel the most advantageous route, with four Indian observers and a sheriff on horseback in attendance. The surprise and disgust of the Indians as the affair became an endurance marathon was registered by their dropping out. Even two of the runners could not make it. But by noon of September 20th, the third had covered sixty miles, finishing beyond the Blue Mountains. The surveyors who followed added even more land to the Walking Purchase. The Penns were pleased; this territory plus other Indian claims gathered by negotiation over the past few years doubled the amount of land open to settlement. The Indians did not protest; Nutimus reappeared in Philadelphia for his ceremonial visit, as did Sassoonan. The Forks of Delaware and Tulpehocken were open for settlement. Europeans flooded the remainder of eastern Pennsylvania, unaware of the concealed resentment of the natives.

The intruders were oblivious to the problems created, and the fortunes made, by their presence because their desires were simple, their concerns parochial, and their constant movement hardly a matter of reflection. James Magaw, a Scotch Irishman who had recently settled in the Cumberland Valley, wrote back to his brother John, east of the Susquehanna:

We was three days on our journey coming from Harrisses ferry here. We could not make much speed on account of the childer; they could

By the mid-eighteenth century there was a striking divergence between country life (Bertolet-Herbein Log House, 1738, above) and city existence (Elfreth's Alley in Philadelphia, left). (above) *Courtesy of Irwin Richman and the Pennsylvania Historical and Museum Commission.* (left) *Historical Society of Pennsylvania.*

not get on as fast as Jane and me. I think we will like this part of the country when we get our cabbin built. I would have put it near the watter but the land is lo and wet. John McCall, Alick Steen and John Rippey bilt theirs near the stream. Hugh Rippey's daught Mary berried yesterday; this will be sad news to Andrew Simpson when it reached Maguire's bridge. He was to come over in the fall when they were to be married. Mary was a very purty gerl; she died of a faver, and they berried her upon rising groun, north of the road or path where we made choice of a peese of groun for a graveyard. She was the furst berried there. Poor Hugh has none left but his wife, Sam and little Isabel. There is plenty of timmer south of us. We have 18 cabbins bilt here now, and it looks a town; but we have no name for it. I'll sent this with John Simpson when he goes back to paxtan. Come up soon, our cabbin will be ready to go into in a week and you can go in till you get wan bilt; we Have planted some corn and potatoes. Dan McGee, John Sloan and Robert More was here last week. Remember us to Mary and the childer, we are all well. Tell Billy Parker to come up Soon and bring Nancy with him. I know he will like the country. I forgot to tell you that Sally Brown was bit by a snaik, but she is out of danger. Come up soon.

Loneliness, sickness, and death were the recurrent themes of the frontier, movement and progress the choruses of survival.

The Scotch-Irish, who usually landed in New Castle, moved west or northwest. By 1720 there were settlements along the Susquehanna, one near the disputed boundary with Maryland, and the other halfway between Lancaster and present-day Harrisburg. Some settlers continued west to Gettysburg, reached by the early 1730s, while others moved north on the west bank of the Susquehanna (Logan having pushed them out of the Conestoga Valley) to the Donegal and Paxton regions. There was also a settlement of Scotch-Irish established near present-day Allentown in 1727, providing another reason for obtaining the Forks of Delaware area. Germans, having built communities along the Pequea and Conestoga Creeks before 1720, also moved north up the Schuylkill from Philadelphia, along with English Quakers and Anglicans. The more southerly inhabitants had, by 1730, crossed the Susquehanna, traveling along Codorus Creek southwest to Hanover and even beyond. In the north, Germans spread throughout the region south of Blue Mountain. By mid-century, the extreme southeast portion of the province was largely English, the far west mainly Scotch-Irish, the middle area German, though there were large numbers of English everywhere but Cumberland County, a Scotch-Irish stronghold, and Berks County, filled with Germans. In Lancaster and York counties the Scotch-Irish and Germans were about evenly matched. There were substantial numbers of Germans in Northampton County and in the older counties of Bucks and Philadelphia as well.

The division of the interior into counties and the laying out of towns to serve as county seats and commercial centers was a necessary though sometimes delayed consequence of westward migration. After 1682, when William Penn had divided the Delaware Valley into Chester, Philadelphia, and Bucks counties, no more counties were created until 1729, at which time the three local units served about forty thousand people, only twenty-five thousand of whom lived within thirty miles of Philadelphia. In 1728 settlers on the east bank of the Susquehanna petitioned for a new county, complaining of their remoteness from the county seat (Chester was ninety miles distant) and the absence of law and order. Governor Patrick Gordon consulted with the Assembly, which consented to the division of Chester County and the choosing of four new assemblymen from Lancaster County (Chester, Philadelphia, and Bucks each had eight members and the city of Philadelphia had two).

The location of the town of Lancaster provided another illustration of the connection between public service and private gain. Although several county officials who owned land at Wright's Ferry on the west bank of the Susquehanna viewed this spot as the logical place for a county seat, the site chosen was ten miles east of the river and a mile north of Conestoga Creek; the closest wagon path was four miles distant. In its favor was its central location and the presumption that the tract belonged to the proprietary family. Hence, with the approval of the governor and the Council, Logan sent one of his surveyors to lay out 1,000 acres, and the site was approved May 1, 1730. It was then revealed that the land belonged to Andrew Hamilton, speaker of the Assembly and prothonotary of the Supreme Court, whose connection with the proprietors obviously had secured him the property. Hamilton, also the architect of the Province House (later Independence Hall) in Philadelphia, designed the grid plan with central square and courthouse, in addition to selling lots in the town.

After the establishment of Lancaster County, it was two decades before the Assembly acted again. York and Cumberland counties, both west of the Susquehanna, were set up in 1749 and 1750 respectively, each having two representatives to the provincial legislature. In 1752, thirteen years after inhabitants in the remote parts of Lancaster and Philadelphia counties petitioned for a new local unit, the counties of Berks and Northampton were created with one representative apiece. Strong anti-German feeling at the time was probably responsible for such blatant underrepresentation.

The formation of towns, a proprietary or private rather than legislative function, moved more quickly than the creation of counties. The Penns were responsible for all county seats founded before the Revolution: York (York County), Reading (Berks), Carlisle (Cumberland), Easton (Northampton), Bedford (Bedford), and Sunbury (Northumberland). Their guiding principles of town placement were centrality within the county, distance from Philadelphia (none was closer than fifty-five miles; towns in the original three counties had failed to flourish due to the port city's preeminence) and from one another (none closer than twenty-four miles), and relationship to the trading area (York and Carlisle were on the eastern sides of their respective counties because proximity to Philadelphia was a way of meeting the competition of the Baltimore merchants).

Town surveys varied little, the gridiron pattern with central square prevailing everywhere. Holders of the square lots were required to build houses or forfeit their property. The proprietor reserved lots to himself for speculative purposes, however, and collected rents from other lot holders. Although this policy was not objected to, townspeople did complain of the proprietary policy of taking land around the town and not providing places for pasturing, or gathering of fuel and construction materials. The virtue of the Penns' policy of placement and management was evidenced by the growth of the proprietary towns, certainly not the happy fate of some of the hoped-for urban centers promoted by private individuals, whose sites lacked the courts, markets, and fairs, as well as the placement principles, of their competitors.

Less than a decade after the establishment of Lancaster, Thomas Penn openly favored the founding of two towns, one west of the Susquehanna and the other northwest of Philadelphia on the Schuylkill. York was surveyed in 1741, on the manor of Springettsbury, after which interested persons applied for lots. Reading, however, was located on private land, and it took about six years for Penn to gain title, three more for the survey and offering of lots in 1749. Three years later it was selected county seat of Berks. Carlisle and Easton were surveyed in 1751 and 1752, after Cumberland and Northampton counties were organized. Shippensburg was more central in Cumberland County, and the first courts were held there, but Carlisle had better connections with Philadelphia by way of Harris' Ferry. Unlike more eastern towns, Carlisle was for a long time a supply depot for traders and soldiers, a center for the legal business of the western areas, a town of innkeepers rather than craftsmen. Easton was on the eastern edge of Northampton County, where the Lehigh poured into the Delaware, but its location was deemed important as a link between Philadelphia and New York. It grew slowly and proved to be a poor proprietary investment.

With the enlargement and organization of the interior came also a settlement of the boundary dispute with Maryland (after much legal dispute in England, a temporary line was run in 1738 which ultimately was made permanent) and a reform in the policies and practices of the land office. Thomas Penn, a man almost compulsively devoted to method, wanted both order and revenue. During this period Penn regularly attended meetings of the Board of Property, making certain that records were accurate and complete. Logan, who had found in apparent chaos a source of private aggrandizement, was consulted but not trusted by the young proprietor. By doubling the amount of soil open to settlement, the land office took in over £90,000 between 1732 and

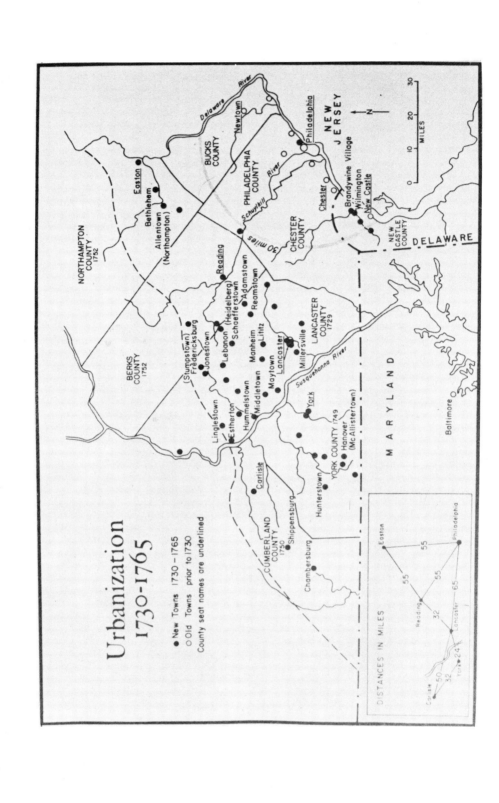

Urbanization
1730-1765

● New Towns 1730-1765
○ Old Towns prior to 1730
County seat names are underlined

Bethlehem was an exception to the pattern of proprietary town planning, as well as to conventional canons of provincial life. Founded by Moravians in 1741, the town had an economic and social structure based on religious communitarianism and separation of peoples by age and sex. (above) *From James T. Lemon,* The Best Poor Man's Country, *copyright The Johns Hopkins University Press.* (below) *Archives of the Moravian Church.*

1741. Penn agreed to the practice of allowing settlement to precede a land warrant and, on the recommendation of one of his agents in Lancaster County, accepted and put into practice the idea of installment buying.

Thomas Penn had come to America for economic reasons, and he was now getting a revenue from the soil, largely, it would seem, from land sales rather than quitrents, which were still resented. Settlers continued to be affronted, as well, by the proprietary policy of setting aside land for speculative purposes: Penn reserved 150,000 acres during his nine-year stay in the province; from 1683 to 1773 about 550,000 acres were held by the proprietors. After Penn's departure, these problems continued to haunt the land office. In addition, receipts increased only slightly (from £10,000/year during the 1732 to 1741 period to £12,000/year from 1741 to 1755), quitrents went farther and farther into arrears, and there was no really effective way to collect them. And, although immigrants coming through Pennsylvania were traveling down the Cumberland Valley into the backcountry of the southern colonies, the thousands of Germans and Scotch-Irish annually entering the province, supplemented by the growing native European population, put increasing pressure on Indian lands. The large purchase in 1749 of real estate between Blue Mountain and the north branch of the Susquehanna was unattractive until that territory was exempted from quitrents six years later. The 1754 purchase of soil beyond Blue Mountain and west of the Susquehanna was subject to Indian raids for several years, after which settlement again moved forward.

The man Thomas Penn chose to administer his policies, taking over James Logan's post as provincial secretary and, hence, secretary of the land office, was Richard Peters. An Anglican priest who had come to Pennsylvania in 1735 and attached himself to Christ Church, Peters moved in social circles which put him in contact with the humorless, cold, and friendless Penn, who "threw off" the Quakers in the early 1740s but did not join the Church of England until a decade later. The young curate, only three years Penn's junior, became his comrade and, somewhat later, his employee, holding the job as secretary from

1737 to 1761, when Peters returned to the church. His secular employment was not an aberration, for Peters had studied law before entering the priesthood, and he proved to be not only hard-working but astute in handling proprietary matters. Though he was inconsistent, even unstable, and sometimes a malicious gossip, Peters' gregariousness and sincerity gained him friendships with most non-Quaker provincial leaders during his tenure. Penn relied on his opinions and, though always resistant to the delegation of authority and insistent on knowing even the smallest details, gave Peters considerable autonomy, rivaled only by that extended to Andrew Hamilton's son James.

Andrew Hamilton was the dominant figure in Pennsylvania's political life during the 1730s. He served as speaker of the Assembly from 1729 to 1733 and again from 1734 to 1739. His refusal in 1738 to give the conventional speech, modestly denying his fitness for the office, was a milestone in the growth of the speaker's power. And in his farewell address he made it clear that the material progress of the province was not the consequence of natural bounty but "the excellency of our constitution, under which we enjoy a greater share of civil and religious liberty than any of our neighbours . . . instead of triennial assemblies, a privilege which several other colonies have long endeavoured to obtain, but in vain, ours are annual. . . . we sit upon our own adjournments . . . and are not to be sent packing in the middle of a debate." Hamilton's claim that Pennsylvania had "no officers but what are necessary," and those hard-working and popularly chosen, was probably meant to be judged by his own career: speaker of the Delaware as well as the Pennsylvania Assembly, attorney general, and judge of the vice-admiralty court.

Yet in his attribution of this constitution to "the wisdom of Mr. Penn . . . [who] reserved no powers to himself or his heirs to oppress the people" and his conclusion that "our own interests should oblige us carefully to support the government on its present foundation," Hamilton showed his attachment to the proprietary interest. This connection was carried on by his son James, who—in addition to serving in the Assembly in the late 1730s, in the lucrative post of prothonotary of the Supreme Court after his father vacated it in 1733, and as mayor of Philadelphia and a member of the Council—was deputy governor from 1748 to 1754 and again from 1759 to 1764 and acting governor twice in the early 1770s. In 1734 Hamilton's daughter Margaret married William Allen, Jr., who was already closely allied to the proprietary interest.

The same age as Richard Peters, Allen was born in Philadelphia and baptized a Presbyterian. His father, a modestly wealthy Scotch-Irish merchant, and his mother were related by marriage or service to William Penn. Although his father never entered politics, he did provide the capital and the commercial connections which allowed his son to become one of the wealthiest men, if not the wealthiest, in Pennsylvania. From his sojourn in England and the Continent in his youth, William Allen received a modicum of education, a preference for genteel living which led him to both ostentation and generosity, and an important association with the proprietors (Logan frequently mentioned him favorably in letters). He loaned money to the Penns, represented them before the Duke of Newcastle, and relieved William Penn, Jr., of 10,000 acres, his first venture in a distinguished career of land speculation. Although commerce and mining engaged a substantial portion of Allen's business energy, his largest investments were in real estate; his fortune, valued at £100,000 at his death, was mostly land. The ingredients of his success were a confidence as large as his portly physique, an almost inerrant eye for successful ventures, and a recognition of the importance of political maneuver to private fortune.

Allen entered politics with ease. On his brief return from London to settle his father's will, he was elected to the Common Council of Philadelphia in 1727. On his second and more permanent homecoming, he was promoted to alderman in the Council and chosen for the Assembly from Philadelphia in 1730. In 1735 he served as mayor of Philadelphia, and six years later he was chosen recorder to replace his father-in-law. His committee activity in the Assembly involved legal work (he had read law at Middle Temple), land matters, and financial problems.

Allen's early career was paralleled by that of a man destined to

Isaac Norris II.
*Historical Society
of Pennsylvania.*

James Hamilton.
*Independence National
Historical Park.*

Richard Peters.
*Pennsylvania Academy
of Fine Arts.*

be his constant rival in provincial political life, Isaac Norris II. He entered the Common Council of Philadelphia with Allen, was chosen alderman with him, but was not elected to the Assembly until 1735. Three years Allen's senior, Norris was born a Quaker and was always active in the Society. Isaac Norris, like William Allen, Sr., was a successful merchant, but unlike the elder Allen he was drawn into politics, serving as justice of the peace in Philadelphia and also its mayor, member of the Council after 1709, and assemblyman frequently after 1710 (in 1712 and 1720 he was speaker). Married to the daughter of Thomas Lloyd, the senior Norris served as adviser to and attorney for William Penn, who named him a trustee in his will. He trained his son in the family shipping business, which involved travel through the colonies and to England. When he fell ill in 1734, his son returned from London and, after his death a year later, replaced him in the Assembly. Isaac Norris II was reelected in 1737, again from Philadelphia County, and from 1739 to 1765 he served continuously in the legislature. In 1739 he married James Logan's daughter, Sarah; his father-in-law considered him the most learned man in Pennsylvania, save for Richard Peters.

Norris entered politics as Logan exited, entered not only with new men—Allen, James Hamilton, Secretary Peters, and Benjamin Franklin, clerk of the Assembly—but also as a fresh issue and an altered political alignment dominated the scene. Logan's final executive duty was as president of the Council which, after Governor Gordon's death in 1736, took charge until Governor George Thomas' arrival two years later. (Logan remained on the Council until 1747, when his son William replaced him.) Thomas, a wealthy planter from the West Indies who also owned property in Pennsylvania, applied for the deputy governor's post on the grounds that his independent fortune would raise him above temptation, almost the opposite rationale from that applied to the appointment of Sir William Keith. Thomas was steadier than Keith though less creative, a man given to administration rather than adventure. He negotiated, with a minimum of conflict, a bill regarding paper money which was acceptable both to him as a proprietary appointee responsible to the crown and to the Assembly. And he managed to get financial support for himself from that penurious body. Thomas was not, however, prepared for the legislature's response to his request for military appropriations, an issue that had long been dormant.

For the past twenty-five years Europe had been at peace. In England, where foreign policy traditionally sought to maintain a balance of power among the Continental states, there was now more consideration given to building economic strength through the empire, a strategy that favored oceangoing commerce uninterrupted by war. Moreover, the principal minister in Parliament, Robert Walpole, saw in the absence of government spending during peacetime a way of removing contention from politics and, thus, maintaining himself in power. But as English and colonial merchants became bolder in their search for products and markets, trading illicitly in Spanish America, Spain exercised the right of search and seizure. Walpole at first tried to defend this practice but finally was forced into declaring war in 1739. The following year the crown called on its American colonies to support an expedition against Spain in the West Indies.

Most of the American provinces responded promptly and obediently to this summons. In Pennsylvania, despite Governor Thomas' statement that funds would be spent only for nonmilitary necessities of troops en route to the West Indies, the Assembly replied that the religious principles of a majority of its members did not allow them to "preserve good Consciences and come into the Levying of Money and appropriating it to the uses recommended." The history of the Assembly's responses to similar requests had not led directly to this adamant refusal.

In 1693 the Assembly had voted on a "bill for the support of Government," an action consistent with the Quaker belief that governments, installed by God, were owed obedience by their subjects. If the money contained in the bill was to be used for military purposes, that was not the Assembly's responsibility, though Quakers did not deny a nation's right to defend itself. The irony was that the Assembly's behavior in 1693 had been conditioned by a desire to obtain broader powers in exchange for an appropriation, powers that it achieved over the next several years. Consequently, when a subsequent royal demand for aid to the war effort was laid before the legislature by Governor Gookin in 1709, that body probably could have directed money to specific purposes and hence assumed responsibility for spending the funds. The Assembly refused to contribute to the Canada expedition which was in the governor's request but did offer a smaller amount as "a Present" to the queen. Faced by a requisition for the same purpose two years later, the Assembly responded with a larger sum "for the Queen's use," fully aware that a portion of it would be diverted directly to military operations. But these martial activities would be conducted outside of Pennsylvania, where the provincial government had no jurisdiction. From a constitutional point of view, Quaker politicians took shelter under their subordinate position in the empire. They had not abandoned the peace testimony but only found a different way to reconcile it with their commitment to the government.

Between the end of Queen Anne's War in 1713 and the beginning of King George's War in 1739, Quakerism was undergoing significant change, symbolized by the fact that when the first quarter of the eighteenth century ended, the first-generation founders of Pennsylvania were dead. What had been a Quaker colony was now a heterogeneous society, with Friends clearly in a minority. And, as their preponderance diminished, they lost their sectarian characteristics. Not that a universalistic view had ever been absent from the Society, but it had been a Quaker universalism, the apocalyptic conceit of every vital Christian group, and it had always been balanced (perhaps contradicted) by the desire to live as a pure community, tolerated by the larger society. Now Pennsylvania Quakers were reflecting rather than reforming their environment. As the wealth and class consciousness of the community increased, it was mirrored in the society of Friends, not only in the elegance of the rich Quakers' life-style but also in the recognition that the economic elite were the religious leaders as well. The two Isaac Norrises stood as testimony to this development. But had there been any doubt about generational succession in 1737 the practice of birthright membership in the Society was accepted by the London Yearly Meeting.

Indeed, there was a problem of keeping younger Quakers within the fold. By the third decade of the century it was recognized that delinquency as defined by the Society, though often not by the provincial government, was sharply rising; far and away the major offense was "marrying out" to a non-Quaker. Whether or not the intrusion of alien groups promoted waywardness, this was perceived to be the case. In 1733 the Philadelphia Yearly Meeting wrote to the London Yearly Meeting: "Greater circumspection appears the more necessary by the great increase of people, not only those born among us, but others of divers nations, customs and manners, which of late years have flow'd in upon us, so that with grief we observe vice and immorality to increase."

Although it was the general practice at this time to attempt to bring the wayward back to righteous behavior, the emphasis on correct conduct and possible punishment betrayed an absolutism of ideology, a lack of flexibility in a culture of change, which could only relegate once-vital beliefs to the status of dogma for a substantial number of Quakers. Membership depended on doctrinal conformity rather than the Inner Light—a logical reaction to the growing number of aliens without and an increasing amount of backsliding within. John Churchman, an itinerant Quaker minister, observed that there were three kinds of Friends: the nominal members, who were satisfied that other Quakers thought well of them; the hypocrites, who censured others but failed to see their own profligacy; and the "humble and bowed," who said little except to lament the state of society or their own weakness. Yet even those who honestly feared straying from the truth were more concerned with behavior than belief.

In politics this stance fostered a united Quaker interest. The factionalism of the early years disappeared, a situation almost announced by the death of David Lloyd in 1731. During that decade when provincial energies were focused on the development of the interior, the friends of the newly arrived proprietor were prominent. But in 1739 Andrew Hamilton stepped down from the speaker's chair to be succeeded by John Kinsey who, in addition to holding that post until his death in 1750, served as clerk of the Philadelphia Yearly Meeting. Described by Richard Peters, hardly an unbiased observer, as gay and flirtatious, hard-drinking and extravagant—the latter quality proved by the embarrassing discovery that he had misappropriated at least £3,000 from the General Loan Office for private use—Kinsey represented the concessions the Society of Friends had made to worldliness. The minority, aware of what was happening, could not effect reform so long as the fear of dissent in the Society and the abhorrence of change without unanimity assumed greater priority than adherence to principle.

An omen appeared at the close of the indulgent 1730s. The peace testimony was one of the remaining vestiges of primitive Quakerism. In September 1739 the Philadelphia Yearly Meeting circulated a letter calling for strict adherence to the testimony, a position adopted by Quakers elected to the Assembly in October and relayed to Governor Thomas in the summer of 1740 in response to his request for funds. Thomas was handicapped in this affair not only by Quaker inflexibility but by the absence of proprietary support in the legislature. William Allen had followed his father-in-law Andrew Hamilton into retirement in 1739, writing to John Penn: "I had served on the Assembly these Nine Years past & as most of our Disputes seem to be at an End & the Province's Affairs upon a very good Footing I choose to Decline being concerned this Year as . . . Mr. Hamilton & several others of our Friends have done." Quakers occupied twenty-two out of thirty-six seats as a result of the 1739 elections.

Legislative recalcitrance, however, did not stand in the way of recruitment of men to serve in the West Indies expedition, and Governor Thomas reconvened the Assembly in late July 1740 to inform it that seven companies had been enlisted in the province and must be supported. Now the Quakers not only reaffirmed their position on military spending but pointed out that servants had been signed away from their masters. John Kinsey, who also served the province as attorney general, gave his opinion that this practice was illegal, speaking to self-interest in the name of liberty and property. With this principle in tow, Quaker politicians made great appeal to Germans who had never previously voted. William Allen, surging back into politics in the 1740 elections as the head of the proprietary interest, was shocked and angered by a stunning Quaker victory at the polls. Thus, a new political alignment emerged, the product of major social forces in Pennsylvania. The Quakers, made to feel their distinctiveness by developments within and without the Society, found allies in a responsive immigrant group. Friends of the proprietors, appalled by Quaker resistance to royal demands, formed a well-defined political cluster. The leaders of both "parties" were, of course, drawn from the economic elite. Class conflict was no more an issue than democratic principles.

But another transatlantic movement, quite unrelated to the war though it also began in 1739, exacerbated the strife in Pennsylvania by stressing religious differences between the two contending groups. The Great Awakening, that widespread and pervasive quickening of spiritual life, affected not only the American colonies but, under different labels, England and the Continent. It was a conservative movement insofar as it brought about a revival of religion in an increasingly secular world; it was a new departure in its focus on individual rather than group piety. In its broadest context it was a reaction to the Enlightenment, the eighteenth-century intellectual revolution grounded in the thought of Bacon and Descartes, Newton and Locke, and later popularized for acceptance by all who could believe that the Western world was emerging from a dark past of ignorance and lethargy into a present of reason and progress. The universe, formerly the mysterious preserve of an inscrutable God, became comprehensible through the understanding of natural law, applicable everywhere since the beginning of time. The Deity was not capriciously manifest in nature but, rather, no longer interfered, having set the world in motion according to rules discernible by man the master of reason. Probably no person in colonial America so well represented this viewpoint as Benjamin Franklin.

The tide of the Enlightenment was resisted by those to whom faith loomed larger than reason, the supernatural more meaningful than the natural. In Europe the reaction was called Pietism, brought to the New World by German sects which most frequently landed in Pennsylvania; in England, it was Methodism, the creation of the Wesley brothers and George Whitefield. It was the latter who inaugurated the Great Awakening in America by undertaking a protracted preaching tour up and down the Atlantic seaboard. He first appeared in Philadelphia in 1739, and Franklin, who became his friend and printer but not his convert, many years later recalled: "It was wonderful to see the change made in the manner of our inhabitants. From being thoughtless or indifferent about religion, it seem'd as if all the world were growing religious, so that one could not walk thro' the town in an evening without hearing psalms sung in different families of every street." Whitefield's success was widespread though exaggerated by Franklin.

The Quakers could hardly be friendly to the Enlightenment's denial of the immanence of God and the permanence of Truth. But, despite their origins in spiritual enthusiasm, Friends remained aloof from the revivalistic preaching and Calvinistic theology of Whitefield and his fellow itinerants. Within a year or two, even the tolerance faded. James Logan, though not the best of Friends, expressed a characteristic opinion when he observed of Whitefield: "It must be confessed that his preaching has good effect in reclaiming many dissolute people, but from his countenancing so very much the most hot-headed predestinarians, and those of them, principally, who had been accounted as little better than madmen, he and they have actually driven divers into despair, and some into perfect madness." If Quakers and evangelists shared a belief in the immediate inspiration of the Spirit, they agreed on little else. And among the Germans, the pietistic Dunkards and Moravians who staged the Awakening had little success among the older sectarian groups, the Mennonites and Schwenkfelders, though they made great inroads into the Lutheran and Reformed denominations, just as Whitefield had reached the Presbyterians and the Anglicans among English-speaking Pennsylvanians, while failing to attract the Quakers.

Evangelism was more effective among church people than sectarians not for theological reasons but because churches had failed to establish the hierarchical institutional structures in

America which they had left in Europe, structures that were largely irrelevant to sects. Not only had the churches tried in vain to recreate an ecclesiastical system above the level of the congregation, but they had been unable to settle a ministry adequate to the needs of a rapidly expanding population. An established clergy was less important to sectarians, and the investment of authority in congregational leaders less necessary. Consequently, popular control was not so threatening. Sectarians, furthermore, were used to existing in the shadow of other religious groups, while church people found the multiplicity of denominations in Pennsylvania confusing, the heckling of their neighbors unnerving (such as the reaction of a Quaker to the baptism of an acquaintance: "Why didn't thee desire the Minister rather to piss upon thy Head . . . that would have been of more effect"), the proselytizing tempting, and religious intermarriage often irresistible.

Indifference and anticlericalism flourished before the Awakening, the evangelists catering to the hostility toward ministers through characterizations of an "unregenerate clergy" while overcoming apathy with the promise of spiritual rebirth. The major consequence of the Awakening was the renewal of organized religion, bringing the laity back into the churches and restoring the authority of the regenerate clergy. In so doing, the Awakening ultimately fostered denominational self-awareness. The Quakers and their German sectarian allies held aloof from the Awakening as they did from war. They faced revitalized church groups, conscious of their religious distinctiveness and willing to take up arms for the crown and the proprietors.

In the early 1740s the division between sect and church groups was strongly felt and politically expressed. It was evident even in the Assembly's choice of a representative in London. Not until 1730 had governor and legislature agreed on maintaining a permanent agent, at which time Ferdinando John Paris—a solicitor for the Penns with a tested reputation for doing well by his clients—was hired. Although he performed capably, he was replaced in 1740 by Richard Partridge who, like Paris, had experience representing other colonies and, in fact, appeared several times with Paris in Pennsylvania's behalf. Unlike Paris,

Partridge was a Quaker, brought up in New England and a strong proponent of the colonists' interests. He had known John Kinsey when the latter was speaker of the New Jersey Assembly and Partridge its agent. He also had the backing of Isaac Norris II and of Israel Pemberton, a better and only slightly less powerful Quaker than Kinsey during his service in the Assembly in the 1730s and 1740s. When a letter written by Governor Thomas in October 1740 on the defenseless state of the province reached the Board of Trade, depicting the Quakers and their tactics in quite unflattering terms, Partridge surreptitiously secured a copy and circulated it among Friends in London and in Pennsylvania, where it was used to influence the election held in the fall of 1741.

Again the proprietors' friends made a bid for power, the contest becoming so heated that James Hamilton came to blows with Israel Pemberton. Again the Quakers scored a victory. The fisticuffs which distinguished the election were but a warm-up for the title bout, which occurred when voters went to the polls in 1742. The proprietary group had attempted to defeat their opponents by petitioning the Board of Trade to have Quakers disqualified from elective office in time of war. Richard Partridge's news of the failure of this strategy arrived in the province immediately before the October 1 election, adding desperation to a situation in which nerves were short and tempers ran high. It was rumored that Quakers would import unnaturalized Germans to vote, and that Allen and his followers had hired armed sailors to drive Friends from the Court House, the polling place at Second and Market streets in the midst of taverns and close by the wharfs. There was sure to be a mob scene because inspectors, who judged the legality of the election, would be chosen by the number of men who lined up behind each of them as the sheriff called off names of candidates. Inspectors could determine elections, since they were empowered to inspect the "secret" ballots of voters. In Philadelphia, each elector walked to the second-story balcony of the Court House to drop his folded ballot in the box, having to pass before the inspectors at the landing of the stairway.

William Allen attempted to avert confrontation with a compromise giving the proprietary and Quaker contingents each four inspectors, but confident Friends rejected the proposal. (Allen, in addition to being an interested party, as recorder of Philadelphia was required to maintain the peace.) On election morning Quakers saw sailors everywhere and demanded that Allen disperse gathered "strangers." Meanwhile, Israel Pemberton tactlessly warned one Captain Mitchell against demeaning himself by heading a mob of mariners, and for his persistence Pemberton was threatened with a cudgel. Again Allen was bluntly approached, this time responding angrily that "Sailors had as much right to walk the streets as the unnaturalized Dutch." At ten o'clock the sheriff opened the elections at the Court House, and it soon became apparent that Allen was receiving few votes, while Isaac Norris pulled many. Suddenly some fifty to seventy sailors appeared, swinging clubs to clear out the Quakers. The sheriff quickly issued constables' staffs to willing citizens, who drove back the marauders at some physical cost. The sailors were more successful in their second assault, some of the Quakers retreating to the safety of the Court House, which was also attacked. Allen vainly tried to quell the riot by going among the sailors, telling them "they were a Parcel of Villains," but only a counter effort by armed Quakers and Germans ended the fracas.

This violent outbreak, despite lack of evidence that it was the work of Allen or his followers, spelled disaster for the proprietary group. Not only was the immediate election lost, but politicians associated with the Penns lived under a cloud for the next decade. Allen, who sued Israel Pemberton for calling him a plotter, had to face John Kinsey as opposing counsel and found the investigation of the riot turned over to the obviously biased Assembly. His humiliation could be seen in his failure to gain reelection to the Assembly for the following fourteen years. And the program of the proprietary supporters had stalled. Not only had their petition to bar Quakers from the legislature failed, but there were still no funds for the war effort and the governor had gone unpaid for more than two years.

The rout of the proprietary interest gave the Quaker politicians an opportunity to effect a compromise with the governor on their terms. There were pressures from within the Society to reach an accord on the issue of military appropriations. A prominent English Friend had recommended to Israel Pemberton in 1740 that the Pennsylvanians follow the practice of their English brethren: "to pay Caesar his Due, and to let the Government do therewith as they judge best for the Good of the Country." The following year James Logan sent a letter to the Philadelphia Yearly Meeting reiterating a position he had announced decades earlier: civil government was founded on force and Friends ought not engage in it. Though the meeting disregarded his message, there was soon afterward a move in Chester and Bucks counties to replace radical assemblymen with more moderate types. Nor could Quaker politicians be impervious to the clear disapproval of the crown regarding their position on military matters. In particular, a scathing indictment of the Pennsylvania Assembly was made by the Board of Trade in February 1742.

John Kinsey, whom Richard Peters referred to as "the Hinge on which the Quaker Politicks all turn," in early 1743 approached Governor Thomas on reaching a peaceful settlement of differences. The governor had refused to sign Assembly bills while his salary was withheld; his signature on each piece of legislation would, part by part, restore the money due him. Furthermore, Kinsey still resented his dismissal from the post of attorney general in October 1741, which was Thomas' reaction to Kinsey's statement that he would serve as speaker without the governor's approbation since he was the legislature's choice—thus going a step beyond Andrew Hamilton in augmenting the power of that position. Now Kinsey asked for and received appointment as chief justice of the Supreme Court, an obvious political plum but one for which he was qualified. Even Thomas Penn had remarked: "Tho he has been in with a party I always took him for an honest Man, & Capable of Doing Service [as attorney general] being the only person now in the Law, that has been long acquainted with the Constitution & People of the Province."

Despite this turnaround in relations between the executive and legislature, the Assembly was slow to respond to continued requests for military funds, even after the declaration of war on France in June 1744. It would not contribute to the expedition against Louisbourg being organized by Governor William Shirley of Massachusetts, and when it finally did respond to a demand for a contribution to the defense of Nova Scotia in January 1745, the money (£4,000) was voted "for the King's Use" and designated specifically for the purchase of "Bread, Beef, Pork, Flour, Wheat or other Grain . . . within this province." Franklin's witty recollection that Governor Thomas understood "other Grain" to mean gunpowder was probably apocryphal but, as usual, the philosopher grasped the larger meaning of the gesture. His characterization of the Quaker politicians struck at the Society's dilemma: "They were unwilling to offend government, on the one hand, by a direct refusal [to grant aids for military purposes]; and their friends, the body of the Quakers, on the other, by a compliance contrary to their principles; hence a variety of evasions to avoid complying, and modes of disguising the compliance when it became unavoidable." Logan had come down strongly on the side of government support while the Pembertons had attempted, and failed, to elect a stronger pacifist slate in Philadelphia County in 1744. The Kinsey forces were between the extremes, edging in Logan's direction.

It was Franklin who forced the decision on Quakers to move farther from pacifism. In May 1747 Governor Thomas retired for reasons of health, and his place was taken by Anthony Palmer, oldest member of the Provincial Council. Neither that body nor the man heading it had recently played a prominent part in provincial politics, but decisive leadership was necessary with the threat of Spanish and French privateers sailing into Delaware Bay and up the river. Franklin saw the opportunity and published *Plain Truth*, a pamphlet that emphasized in several ways the common interests of Pennsylvanians: the importance of defending the western frontier and the eastern coast; the general benefits of trade, endangered by foreigners; the crucial need to defend "the middling People, the tradesmen, shopkeepers, and Farmers of this Province and City," who had been neglected by "those Great and rich Men, Merchants and others, who are ever railing at the Quakers for doing what their Principles seem to require . . . but take no one Step themselves for the Publick Safety." Praising the "fierce fighting Animals" from the British Isles and the "*brave* and *steady* Germans," Franklin called for the organization of a militia on a voluntary basis.

Franklin did not censure the obstructionist Friends, noting only that their pacifist principles need not prevail when they composed a minor part of the population. But Gilbert Tennent, a leader of the Great Awakening and the most important Presbyterian minister in Philadelphia, wrote a tract on the "rightfulness of lawful defense" that was clearly aimed at faulting the Society. Meanwhile, in the spring of 1748 foreign privateers were in Delaware Bay. The Quaker politicians had to act. John Kinsey promised Palmer and his Council that the Assembly would support action "for the Good of the Province," and he expressly approved military measures. The Assembly carried through on this promise to the executive. Furthermore, some Quakers privately initiated subscriptions to a fund to be used at Palmer's discretion in "emergency situations." In deciding to favor support of the government over the peace testimony, Friends situated responsibility for defense in the executive rather than the legislature. They did not underwrite the taking up of arms.

In this situation there were two dissenting viewpoints which forecast future conflict. John Churchman, a ministering Quaker, spoke of government as the instrument of God (a view William Penn had discarded) and the peace testimony as more important than any obligation to the imperial government or to religious groups that sanctioned war. And Thomas Penn, despite the fact that the voluntary militia foundered when peace broke out, was certain that Franklin's *Plain Truth* had "done much mischief." He feared that "the people of America are too often ready to act in defiance of the Government they live in, without associating themselves for that purpose." Penn quite disapproved of the very sort of associations that Franklin created, once accusing the Assembly of irresponsibility for appropriating money to such projects as "hospital, steeple, bells, unnecessary library with several other things." Penn had only uneasy concern for Franklin, writing to Richard Peters in June 1748: "He is a dangerous Man and I should be very Glad he inhabited any other Country, as I believe him of a very uneasy Spirit. However, as he is a Sort of Tribune of the People, he must be treated with regard." Dissension within the Quaker ranks and the emerging rivalry between Benjamin Franklin and Thomas Penn, chief proprietor of Pennsylvania after the death of his brother John in 1746, set the stage for the-1750s.

8

PRUNING: INDIAN AFFAIRS, POLITICS, AND QUAKER REFORMATION

In 1748 Benjamin Franklin took on "a very able, industrious, and honest partner, Mr. David Hall, with whose character I was well acquainted as he had worked for me four years." In a partnership that last eighteen years, Hall ran the business while Franklin planned to spend the rest of his life engaged in "philosophical studies and amusements," or so he recalled. "I proceeded in my electrical experiments with great alacrity; but the publick, now considering me as a man of leisure, laid hold of me for their purposes, every part of our civil government, and almost at the same time, imposing some duty on me." Franklin's recollection did justice to the pull of public affairs on his life but hardly to the importance of his work in science.

In the age of the Enlightenment great emphasis was placed on description and classification, since the discovery of external facts had to precede their orderly arrangement which in turn would yield the natural law underlying the facts. Natural history was therefore of tremendous interest in the Western world, and the novelty of the American environment compensated for the lack of libraries and other accouterments of accumulated learning to be found in Europe. There was an intellectually dynamic group of natural scientists who traded ideas and information across the Atlantic in the eighteenth century, and no colony matched Pennsylvania's vigor in the field. James Logan, with the largest colonial library of scientific titles, was internationally known as a botanist, and encouraged a young Quaker named John Bartram, the "wonderful Natural Genius" of the American plant world. Cadwallader Colden, not technically a natural scientist nor a Pennsylvanian but a New York historian and philosopher, was also urged on by Logan, his wife's cousin, when he visited Philadelphia.

Franklin, too, worked in Bartram's behalf, unsuccessfully attempting to raise money for a botanical expedition. He responded kindly to Colden's rustic work on gravitation, and his Library Company was the initial step toward Colden's suggestion of an intercolonial scientific society. In 1738 John Penn presented the company with a "costly Air-Pump," and the proprietary family contributed other scientific apparatus. When Franklin proposed an American Philosophical Society, it was with Bartram's strong assistance, though Logan, by now cool toward Bartram, refused to participate, thus depriving the struggling institution not only of patronage but his own ideas and his European connections. Support did come from Dr. Archibald Spencer of Edinburgh, who lectured through the colonies on medical matters and electricity and encouraged the society, but to no avail. The scientific community in the colonies was too frail to support it.

Soon afterward, probably in 1746, the Library Company received a glass tube for conducting electrical experiments, as well as German writings on the subject, all of which fascinated Franklin. The sender was Peter Collinson, a London Quaker merchant who, more than any other European, made certain the scientific efforts of Americans were given an audience and rewarded abroad. He soon heard from Franklin concerning the "electric tube. . . . I never was before engaged in any study that so totally engrossed my attention and my time." The Philadelphian promised to send the results of his work, which Collinson passed on to friends, read to the Royal Society of London, and published in 1751 as *Experiments and Observations on Electricity*, supplemented in 1753 and 1754 with more letters. Collinson provided Franklin with an international audience, which led to a reputation, honorary degrees from American colleges, and fellowship in the Royal Society. For Franklin's electrical discoveries came when interest in the subject was high, his lightning rod demonstrated the utility of knowledge, and his American origins served as a reproof to Old World scholasticism.

In truth Franklin, unlike the students of natural science, was at a disadvantage in his environment. While he appeared interested in nature, the questions he raised revolved about storms and earthquakes rather than flora and fauna. In the Junto he raised such questions as: "Is sound an entity or a body?" His interests led him to natural philosophy, which meant the Newtonian system and required a mathematical understanding, not part of his background. Formal learning and libraries, where the accumulation of past knowledge could be found, were important to experimentation in physics. Franklin's belief in the free exchange of ideas, which made him turn naturally to college teachers with mathematical training, helped compensate for his deficiency.

In his willingness to publish his work, admit his errors, and accept better explanations than his own, Franklin stood in almost vivid contrast to the man he and other eighteenth-century natural philosophers were most beholden to—Sir Isaac Newton. It was probably less an index to the difference between the scientific worlds of England and America than between their respective childhoods that the foremost natural philosophers of the two places were so different. Newton, whose father died before his birth and whose mother put him out to a grandmother and uncle two years later, was not only starved for family affection but friendship. His premature birth and consequent physical weakness appeared to have subjected him to boyhood taunts and humiliation from which he could not recover. The solitary, lonely boy became a suspicious man, isolated, intense, introspective. (Franklin, who seemed able to gain access to anyone, was unable to see Newton during his first trip to England.) After his first published work on light and color created a controversy, Newton was cautious about publishing, though the security which came from recognition altered this behavior in his later years.

Newton stood alone among the scientists of his age, his creative ability unrivaled. Franklin was an extremely talented disciple.

Though Newton had done practically no work in electricity, the Philadelphian could use the Newtonian method. And, like Newton, Franklin had the dexterity necessary to build his equipment. The candor with which he described his experiments —what he planned to do, the apparatus used and the operations performed, the relationship of the results to the working hypothesis—and the homey language he employed were expressive of the flesh-and-blood Franklin. Similarly, the forbidding Latin prose of the *Principia* (speculation) and the *Opticks* (experimentation)— neither of which revealed the process by which their author developed his ideas—was a guide to the personality of the inaccessible Newton, a man mysterious in his own time.

Although he served as master of the mint and in Parliament, scientific work was the reality of Newton's life. He was schooled to it, and his absent-mindedness concerning anything but his absorbing occupation was notorious. Franklin, however, had already forged a successful business career when in the 1740s he began to talk of "leisure to cultivate the finer arts and improve the common stock of knowledge" while delving into the scientific literature that would enable him to frame the questions for his experiments at the end of the decade. Probably the very lack of learned associates, such as clustered around Newton, help to account for the simplicity of Franklin's explanations of his experiments, as he tried to make himself understood to a lay audience. The work itself was not naive, however, for Franklin extended the boundaries of natural philosophy by dealing with the constitution of matter, the relationship between the composition and physical properties of bodies, and the variant behavior of different kinds of matter. Though Franklin's single fluid theory of electricity, the ideas of positive and negative attraction, and the empirical proof of the constant existence of electrification in nature (the lightning experiments) were great contributions, he went beyond even these accomplishments to postulating general principles that supplemented Newtonianism.

Yet throughout these several years devoted largely to science, Franklin never lost touch with the audience he originally found with his newspaper, later with his projects, and finally with his politics. His obsession with experimentation diminished as he answered the weighty questions which he ingeniously framed. If "the publick . . . laid hold" of him, as he said, he was not an unwilling captive. Although Franklin was unable to sustain the American Philosophical Society, he was instrumental in the founding in 1751 of the Pennsylvania Hospital, an obvious demonstration of the practical uses of science. Having written the record of provincial legislation for fifteen years, he stood for election to the Assembly from the city of Philadelphia in 1751 (he was already a common councilman and alderman), winning and holding his seat until 1764, while his son William took over his post as clerk. ("I was at length tired with sitting there to hear debates, in which, as clerk, I could take no part, and which were often so unentertaining," he later recalled.) It would be a new role for Franklin, who up to this time had drawn his own agenda, operating outside the established political order, and who had stayed aloof from partisan quarrels, maintaining friendships with every powerful interest or person, not even admitting a religious affiliation.

Franklin entered provincial politics in the wake of some major changes in personnel. In 1748 James Hamilton, a former assemblyman, was designated deputy governor. It was a wise proprietary appointment, with Franklin expressing the popular sentiment in his observation that "we esteem him a benevolent and upright, as well as a sensible man." In 1750 Speaker John Kinsey died, embarrassing the Society of Friends when his financial peculations were revealed but in no way diminishing the Quakers' political power. His successor was Isaac Norris II, frequently referred to as "The Speaker" because he remained in the chair until 1764, a man who had plunged into politics after the untimely death of his wife, Sarah Logan, in the early 1740s. His life during that decade had been further troubled by his brother's demise and a quarrel with his father-in-law, James Logan, who died in 1751.

Logan, for half a century a power, often the power in Pennsylvania politics, respected his son-in-law's intelligence, but he felt the need to apologize to the Penns for Norris' politics. (Richard Peters, who now handled the bulk of proprietary affairs, wrote in 1750 that he "used to settle all matters with Mr.

Kinsey previous to their being laid before the house & coud tell what woud & what woud not be done but now I have not a creature to speak to that can carry a point.") By 1750, however, Norris spoke for the larger wing of the Quaker party, some of his constituents embracing Logan's position on defensive warfare, others at ease with Franklin's concept of a voluntary militia.

Neither of these viewpoints was acceptable to the faction of Friends whose commitment to the peace testimony would not admit the establishment of any sort of military force in the province. Israel Pemberton, Jr., later known as the "King of the Quakers," was the acknowledged leader of this contingent. His outspoken charges against executive action led Governor Thomas to issue a warrant for his arrest in 1739; his tactlessness in dealing with the "lower sorts" played no little part in provoking the election riot three years later. Despite some suspect business dealings, the Pemberton family was noted for its adherence to strict Quakerism. Israel's brother John was a ministering Friend, though James would sit in the Assembly, and at mid-century Israel curtailed his commercial activities to devote himself to religious concerns and put his principles into politics. He succeeded John Kinsey as clerk of the Philadelphia Yearly Meeting, holding the office as long as Norris held the speakership. Thus Kinsey's control of the key religious and political positions, not always ethically compatible, was now divided between two men. (Kinsey's third post, chief justice of the Supreme Court, went to proprietary supporter William Allen.) Neither Quaker leader, however, doubted that the Assembly should play the ascendant role in provincial politics.

In 1751 the legislature was as strong as it had ever been, its accretion of power having taken place gradually and, often enough, unintentionally over the past decades at the expense of the proprietors. Thomas Penn fully recognized his family's loss of strength, was convinced that the Assembly always acted with malicious intent, and saw the legislature's virtually independent authority in provincial finance as the key to control. "There is nothing but the power of appropriating the Publick Money that can give those People any weight," he informed Governor Hamilton in 1751, implicitly promising to make money rather than war the issue that inflamed relations between executive and legislature in the early 1750s.

From the very beginning there had been a scarcity of specie in Pennsylvania, caused mainly by the unfavorable balance of trade with England. Although barter was resorted to in the 1680s and 1690s, it was inadequate to the problem. Another expedient used at that time was raising the rate of exchange on currency to draw money into the colony, but the Assembly's activity was blocked by a royal proclamation in 1704 fixing the rates of foreign coins in the colonies (Isaac Newton, master of the mint, drew up the rates), a move confirmed by act of Parliament four years later. Complaints about the dearth of money in circulation increased with the arrival of immigrants who made the problem more acute, leading to a third solution—paper money. In 1723 the Assembly issued £15,000 in bills of credit and set up a loan office with four trustees at Philadelphia. Amounts from £10 12s. to £100 could be borrowed for eight years at 5 percent interest, the loans secured by mortgages on borrowers' estates. Later in the year £30,000 more was issued on the same terms. It was generally agreed that inflation of the circulating medium led to a revival of trade in the province.

Nevertheless, the Board of Trade did not favor paper money, causing colonial governors to shy away from it. It took almost a year and Franklin's tract on currency ("As bills issued upon money security are money, so bills issued upon land are, in effect, coined land.") for the Assembly to reach an agreement with Governor Gordon in 1729 on the issue of £30,000, which Franklin printed. In 1731 £40,000 more came out, and in 1739 an Assembly act provided for the reissue of £68,889 15s. then outstanding, as well as the new printing of £11,110 5s., putting £80,000 into circulation. By this time the Board of Trade was presenting Parliament with a report on colonial currency in response to agitation from English merchants. Within a few years legislation was presented which would have stopped the issue of bills of credit as legal tender, with a clause giving royal instructions the force of law. The Pennsylvania Assembly, alarmed as were other colonial legislatures, feared that passage would be "destructive of all their Liberties, and likely to be attended with the most dangerous consequences to all the King's Subjects in America." The parliamentary legislation failed, and Governor Thomas agreed to the reissue of the £80,000 put in circulation in 1739, as well as to the printing of £5,000 more to finance a military expedition to Canada. In 1749 it again appeared as though Parliament would prohibit all American colonies from using paper as legal tender, but the Currency Act of 1751 forbade only the New Englanders from emitting paper currency.

Thomas Penn, however, would not let the Pennsylvanians off so easily. Having vowed to reduce the power of the Assembly when he came into possession of three-quarters of the proprietary estate in 1746, he focused on the legislature's monetary affairs. He recognized that when the Assembly issued paper money, it collected the interest, an average of £3,000 annually, for which it was accountable to no one. It also took in another £2,500 to £3,000 annually through a manipulation of excise rates which, raised high enough, yielded a considerable sum over that needed to retire the paper money in circulation. Only a month after the Currency Act omitted Pennsylvania from its control, Penn instructed Governor Hamilton that he was not to approve "any Paper Money or Excise Law" which did not allow him a determination in the expenditure of its produce, an obvious encroachment on the Assembly's strength.

Penn's perspicacity in pinpointing a source of legislative power did not extend to an understanding of legislative pride. The first Assembly in which Franklin sat passed a bill in February 1752 for the issue of £40,000 in paper which Hamilton refused, as he continued to refuse money bills for the next year and a half. The Assembly, for its part, rejected Hamilton's assertions that the province had sufficient currency and that a new bill would provoke retribution from London, perceiving instead that the governor was acting on instructions from the proprietor. One of the proprietary supporters informed Penn that if his instruction to the chief executive regarding control of any money bill's produce were known, the "Governor and his Friends would be publickly branded as Deliverer's up of the People's Rights," while William Allen urged Hamilton to conceal his instruction.

Perplexed by his dilemma, Hamilton resigned in February 1753, effective a year from his letter's receipt, warning that whoever tried to restore "the Balance of Power in the Proprietor's Scale" would be left "standing simply, exposed to the resentment and reproaches of the whole province." Penn backed off, rescinding his instruction, and Hamilton promised to approve a new issue in August 1753. But his stipulation, the so-called suspending clause, that the money bill could not become law until it received royal approval made him the object of the Assembly's wrath, the members of that body rightfully feeling they had been thwarted again.

The conflict in Philadelphia was matched by the outbreak of hostilities with France in the western part of the province, a collision whose background could be viewed in the perspective of Pennsylvania's Indian relations. This situation could only increase friction between the Assembly and the proprietor. Not only was control over the conduct and financing of Indian affairs contended, but the thorny problem of military appropriations was raised again. The Indians in the Ohio Valley, who united with the French to fight the English in 1754, had recently regarded the Pennsylvanians as "brothers," just as they referred to the Iroquois as "uncles." This connection, better known as the covenant chain, was in the 1730s broken up by James Logan when he convinced Schickellamy, the representative of the Six Nations resident in Shamokin, to sacrifice the Lenape and Shawnee lands in favor of advancing white settlement.

A third party to this new arrangement, the man who would carry the burden of Pennsylvania's Indian negotiations over the next few decades, first appeared in Philadelphia as Schickellamy's interpreter in 1731, where he met Logan. Conrad Weiser, born in Württemberg in 1696, left Germany with his widower father and eight brothers and sisters. Eventually he reached New York, settling on Livingston Manor. Two brothers were apprenticed on Long Island, a third died, and the father remarried a woman unable to keep the family together. When its remnants moved to Schenectady, sixteen-year-old Conrad was sent to a Mohawk village to master the language. Meanwhile, the Palatines were not getting along with the New York authorities and, on Governor William Keith's invitation, some of them moved to Pennsylvania. In 1720 Conrad married; nine years later he took his wife and four children to Tulpehocken. Apparently he had already met Schickellamy.

Through the 1730s Weiser kept his contact with the Indian leader and grew increasingly close to Logan, though his uneasiness with the Walking Purchase drove him into the religious cloister at Ephrata, where he had been baptized a couple of years earlier. (Weiser, already the father of nine children, became a celibate known as Brother Enoch, the name signifying a soul in paradise and a body in the flesh; he later fathered five more children.) He remained in virtual seclusion until, spent by his spiritual orgasm, he was lured back into provincial affairs by a personal visit from Governor Thomas. By 1741 he was in league with Logan to defeat an assemblyman from Lancaster County who represented the Quaker interest. A year later he was in Philadelphia "interpreting" the Walking Purchase to the Six Nations. Nutimus, the Lenape chief in the Forks of Delaware area, had protested against the invading white settlers. He was in turn reminded by Governor Thomas of English numerical superiority and humiliated by the Iroquois, who subjected the Lenape to ridicule while commanding them to vacate the region. It was this operation of the Six Nations–Pennsylvania alliance which made the eastern Indians, now forced into the Ohio Valley, realize that their "uncles" and "brothers" could no longer be trusted. One Delaware, Teedyuscung, later remembered that at this conference in 1742 he had been taken by the hairs of his head and shaken.

In 1744 in Lancaster Weiser and other officials of Pennsylvania, Maryland, and Virginia met with chiefs of the Six Nations and negotiated a treaty ceding Iroquois land in the Ohio Valley to the English colonies and concluding an alliance between the two parties. In resolving this venerable conflict over real estate and friendship, the Six Nations mistakenly thought the recognition of their land claims and of their right to speak alone for the Shawnee and Lenape who had retreated into the Ohio Valley was a token of their augmented power. Instead, they had now to explain their behavior to their former Indian subjects. Speaking in behalf of the English and especially the Pennsylvanians was a sign of declining strength from the time when the Iroquois spoke for the united covenant chain. The so-called Long Peace was the work of Sir Edmund Andros, who created in the seventeenth century the chain which promised protection; William Penn, who respected the Indians' tenure rights; and even James Logan, so long as trade was profitable and, thus, sustained the Indians. It was endangered when protection was no longer forthcoming, when the proprietary family became land grabbers, and when settlers disrupted the fur trade. The French who, unlike the English, built many forts but few towns, became more attractive allies to the Indians. Indeed, the very proximity of the French made them more dangerous as enemies than the English; it was important that the French be friends.

Discontent in the Ohio Valley was fed by the arrival of such Indians as Pisquetomen, whom Logan, Weiser, and Schickellamy tried to block as the successor to Sassoonan at Tulpehocken. (Later, in 1751, the Pennsylvania Council without even consulting the Iroquois told the Ohio Lenape to choose a successor to Sassoonan. The Six Nations, having little alternative, consented to the choice of Shingas, the younger brother of Pisquetomen.) Matters were complicated by the adventurer George Croghan, who plunged into the Ohio country in the mid-1740s, provoked some resident Indians into an attack on the French, and, despite Weiser's denial of Pennsylvania's responsibility for his actions, was financially rewarded by the Council. Croghan, though he acted selfishly and with abandon, garnered a reputation as a good negotiator with the natives and became more and more involved in the province's conduct of Indian affairs. The Assembly was sobered by Franklin's calculation in 1751 that expenses of Indian relations had doubled or trebled with Croghan's entrance.

Up to this time, the provincial government had dealt with the Ohio Indians only through the Six Nations. But Weiser himself was soon recommending that the Ohio tribes be dealt with independently of the Iroquois, a policy the provincial government quickly adopted. Indeed, the attitudes of all the principles were changing. When Weiser visited the Six Nations' council in New York in 1750, he discovered a new chief sachem who was pro-French. Hence, the Ohio Indians became even more important to the English.

The reorientation of the Iroquois was directly related to the French promise not to settle in the Ohio Valley without permission of the Six Nations. But this pledge was broken in 1752 by the new French governor, the Marquis Duquesne, who began building a chain of forts from Lake Erie to the forks of the Ohio River (present-day Pittsburgh). Duquesne was reacting to the Ohio Company of Virginia's determination to place settlers south of the Ohio forks, a move triggered by an agreement between the Virginians and Ohio Indians at Logstown (south of present-day Pittsburgh) in 1752. Not only had the Iroquois been cast aside, but the Ohio Indians saw they too would be caught in the European pincers. Representatives of the Ohioans met with Franklin, Peters, and Norris at Carlisle in 1753, presented their case, and asked the Pennsylvanians to restrain the invading settlers, but got no satisfactory answers. Frontiersmen could not be controlled from Philadelphia, almost two hundred miles east of the farthest settlement. Military solutions were tried. The worried Virginians sent George Washington into the Ohio Valley. After a surprise attack on the French, he assured the Indians that the English intent was "to put you again in possession of your lands, and to take care of your wives and children, to dispossess the French." Washington's subsequent defeat was a sign that France, in fact, controlled the Ohio region.

The French and Indian War thus began in western Pennsylvania, spreading to Europe two years later where from London's perspective it was referred to as the Great War for the Empire. The French had Ohio Indians on their side but, though militarily well organized, could boast a population of only sixty-five to seventy thousand. Approximately fifteen times as many people lived in the British colonies along the Atlantic seaboard as in New France, but the English forfeited the advantage of numerical superiority in discord among themselves and alienation of the Iroquois. Both of these problems were faced but not really solved when, at the instigation of the Board of Trade, representatives of seven English colonies met at Albany in June 1754.

Pennsylvania's representatives at this congress were Benjamin Franklin, Isaac Norris, Richard Peters, and John Penn, grandson of the founder. Conrad Weiser was also in attendance. Of these men, Franklin was by far the best equipped to deal with imperial issues. He had published not only the *Pennsylvania Gazette* but also papers in South Carolina and Rhode Island, in addition to being distantly involved with the gazettes of New York, Connecticut, and Antigua. He was the public printer for Delaware, New Jersey, and Maryland. Indeed, as a printer he looked beyond the colonies to England and the Continent, which received more news space in his *Gazette* than the Pennsylvania backcountry. As a scientist his contacts were also intercolonial and transatlantic; for his work he received recognition from Harvard, Yale, William and Mary, and the Royal Academy. Having been deputy postmaster at Philadelphia since 1737, he was appointed, jointly with William Hunter, publisher of the *Virginia Gazette*, deputy postmaster general for the colonies, a post he held until 1774. While most Pennsylvania politicians were inward-looking and almost incestuous, Franklin had an outward view. But he hardly differed from his colleagues when looking at the Indians.

His allegiance in the backcountry, a region now embracing about three-quarters of the province and containing almost half of its 150,000 inhabitants, was to the advancing settlers rather than the retreating natives. Never did he question the wisdom of the westward thrust. "So vast is the territory . . . that it will require many ages to settle it fully," he wrote in 1751. In the Assembly his concern with the Indians revolved about the financial burden of dealing with the aborigines. He was on the committee which, ten days after he entered the legislature, requested of the proprietors that they pay a designated share of Indian expenses; the answer, arriving well over a year later, was negative. In the autumn of 1753 Franklin had his first taste of negotiations with the natives, having been chosen with Speaker Norris and Council Secretary Peters to journey to Carlisle. Franklin's recollection many years later was not of the content of the talks but of the behavior of the Indians after the discussions, when they were drunk on the white man's liquor: "Their dark-colour'd bodies, half naked, seen only by the gloomy light of the bonfire, running after and beating one another with fire-brands, accompanied by their horrid yellings, form'd a scene the most resembling our ideas of hell that could well be imagin'd. . . . if it be the design of Providence to extirpate these savages in order to make room for the cultivators of the earth, it seems not improbable that rum may be the appointed means."

Given Franklin's sentiments, it was altogether fitting that the few Iroquois who bothered to attend the meeting at Albany went home professing friendship and laden with thirty wagons full of presents but without satisfactory answers to their questions about land encroachments. (Though John Penn did at this time purchase from them real estate on the west bank of the Susquehanna in the southern part of the province.) And the colonists went home carrying a Plan of Union devised by Franklin. He had been considering this project at least since 1751, when he wrote to a friend that past attempts at intercolonial unity had failed because governors for various reasons could not provide the cement. He did not, however, propose that assemblies take on the task but described, instead, his own mode of operation: intelligent men with "a reasonable scheme" would act as ambassadors to "the leading men," getting them to promote the "voluntary union." His idea was that representatives of all colonies would form an intercolonial council of Indian affairs and defense, presided over by a governor appointed by the crown but financed by the colonies.

The Albany Plan of Union differed little from his earlier proposal: a royally designated president general would have veto power over but could neither prorogue nor dissolve a colonially elected Grand Council which would handle the matters of war and peace, military forces, Indian treaties and trade, land purchases and the establishment of new colonies, and, finally, the levying of taxes for support. Neither the ministry in London nor any of the colonial assemblies would accept the plan. Norris presented it to the Pennsylvania legislature when its author was absent! A disappointed Franklin wrote: "Every Body cries a

Union is absolutely necessary. But when they come to the Manner and Form of the Union, their weak Noddles are presently distracted."

Up to this time, Franklin had experienced success in private and public life not effortlessly but easily. With some exaggeration it could have been said that his career was a parable of Pennsylvania's eighteenth-century growth. He was now, like his adopted colony, rather suddenly face to face with the harsh realities of international politics and intercolonial jealousy. Franklin, a tolerant and optimistic man, saw all conflict as reconcilable. And, indeed, it had been in his Philadelphia where, if institutions did not provide solutions, he provided institutions. His strong commitment to utility and efficiency was not an attitude compatible with the petty intricacies of politics, yet his first years in the Assembly were untroubled as he blithely, or so it seemed, ignored factionalism.

He had friends everywhere, regarding political life as a matter of personal relationships rather than structures and theories. William Allen, chief justice and a bulwark of the proprietary interest, was his most generous patron, donating the lion's share for the academy and the hospital while also supporting the Library Company and German charity schools. Despite Thomas Penn's wariness regarding the voluntary Association in 1747, he and Franklin maintained an amicable relationship through intermediaries. That Franklin simultaneously continued his friendships with prominent Quakers was evidenced by his occupation of an Assembly seat that was virtually the preserve of Friends. Significantly, it was Franklin who accompanied the Quaker speaker of the legislature and the proprietary secretary to Carlisle and Albany.

After the Albany Congress provincial politics were altered by the convergence of events and personalities that inflamed old issues to produce a new alignment. Governor Hamilton apprised the Assembly of Washington's defeat at Fort Necessity in August 1754, but he was unable to reach an agreement with the legislature on how to raise a requested appropriation for the king's use. In October Robert Hunter Morris, a New Jersey proprietor who was viewed as an avaricious landlord and a "great stickler for prerogative," arrived as Hamilton's replacement and with Hamilton's instructions: no paper money would be issued without proprietary control over expenditure. This fact was leaked to the Assembly by its agents in England, and the new governor ran into the same impasse as his predecessor, although now the legislature resorted to a petition of grievances to the crown. Franklin, just returned from a tour of the northern post offices, observed: "The Assembly ride restive and the Governor, tho' he spurs with both Heels, at the same time reins in with both Hands, so that the Publick Business can never move forward."

Franklin, ever the expediter, saw special need for action with the arrival of Major General Edward Braddock, an English soldier determined to drive the French from Fort Duquesne while forces from New York and Massachusetts assaulted enemy strongholds farther north. To deal with the unresolved conflict in Philadelphia, Franklin again willingly violated established procedures and found "a Method of doing Business without the Governor" by a complex scheme for raising money for New England's troops while delaying payment and ensuring interest to creditors. Braddock, meanwhile, had bogged down in the backcountry, lacking the necessary foodstuffs, horses, and wagons to move on. Franklin, as emissary of the Assembly, traveled into the vicinity and ingeniously procured the necessary supplies. He also warned the English general of the danger of "Ambuscades of Indians," but the fearless Braddock, when he encountered the friendly Lenape and Shawnee, assured them that no savages would have the Ohio soil and, furthermore, he "did not need their Help and had No doubt of driveing the French and their Indians away." He was killed in battle and his forces destroyed in early July 1755.

Braddock's defeat, thrown into relief by the simultaneous failures of the New York and Massachusetts onslaughts, clearly placed Pennsylvania in a more dangerous situation than it had ever before faced, and the Assembly responded with a grant of £50,000 for defense. This huge sum was to be raised in an unprecedented manner through a land tax. Governor Morris, acting on instructions from Thomas Penn, would not sign such a bill unless proprietary estates were exempted. In view of the huge arrears in quitrents, Penn's precarious financial state, and his knowledge that the Assembly would assess the land, his position was understandable. Yet under the circumstances, it was highly impolitic. The Assembly reacted predictably, and Franklin stood squarely with his colleagues, vehemently attacking Morris as a "Knave" a "Fool," and a "Liar." Somewhat more gingerly, he took on the proprietor: "How odious it must be to a sensible manly People to find him who ought to be their Father and Protector, taking Advantage of Publick Calamity and Distress, and their Tenderness for their bleeding Country, to force down their Throats Laws of Imposition, abhorrent to common Justice and common Reason." Not even the Philadelphia philosopher was immune to the partisanship of Pennsylvania politics.

Hard on the heels of this confrontation came the news that bands of Ohio Indians had massacred settlers in the Tulpehocken and Forks of Delaware regions. Angry frontiersmen appeared in Philadelphia. The proprietor quickly granted £5,000 for defense, while the Assembly voted £55,000 but excluded the proprietary lands from taxation. Franklin's bill creating a voluntary militia was accepted by the Assembly, with four Quakers dissenting, and by the governor, though with hesitation. This was the first legislated armed force in the province. Franklin himself did a stint as regimental colonel in the Lehigh Valley.

With the continuation of Indian attacks along the frontier, Morris and his Council prepared a declaration of war, against which only James Logan's son William protested, and offered a bounty on scalps. A Quaker petition opposing these bellicose measures, signed by Israel Pemberton, who was William Logan's cousin, and other of Philadelphia's weightiest Friends was ignored. The Assembly was not consulted until after the declaration was issued on April 14, 1756. But this flurry of governmental activity could not disguise two salient facts: the split between the executive and the legislature was not mended by the external threat, and the province was officially in violation of pacifism for the first time in its history.

On June 4, 1756, despite Morris' suspension of hostilities a day earlier, James Pemberton and five other Quakers resigned their

INDIAN MEDAL

This medal represents William Penn, or as the Indians call him, Brother Onas, at a Council fire offering the Calumet of Peace to an Indian Chief and pointing at the Sun as characteristic both of the Purity and durability of the Friendship which the Friendly Association designed to promote.

James Pemberton (above) and other Quakers looked back to William Penn's example of dealing with the Indians when they formed "the Friendly Association" (left). (above) *Friends Historical Library of Swarthmore College.*

Assembly seats, unable to serve when "the present Situation of Public Affairs call upon us for Services in a military Way." In July Israel Pemberton gathered Friends who believed that the Society should intercede in making peace with the Indians rather than letting the government carry on negotiations alone. By the late autumn, with subscriptions gathered largely from Quakers (but also from Mennonites and Schwenkfelders), "The Friendly Association for Regaining and Preserving Peace with the Indians by Pacific Measures" had been launched.

Already the first of several conferences with the Indians had been held at Easton, and Pemberton, king of the Quakers, had met Teedyuscung, king of the Delawares. The latter's pathetic life was a constantly unsettling reminder that the European and aboriginal cultures had met but never mixed, except to the mutual degradation of both. His habitat twice engulfed by advancing white settlement, an erstwhile Christian convert and frequent drunkard, Teedyuscung was now heard as the spokesman for the former Iroquois tributaries, protesting the overlordship of the Six Nations, whom the English feared to provoke lest they form a French alliance, and corruption in proprietary practices of land acquisition, most notably the Walking Purchase, which inevitably led to the Indians striking back.

Franklin was initially skeptical of the Quaker effort: "I do not believe we shall ever have a firm peace with the Indians till we have well drubbed them." But he ultimately appreciated the use of Teedyuscung in the Assembly's battle against the proprietory. So did Richard Peters, who observed that "Israel Pemberton and the Association will mold, fashion, turn, twist and manage matters at the ensuing treaty as they please." The proprietary position was that Quaker pacifism invited the Indian raids. At the second Easton conference, Franklin and Pemberton dined with the newly arrived governor, Captain William Denny of the British Army, a silly man, anxious to oblige, and perhaps especially susceptible to Franklin who had recently visited the new commander in chief of North America, Lord Loudoun. The new governor apparently accepted Teedyuscung's interpretation of proprietary policy. Only later was he notified that the British ministry was hostile to Quaker poaching in the governmental preserve of Indian affairs.

The following year at Easton, despite Denny's erratic behavior in the face of contending interests, a peace agreement was reached with the Delawares, a compact promising to preserve their place in the Wyoming Valley. At the third Easton conference in the early autumn of 1758 there were in attendance some five hundred Indians, many of them Iroquois, and a treaty was signed settling all outstanding disputes except the Walking Purchase and affirming the dominance of the Six Nations, a setback for Teedyuscung and his Quaker allies and a sign marking the decline of the Society's influence on Indian affairs.

Meanwhile, the locus of power in the Quaker party in the Assembly had shifted in the direction of Franklin, though the party itself remained as hardy as ever. With the resignation of the six pacifist Friends in June 1756 Franklin and the Quaker politicians had chosen a half dozen moderate Anglicans as replacements, "mere Franklinists" in the words of Richard Peters. After Franklin and men from the proprietary interest had agreed upon a Philadelphia County slate for the October election which included two proprietary candidates, the Quaker Yearly Meeting urged and accomplished the latter's defeat. Only the frontier counties of Northampton and Cumberland returned proprietary members, one of whom was William Allen.

Despite the resignation of four more Quakers after the election, the new Assembly was securely in the Franklin-Norris grasp. One beneficiary of the Yearly Meeting's intrusion in Philadelphia County was Joseph Galloway, "a young nosey Quaker Lawyer" according to Peters, who was soon attached to Franklin. The proprietary forces were in almost total disarray. Peters unrealistically thought that William Allen, had he not been in "so bad an humour," could have put together a "Coalition of his & the Quakers interest," adding that Allen had "an irreconcilable aversion to Mr. Franklin." True enough, Allen was characterizing his former friend as a "very artful insinuating fellow." Franklin was too secure to worry. Not only did he have a firm alliance with the Quakers, but Friends were not likely to find common interest with the proprietary men who had been pushing them aside in government posts, on the boards of prestigious private institutions, and even in positions of economic prominence. Thus entrenched, men attached to the proprietary interest relied on the governor as a bulwark against the Assembly. Franklin, believing that the harmonious operation of government depended on the removal of proprietary obstacles and confident of his power in Pennsylvania, left the province in February 1757 on a legislative mission: to present the Assembly's case in London.

If Quaker political power was secured through a firmer bond with Franklin and other sympathetic non-Quakers in the Assembly, it was no sign that the Society was untouched by the implications of waging war. Pacifism was a delicate but badly defined subject for Friends, and its consideration in mid-century threatened schism to a sect that had suffered the throes of division several times in its brief history and was anxious to avoid further fragmentation. Quakers in England, excluded from the corridors of power, were comfortable following George Fox's Scriptural dictum: "To Caesar we give unto him his things, and to God we give Him his things." But Friends in mid-eighteenth-century Pennsylvania were not impotent. Though in 1711 Quaker politicians had been able to avoid the issue of pacifism by assuming they had no direction of funds spent outside the province and not managed by them, this claim could not be made in the 1750s. Rather, the legislature's quest for power had led to the very control of appropriations which had previously been lacking.

Thus, in July 1755, when the Assembly had voted to raise £50,000 by a property tax, it appointed Speaker Norris, a prominent Quaker, to manage expenditures. Conscientious Friends, including John and Israel Pemberton, protested the bill to the legislature in November. Receiving little sympathy, these same scrupulous Quakers issued an "Epistle of Caution," un-official but carrying considerable weight nonetheless, declaring their resistance: "As we cannot be concerned in wars and fightings, so neither ought we to contribute thereto paying the Tax." The Philadelphia Yearly Meeting in September had been unable to reach a consensus on this matter. Clearly, Quakers in Pennsylvania were divided among themselves as well as from their English brethren.

And the divisions were complicated by other considerations. In England, the Pennsylvania Friends were attacked in *A Brief State of the Province of Pennsylvania*, a tract issued in early 1755 by the Anglican provost of Philadelphia's Academy, Reverend William Smith. Having arrived in New York in 1751 after four years at the University of Aberdeen, with no degree but opinions on everything, the twenty-three-year-old Smith was drawn into pamphlet warfare on education and attracted the attention of both Penn and Franklin. The latter, acting in consort with Allen and Peters, got Smith his academy appointment. Shortly thereafter Smith wrote his anti-Quaker tract, which Franklin for a long time did not recognize as his protégé's work, accusing Friends in the Assembly of blocking defense appropriations in deference to their principles. The charge was not only false but exculpated the proprietor, whom Smith had conferred with on his brief return to England to be ordained in 1753–54. Following Penn's advice, Smith then petitioned the crown to intervene and save the Pennsylvanians; in *A Brief State* he had already advocated a test oath for the province to eliminate Quakers from government.

The defeat of Braddock had awakened the Privy Council to the defenseless state of Pennsylvania. Explanations were needed and pacifists might be blamed. At this point some substantial London Quakers intervened, alarmed by a military situation which threatened their imperial economic interests and a political development which menaced their Pennsylvania coreligionists. (English Friends had gotten into the habit of advising and protecting Pennsylvania Quakers through the London Meeting for Sufferings and, especially, its subcommittee on parliamentary and colonial affairs.) A promise was made to the president of the Privy Council that Friends in Pennsylvania would voluntarily withdraw from politics for the duration of the war, a pledge that would be ensured by sending two members of the Society to the colony. Provincial Quakers were quite unaware that the Privy Council considered disqualifying them from government, while English Friends seemed oblivious to the split in the Society in Pennsylvania, an almost inexplicable breakdown in communications in view of the fact that John Fothergill, one of the prominent Londoners who had dealt with the Privy Council, was the brother of Samuel Fothergill, whose two-year preaching tour among American Friends had begun in 1754.

Indeed, it was Samuel Fothergill who catalyzed the thinking of conscientious Quakers with the power of his word. One of them reported: "Such, indeed, was the force of divine evidence which attended him, that Friends' minds were seized with awful dread, and had to say to each other, after meeting,— Is this the last warning that we are to receive? it seems so like that of Jeremiah to the Jews, just before the destruction of Jerusalem." His apocalyptic message, so reminiscent of George Whitefield and the Great Awakening, a movement logically attractive but denominationally threatening to Quakers a decade earlier, quickened the sense of togetherness among a new generation of Friends. Some of them were destined to political and religious leadership by virtue of family and wealth, such as Israel, James, and John Pemberton, or John Reynell, a prosperous merchant; another was the intense Quaker convert and teacher, Anthony Benezet; of less illustrious families were the two most effective ministers—John Churchman, whose chiliastic prophecies stood in contrast but not contradiction to the itinerant whose behavior was more persuasive than words, John Woolman. Fothergill described the emergent leaders: "A noble seed, of several classes respecting age, though too few of the aged amongst them, [they had] . . . kept their garments clean, and . . . hands . . . strong."

These men saw spiritual decline in the compromises Quakers had been drawn into during their years of political, economic, and social dominance in Pennsylvania. Israel Pemberton wrote to his brother John in 1751 of "that degeneracy & declension which hath been Long standing & I fear still increases." They called for a rejection of worldliness and a return to purity. The dilemma they addressed themselves to was age old in Christianity, stemming from a dualistic concept of the church: it was both the invisible gathering of all souls which were united to God, irrespective of time, place, or petty denominational bickering, and the visible congregation. The first idea summoned a universalist outlook; early Quakers spoke of their religion as the Truth, not the Society, believing that all men should embrace verity. The visible congregation was the manifest evidence of the Truth in action, however, whose purity could best, and perhaps only, be achieved through isolation. English Quakers, following Penn, had requested toleration, since isolation meant existing at the sufferance of society. It was at that time that Friends abandoned their proselytizing, though some of them suggested that the abdication from universalism could be compensated by engaging in social reform. Even in Pennsylvania Quakers carried on little missionary work among Indians and Negroes, and other alien groups were treated as outsiders by the practice of conferring birthright membership on the children of Friends. Clearly the emphasis was on the visible congregation, whether it was conceived as pure and isolated, pure but with an obligation to reform society, or pure in preparation for leadership in the millennium.

The Puritans in Massachusetts Bay held the same two views of the church as did the Quakers and, likewise, could reconcile them only in favor of the visible congregation with its this-worldly bias, including special status for the children of the elect. The decline of piety was a recurrent theme of sermons in late seventeenth- and early eighteenth-century Massachusetts, but the word was insufficient to the deeds. The Great Awakening provided the best hope for reformers, but the ouster from his congregation of Jonathan Edwards, the movement's leading proponent in New England, symbolized the preference of Puritans for a Yankee life. Even the ideal of sectarian purity was rejected for a church coextensive with society, compromising and worldly in its outlook.

The disciples of George Fox in Pennsylvania followed a pattern established by the New England Calvinists, taking on the characteristics of a church down to the mid-1750s, only to turn abruptly back to their primitive sectarian traits. This unusual about-face could probably not have occurred if the preachings of conscientious Friends, accentuated by Samuel Fothergill, had not been so dramatically illustrated in the Quaker politicians' approach to the French and Indian War. Now there was no denying that the peace testimony was violated. Even John Fothergill in England could interpret the initial resistance sympathetically: "It was not altogether the payment of the tax but that the tax should be raised, directed and the use allowed by an assembly the major part whereof were of our profession that gave the offense." However, after the resignations of James Pemberton and five other assemblymen for conscience sake in June 1756 and four more Friends at the direction of the London Yearly Meeting in October 1756, the "major part" of the legislature was no longer Quaker. When Friends refused to pay a property tax in 1757 it was clear that Quaker consciousness had been raised to a level at which no war levies would be paid.

In England, where Friends did pay taxes to support the war with France, they might have censured their brethren overseas but for the fact that English rural Quakers were sympathetic to the conscientious Pennsylvanians, raising the specter of a split between city and country members at the London Yearly Meeting. In Pennsylvania, consequently, compromising Friends led by Isaac Norris in the Assembly had to face the reformers alone. And the latter occupied positions of power in the Society, whose hierarchical structure lent itself to control by a small interest group. Israel Pemberton, who only once stood successfully for an Assembly seat, nevertheless was a political as well as a principled person, capable of using the inherent strength of the Society for his purposes. Not only could he draw upon unifying forces within—the Yearly Meeting and the traveling ministry which favored reform—but he could exploit the internal tensions as well.

Members of the Society were merchants and artisans and farmers, having different styles of life, values, and economic interests. Local meetings reflected this variety and perpetuated it by demanding a Quaker's primary loyalty and binding him to his fellows by mutual aid which did not often or easily reach beyond the immediate group to others within or outside the Society. At the local meeting it was understood that some members had more right to speak than others which, given the religious sensitivities of the meek (who might hesitate to talk for fear of misinterpreting the spirit and offending God), left leadership to the strong, those who had succeeded in the world. At Yearly Meetings, where regionalism and class differences might have been faced and resolved, usually less than 1 percent of the total membership attended, though the gathering was open to all. Again, control was in the hands of wealthy lay activists. They made up the Yearly Meeting's correspondence committee, separate from the visiting committee for ministers, who were almost never from aristocratic families. This elite served its own interests by drawing up an Assembly ticket or recommending economic policy.

But as the economy became more complex, and particularly when commerce suffered, the elite divided between conservatives and liberals, the latter favoring business expansion, breaking away from the Society's strictures, and looking beyond the Quaker mercantile network for wealth. In 1746 Israel Pemberton had a brief fling at the French West Indies trade, largely the preserve of New Englanders and non-Quaker Pennsylvanians such as William Allen, lost a ship, and constricted his operations to the British islands. When several Quaker merchants engaged in the French trade after 1756, meetings led by the Pembertons tried to pressure them out of it. During the 1740s Israel Pemberton made a fortune in commerce and, although he was not hurt by the mid-century business slump that affected merchants unevenly and thus sharpened conflict within the Quaker elite, he recognized that trade was becoming more precarious and less profitable. In 1750, as he was devoting more of his energies to the Society, he was also investing more of his money in land, mortgages, and bonds, betraying a mentality of economic retreat while other merchants called for paper money and inflation. It was, of course, precisely at this time that Quaker power was divided between Pemberton and Norris.

To the conservative Quaker mentality, which saw a dichotomy between moral and secular worlds, this division was quite logical. Primitive Friends, alienated from English society, drew the same dualistic distinction, isolating themselves in purity (thus ensuring that the visible congregation was saintly) but simultaneously charging into the corrupt world with apocalyptic messages. Conscientious Quakers in the mid-eighteenth century saw in the founding of the Society a golden age, while provincial historians discovered the same qualities in the colony's beginnings. Samuel Smith, a New Jersey Quaker merchant, wrote but did not publish a history of Pennsylvania from materials which came down to him through the hands of David Lloyd, Isaac Norris, James Logan, and John Kinsey. His manuscript was inherited at his death in 1776 by Robert Proud, a soured Quaker schoolmaster who had come to the province in 1759, in time to witness the controversy in the Society. He, too, wrote a history. Both accounts assigned William Penn to almost saintly status, but where Smith's was bland fare thereafter, Proud's disposition fit perfectly the theme of decline so pervasive among his contemporaries, the alienated and conscientious Friends who resembled the first publishers of Truth.

Their conservatism was consistent with this theme. Fear of change and evidence of decline were inseparable, while misfortune was to be expected; it was the reminder of declension, God's way of arresting the backsliders and bringing them back to Him. Thus, John Woolman referred to a smallpox epidemic as "an assistant in the cause of virtue." And Israel Pemberton informed John Fothergill that "infinite wisdom is directing us to a more inward self denying Path than we or our most immediate Predecessors have trod in—it seems at times as if our Enemy were employ'd to instruct us in this lesson, at least their unjust Treatment should . . . tend to alienate us from the desire of seeking the Friendship or honour of Men." Quakers were to forsake worldly ties, simultaneously strengthening themselves and the Society through a return to purity, to the golden age.

Friends, however, were not of one mind but two, those who saw the crisis and those who did not. And the meeting, ever fearful of schism, was governed by consensus, the inertia of almost unanimous consent. When the issue of paying a property tax to support the war was about to come before the Yearly Meeting in 1757, Israel Pemberton counseled caution and a committee which included prominent pacifists judged "that it is not proper to enter into a public Discussion of the Matter, and . . . that Friends every where endeavour to have their minds covered with fervent Charity towards one another." But at the same gathering a year later, when the question was one of directly supplying a military expedition, it was unanimously affirmed that no Friend should engage in the practice or occupy a public office that caused him to persuade others to obey "any act which they may conscientiously scruple to perform." Although the penalty for Quaker officeholders was not disownment and furthermore, no Friends in politics were disciplined for officeholding per se before the American Revolution, still there was open displeasure that the issue had been forced and consensus taxed. John Fothergill informed Israel Pemberton: "From what I hear, some amongst you are straining at gnats, and swallowing camels. Rigorously insisting upon points which are disputable."

An earlier effort at unity through purity had taken place in 1755, when a new discipline was drafted by a group of Friends that included John Churchman, John Woolman, and Samuel Fothergill. During the next year prosecutions for breach of discipline increased 75 percent in the six largest meetings, indicating a real turnabout in the Society. In the quarter century after 1730, when the Society increasingly took on characteristics of a church, ethical behavior steadily declined but delinquents were pardoned. After 1755 delinquency rose sharply, as did punishments. Probably as high as 22 percent of Friends in 1760 had been disowned by the time of the Revolution; the rate was lower in Philadelphia than in rural areas, showing the persistence of regionalism. The sense of impending disaster made it essential that the elect be clearly defined. Quakerism again took on sectarian characteristics, a religious transformation without historical parallel. But it was apparently achieved at some cost. The anxiety engendered by an apprehension of doom and compounded by a fear of discipline must have been related to the decline in the reproductive capacity of Quakers. In "Observations concerning the Increase of Mankind," written in 1751 by Benjamin Franklin and later quoted with approval by Thomas

Malthus, the economic basis for population growth was argued. Among Quakers, psychological conditions led in the direction of smaller families than those of their fellow Americans, a biological development in keeping with an ecclesiastical trend.

But despite the sense of crisis, the mentality of retreat, the urge to purity, conscientious Quakers could not forsake the world. Initially, they thought their values would prevail. John Churchman addressed the Assembly in 1748: "They who hold different principles and are settled in this government, can have no just cause of reflection if warlike measures are forborne, because they knew the Charter framed, and the peaceable Constitution, and have ventured themselves therein." But the golden age had not prevailed; the government was in the hands of aliens. Consequently, new approaches to influence were sought. John Woolman's way of showing the Truth by moral behavior was not enough, for it affected only those whose consciousness allowed them to see. Anthony Benezet had a more vigorous plan: "It seems to me that our principles, which, in the present corrupt state of the world, seem to prohibit our meddling with offices, & c., naturally point out to us as a people, rather than others, to serve God and our country in the education of the youth." It was a program that Benezet followed, though it could not help but have a strong parochial flavor since parents determined where their children were schooled.

Furthermore, the crisis was not a generation away but contemporaneous. Direct and immediate action appeared necessary. Conscientious Friends grasped at influence and power by putting their principles into practice through the organization of alternatives to the status quo. Within the Society, the Yearly Meeting's correspondence committee became a Meeting for Sufferings in 1756, controlled by the Pemberton group and, like its English counterpart, provided with funds to lobby and provide legal defense for Quakers. The revival of discipline served the same purpose of transferring power from "wet" to reformist Friends, with traveling ministers transforming urban-rural conflict into a moral debate by molding diffuse sentiment against the urban aristocracy into concentrated opposition. Outside the Society conscientious Quakers organized the

Friendly Association in 1756 to effectuate pacifism by dealing fairly, but extralegally (since foreign affairs were in the government's domain, with the natives).

But the politics surrounding Indian treaties again showed Quakers how difficult it was to preserve purity in worldly endeavors. There was, however, a way to avoid tangling with the government while influencing public affairs, a method utilized so effectively by Benjamin Franklin: the private voluntary society. Quakers were to be found among the members of the Junto, the library and the fire companies, the academy, and the American Philosophical Society. While these were municipal projects, dependent on individual efforts and involving Quakers no more than other Philadelphians, the Society had a tradition of ingroup charity of far greater importance than help extended to outsiders and operating in rural as well as urban areas. Friends who found officeholding repugnant, thus rejecting the union of temporal and spiritual matters which was fundamental to William Penn's "holy experiment," discovered an alternative in voluntary benevolent associations which could put into practice the principles of reformist Quakers without drawing them into complicity with the government or conflict with their "wet" brethren. This second "holy experiment," characterized not by the buoyant optimism of its predecessor but an admonishing moralism born from a feeling of crisis, demonstrated a new approach to working in the world which disdained politics and, in addition, expanded the areas of charity to people previously on the periphery of Quaker consciousness.

Friends who had disregarded the religious needs of fellow Europeans in the early eighteenth century now came to the aid of Acadians deported from Nova Scotia in 1755 for having refused to take an oath of fidelity to George II. The Assembly cooperated in this venture which was largely the work of French-born Anthony Benezet. At the same time aid was extended to refugees, both white and red, who suffered from Indian attacks. Although Quakers had long opposed selling rum and wresting land from the natives, preaching missions were in abeyance after their temporary effects were noted and the outrageous behavior of the savages while drunk was observed.

Then the Friendly Association, as well as the New Jersey Association for Helping the Indians, made overtures on the basis of worldly justice rather than Christian conversion. After some conversions occurred, however, the spiritual interest became predominant. From a focus on ingroup charity, with interest in municipal social services left to individual Quakers, a large number of Friends turned their attention to the Pennsylvania Hospital and the Overseers of the Poor.

These activities put Quakers in the forefront of benevolent activities. But their work with Negroes actually set them apart from their fellow Americans. Friends were forced by the egalitarian implications of their theology and the pronouncements of such leaders as George Fox, who had advocated preaching to Negroes and some form of manumission, to confront the realities of slaveholding and living with blacks. The cultural gulf between Englishmen and Africans raised inhibiting doubts about the latter's capacity to embrace Christianity, yet the belief in moral equality not only made consideration of the slaves' spiritual welfare imperative but posed problems for manumission insofar as the well-being of free Negroes was ignored. The few Quakers who held slaves were puzzled concerning what measures to follow beyond kindness to their subjects, yet by the turn of the eighteenth century attacks on the institution were increasing, causing them to resist. Such polarization of sentiment paralyzed the meeting, with the result that antislavery Quakers turned to the Assembly, where majority rather than unanimity ruled. But the legislature's efforts to end the slave trade were blocked in London; besides, terminating the trade did not solve the proximate problem but only promised to contain its size.

Of the dozen or so condemnations of slavery appearing in the American colonies before 1750, most were written by Quakers, whose arguments went beyond the morality of slaveholding to raise fears of insurrection. Increasing worldliness within the Society did not silence antislavery Friends but, rather, drove them to desperate acts which so threatened the unity of the meeting that several were disowned. Benjamin Lay, not satisfied to have labeled Quaker slaveholders as "a Parcel of Hypocrites, and Deceivers," appeared at meeting in military garb, launched into a tirade, drew a sword which he thrust into a bladder of red juice hidden between the covers of a Bible, and warned that holding a slave was no better than stabbing a man to death. Such eccentric behavior, with its explicit censure of the master, repelled most Quakers. The reform effort which prevailed was gradual and impersonal, advising against certain practices years before sanctioning the disownment of members. The actions of antislavery Quakers had to be compelling rather than repugnant, and no friend was more persuasive in word and deed than John Woolman, whose gentle but intelligent voice was a moving force in the transformation of the Society in the 1750s.

Woolman could claim much of the credit for the decision, made by the Philadelphia Yearly Meeting in 1758, that slave traders would henceforth be excluded from business meetings, a compromise between advice and disownment. Furthermore, the hope was expressed that masters would free their slaves and a committee was appointed to visit slaveholders. Woolman was already ministering to such Quakers, his approach showing respect for both unity and purity, qualities which the reformed Society sought to achieve in balance. In pursuit of the former, he neither attacked his opponents nor published his views until the meeting consented. He discussed slavery almost psychoanalytically, looking for the motive of the master, showing him that holding other men was an act of pride which stood squarely in the way of purity. It was the reverse of brotherhood, for placing the Negro in a degraded position "tends gradually to fix a Notion in the Mind, that they are a Sort of People below us in Nature," whereas Woolman clearly believed that blacks were entitled to the same natural rights as whites. The Pietist was showing the full implications of the Enlightenment to his fellow Americans! And Woolman saw that liberty had to be incompatible with slavery, that the oppressor was confined by his act of oppression. "For while the life of one is made grevous by the Rigour of another, it entails Misery on both."

By 1760 Quakers could see no alternative to the compulsory manumission of slaves, though abolition had as yet not been adopted by the Yearly Meeting and few slaves were freed before 1775. Nor was the prohibition against buying and selling slaves official policy. The slave trade in Pennsylvania was at its high point from 1755 to 1765, and James Pemberton's observation that "the members of our Society Appear entirely clear of being Concernd in the Importation & there are few Instances of any purchasg of them" was apparently more a hope than a fact, in view of the Yearly Meeting's assertion that slaveholding was on the increase. Within a few years Quakers had, in fact, stopped buying slaves, partly no doubt because white indentured servants were again available after a decade of scarcity. And within another ten years, the ideology of the conscientious Friends prevailed in the Society. On the eve of the American Revolution, Friends stood apart from other Americans on the issue of slavery, an unsurprising development in view of the Quakers' image of themselves as a peculiar people, particularly after the reformation of the 1750s. With the exceptions of Woolman, Anthony Benezet, and a few others, Friends probably shared the typical European prejudices against blacks, but they did not need to draw upon the bias of color to define themselves as a group. Nor, of course, could they admit Negroes into the Society.

The clarity of John Woolman's thinking was alarming to most Americans. He depicted the prejudice of pigmentation as the consequence of "the Force of long custom," hence, "the Idea of Slavery being connected with the Black Color, and Liberty with the White: and where false Ideas are twisted into our Minds, it is with difficulty we get fairly disentangled." The musing of Benjamin Franklin was far more congenial to his countrymen: "The Number of purely white People in the World is proportionately very small. . . . I could wish their Numbers were increased. And while we are, as I may call it, *Scouring* our Planet, by clearing America of Woods, and so making this side of our Globe reflect a brighter Light to the Eyes to the Inhabitants of Mars or Venus, why should we in the Sight of Superior Beings, darken its People?" It was not humanitarianism alone which led Quakers to abolitionism, but the added fact that their anguished thinking about identity in terms of benevolence forced them to face the problem of color while other Americans unthinkingly allowed racism to become a parameter of nationality.

9

BUDDING: ROYAL GOVERNMENT, REVITALIZED IMPERIALISM, AND THE EMERGENCE OF NEW POLITICS

On July 26, 1757, Benjamin Franklin made his second entry into London. Almost a quarter of a century earlier he had arrived as the disappointed protégé of a whimsical lieutenant governor; now he was the official agent of a legislature determined to bend the proprietor to its will. Then a nobody, he had been grateful for the advice of a Quaker merchant; now he was a chieftain of the Quaker party and, as deputy postmaster general, a royal official as well. In 1724, alone and poor, he had tried without success to meet Sir Isaac Newton. In 1757, a member of the Royal Society, he contemplated meeting the many friends he had gained through his lively correspondence. Behind him lay the factional disputes of provincial politics, so inimical to his conciliatory nature. That would be the domain of his legislative lieutenant, Joseph Galloway, a handsome, socially prominent lawyer, just the age of William Franklin. Galloway was elected to the Assembly in 1756 through a bit of Franklinian subterfuge, and he had proven to be a trusty aide whose legalistic, provincial outlook could be expected to keep him at his assigned task.

While Galloway wrestled with public affairs and the reformist Quakers confronted their consciences and their colleagues, Franklin confidently strode into the London arena, center of an empire at war. "Mr. Franklin's popularity is nothing here," Thomas Penn wrote in response to Richard Peters' warnings. "He will be looked very coldly upon by great People." The proprietor was referring to politicians, not scientists, and Franklin's experience soon came uncomfortably close to verifying Penn's statement. Lord Granville, president of the Privy Council, informed the Philadelphian that in his opinion the instructions sent to colonial governors had the strength of legislation. Franklin's astonished reply—"I had always understood from our Charters, that our Laws were to be made by our Assemblies, to be presented indeed to the King for his royal assent, but that once given the King could not repeal or alter them"—could not, of course, bridge the transatlantic intellectual gulf which this sentiment symbolized. Furthermore, Granville was the recent ally of London Quakers, who refused to make an all-out effort to help Franklin, uncertain of the wisdom of attacking Penn, with whom they maintained amiable relations.

Franklin's meeting with Penn surpassed misunderstanding; it was marked by mistrust. The proprietor resented the Assembly's grievances against him: that his instructions to his lieutenant governors undermined the work of the legislature and denied that body's exclusive funding powers; that he exempted his estates from taxation. Penn was also rankled by the Assembly's agent, who looked "like a malicious Villain." Franklin observed that the proprietor spoke "as a low Jockey might do when a purchaser complained that He had cheated him in a Horse." Neither side was open to compromise; their differences would have to be resolved by other means.

Franklin's instructions from the Assembly were, should negotiations with the proprietor founder, to turn to the House of Commons, a body which he and his fellow Pennsylvanians believed to be public servants, independent-minded and, thus, open to the virtue of the Assembly's cause. Instead, Franklin found placemen. Richard Jackson, the wealthy barrister who had corresponded with Franklin before his arrival and counseled him during his stay in London, remarked to him: "An Administration will probably for the future always be able to support and carry in Parliament whatever they wish to." It was not surprising, then, that Franklin, who typically disregarded established procedures in pursuit of his goals, went to the top.

Having failed to convince Lord Granville, he sought out William Pitt, "but without success. He was then too great a Man, or too much occupy'd in . Affairs of greater Moment. I was therefore oblig'd to content myself with a kind of non-apparent and unacknowledged Communication thro' . . . his Secretaries, who seem'd to cultivate an acquaintance with me by their Civilities, and draw from me what Information I could give." Franklin, always a keen observer, quickly learned his lesson. The Whitehall bureaucracy—hierarchical, complex, sometimes corrupt—was best dealt with by cultivating connections at its lower and middling levels. The Philadelphia philosopher wrote home that "by working with a Friend who has great influence at the Board, [an agent] can serve the Province as effectually as by an open Reception and Appearance."

In fact, some precedents had already been established. Franklin was filling a post with a history and regularized duties, though in the course of his tenure he left his own imprint. The colonial agent was an information officer, an ambassador, and a lobbyist, necessarily familiar with British politics. Though extraconstitutional, the agency was the only London office at the colonies' disposal. Originating in the seventeenth century and staffed by men of high quality, the colonial agency became a permanent fixture by the English government's demand. Pennsylvania's charter required that the province maintain an agency, and Penn himself filled the post for over thirty years. Although an agent was to represent the entire governmental apparatus of a colony, often he represented only one branch and/or several colonies.

Ferdinando John Paris, appointed agent for Pennsylvania by the Assembly in 1730, already served in that capacity for the East Jersey proprietors and during his career worked for the Maryland House of Delegates, the freeholders of Halifax, Nova Scotia, and absentee landholders in Jamaica. He remained as agent for the Penns when the Assembly replaced him in 1740 with the Quaker Richard Partridge, whose unequaled longevity of forty-five years included service to Rhode Island, the New Jersey lower house, and the Massachusetts Land Bank Company.

Paris had an unusual ability to clear bureaucratic obstacles while Partridge's skill was in obtaining inside information from civil servants whom he wined and dined.

Although some agents, such as Paris and Partridge, might occasionally work in tandem, there was not a history of unity nor a bond of professionalism among agents. Their outlook became as parochial as that of the respective colonies which employed them in the eighteenth century, a degeneration matching the deteriorating vigor of Whitehall. Routine lapsed into sluggishness until the Seven Years War jolted the agency into action. At that time two agents represented the Pennsylvania Assembly, Partridge and Robert Charles. The same age as Franklin, Charles had emigrated to Philadelphia in 1726, married Governor Patrick Gordon's daughter, quarreled with Andrew Hamilton, and returned to Britain in 1739, where he nurtured his political connections, became agent for New York in 1748 and Partridge's colleague in 1754, much to the relief of Thomas Penn, who still employed Paris and regarded Partridge as "weak" and "superannuated." The two men worked together closely and cooperated with Franklin until Partridge's death in 1759 and Charles' resignation in 1761.

Franklin's reputation lent stature to the colonial agency, and he was but the first of several appointees who, during the Seven Years War, raised the quality of the office to its earlier height. Furthermore, Franklin perceived the importance of unity among the agents and promoted it, aided in this effort not only by capable colleagues but also by the common need to apportion treasury reimbursements and consult on military operations during the war. This was useful, though hardly divination of imperial conflicts to come.

His attempts to deal with the anticolonial prejudice of Parliament and the English people through the use of the press was less successful. He, Charles, and Jackson were preparing newspaper releases as early as 1758, not only on the issue of proprietary government in Pennsylvania but also on the matters of war, defense, peace, and territorial acquisition. The following year these men published *An Historical Review of the Constitution and Government of Pennsylvania*, as a result of which "the proprietors will be gibbeted up as they deserve, to rot and stink in the Nostrils of Posterity," according to Franklin, who was disappointed at the poor sale of the volume. But he was not too crestfallen to collaborate in 1760 with Jackson on *The Interest of Great Britain Considered*, whose self-centered but farseeing argument in favor of the retention of Canada was reminiscent of William Penn's *The Benefit of Plantations, or Colonies* issued eighty years earlier. Neither Franklin's work nor Joseph Galloway's *True and Impartial State of the Province of Pennsylvania* (1759) evoked support for the Assembly's case against the proprietors.

If parliamentary sympathy could not be elicited and individual ministers remained aloof, Franklin could still take the Assembly's case before the Board of Trade or the Privy Council, where colonial policy was made and, therefore, familiarity with America could be assumed. Convinced by this time that a victory for the Assembly could be best achieved, perhaps only achieved, by the replacement of proprietary with royal government, Franklin chose to ignore private warnings from Jackson that the Pennsylvania legislature should not expect the ministry or Parliament to uphold its claims. Instead, he informed the Assembly of Jackson's opinion that provincial privileges could only be abridged by an act of Parliament. Jackson's advice not to "drive any of these Points [the disposition of public money and a militia were especially notable], much less all at once to a formal Decision at present, if at all" went unheeded as Franklin, with Galloway's assistance in Philadelphia, brought the Assembly's case before the Privy Council three times between 1758 and 1760.

The first occasion was the result of Galloway's zealous efforts to strengthen his and Franklin's party, which inevitably meant adopting a strong antiproprietary stance. Hanging a bogus libel charge on its favorite enemy, Reverend William Smith, the Assembly under Galloway's direction tried and jailed him, an action which the Anglican cleric appealed to the Privy Council, claiming to be the victim of bigoted Quakers. Franklin's defense of the proceedings was that "the Assembly of Pennsylva. had as full powers as the House of Commons had," but the very fact that the Privy Council would hear the appeal and render a decision betrayed its belief in the inferiority of the colonial lower house to Parliament. The ruling was in Smith's favor, but it was based only on a technicality, encouraging Franklin to appear before the Council again.

The proprietors appeared vulnerable on the issue of Indian relations. Testimony gathered from the Eastern conferences, especially Teedyuscung's charge that Indian attacks along the frontier were the consequence of a proprietary policy of cheating the Delawares—notably, in the case of the Walking Purchase— and his later demand that the crown should take a hand in these matters, was laid before the Board of Trade and the Privy Council. In support of the antiproprietary campaign Charles Thomson, an associate of Franklin and Galloway, prepared for English consumption a strongly antiproprietary tract, *Enquiry into the Causes of the Alienation of the Delaware and Shawanese Indians from the British Interest*. The result was a temporary standoff, in which the Board of Trade decided that the Indian issue should be investigated and resolved in America (in 1762 the Penns were vindicated), while the Privy Council blamed proprietary land policies for arousing Indian suspicions and admonished the Assembly for interfering in the home government's domain of Indian relations.

In early 1759 an abrupt turn of events in Pennsylvania provided Franklin with a third matter to present to the Board of Trade and the Council. Even before he had left the province, the Assembly and Governor William Denny had clashed over the terms of a military appropriations bill, the former demanding that all land, including proprietary estates, be taxed for revenue, the latter confessing that his instructions forbade him to consent to such a measure, a revelation that seemed only to encourage the legislators. Though compromises on raising money were hammered out, each year from 1756 to 1759 the legislature put the executive in the position of vetoing a bill taxing the proprietors. Finally, under pressures from both General Jeffrey Amherst, the English commander in chief who insisted on the urgent need for funds, and Norris and Galloway, who promised Denny arrears in his salary while assuring him that the final responsibility for legislation was not his but the Privy Council's, the governor signed a bill for £100,000 to be raised by taxing all land, including that of the Penns.

The Provincial Council, which had never approved of Denny (William Allen wanted his brother-in-law, James Hamilton, reappointed to the executive post) and had strongly advised against the signing, now sat back impotently while the governor followed up on his capitulation by signing bills designed to curb the power of the proprietary element while augmenting that of the Assembly. In the time it took to replace Denny with Hamilton, the damage had been done, and Thomas Penn had no choice but to fight against the legislation before the home government. And although the Board of Trade reported in Penn's favor, Franklin carried the battle to the Privy Council, where the final decision would be made.

All sides could claim a victory from the result. The Assembly's principle of taxing proprietary estates was upheld, but with significant stipulations. Penn's land would receive minimum assessment; "we have been contending for a Matter of Right rather than Mony," Isaac Norris nonetheless exulted to Franklin. The governor would continue to be paid by proprietary tenants "according to the terms of their respective Grants," a provision which raised fears in Pennsylvania that payment would have to be made in sterling rather than in depreciating paper currency. This situation was threatening not only to individuals but to an economy whose prosperity was dependent on moderate inflation. The proprietors' position was also upheld when the Council repealed all laws but the one granting £100,000, including a paper money act and an act which would have secured control by the legislature over the judiciary. Still, of the three parties involved, the crown was clearly in control, not only by virtue of voiding legislation but, in upholding Penn, through a rebuke to him for not exerting his authority sooner. The analogy of royal to proprietary power was apparent to the privy councillors. The gulf between the crown's and the Assembly's views of the proprietor—too lenient for one, too tyrannical to the other— symbolized dangerously divergent attitudes toward the nature of authority in the British Empire.

With the onset of the Great War in mid-century, Pennsylvania politics had been drawn into an imperial context. The fortuitous meeting of Quaker pacifism and frontier warfare in the Ohio Valley had focused the attention of men in Westminster and Whitehall on Philadelphia. London Friends had sent messages and missionaries in one direction across the Atlantic, explaining to their American brethren the strategy of coexistence with a bellicose government. The Pennsylvania Assembly, still racked by the jealousies and bickering of prewar days, unable thus far to see beyond its rivalry with the proprietor, had sent the most sophisticated and ecumenical member from its midst across the sea in the other direction. But even Franklin had had only minor success in conveying the grievances of his countrymen. His life abroad, though punctuated by meetings with the illustrious and his continued experimenting, had not converted him to cosmopolitanism. "I grow weary of so long a Banishment, and anxiously desire once more the happy Society of my Friends and Family in Philadelphia," he wrote in 1760, when he had two more years to serve before returning. The Assembly, meanwhile, was unchastened by the Privy Council's action and its demeanor toward the governor remained the same.

James Hamilton, who "loved his ease too much, and did not care to have his peace of mind disturbed," according to William Allen, nevertheless accepted appointment as chief executive of Pennsylvania in 1759 on the condition that he could approve laws taxing the proprietary estates. Thomas Penn had agreed to this concession even before the Privy Council decision. Yet despite his permission to accede to the inevitable Assembly demand, Hamilton enjoyed neither ease nor peace of mind as the legislature continued to quarrel with him over the terms of money bills. When Franklin's news concerning the Privy Council's recent assertiveness arrived from England, matters were only made worse. "The Assembly," noted Richard Peters, was "enraged at the Repeal of their Laws. . . . They still think they are in the Right and that the Privy Council and Proprietaries are in a Confederacy against them." The legislature refused to honor the stipulations on taxing proprietary lands despite a pledge made by Franklin to the Privy Council, and Hamilton's increasingly overt threats, moreover, insured the maintenance of a hostile atmosphere. The willingness of politicians to look toward royal government for relief, despite Franklin's bad experience, was owing to this polluted political environment.

Hostilities of a more immediate kind fostered further strife between the legislature and the executive. Although the war in the west had officially ended in 1763, the English and the Indians collided again and again on the seemingly timeless matters of trade and settlement, issues inflamed by French propaganda. Aroused by the visions of a Delaware known to be a prophet and led by an Ottawa named Pontiac, tribes in the Ohio Valley attacked and captured one fort after another in the late spring of 1763. By the summer, Pennsylvania's frontier settlements were under siege, as scalps were taken, buildings burned, prisoners captured. In Carlisle, it was said there existed "not a Stable, Barn, or Hovel of any kind . . . that is not crowded with miserable Refugees." Out of these conditions came hysteria and reprisals. The Assembly attempted to appease the frontiersmen by raising a militia while protecting proximate and friendly Indians by sheltering them in Philadelphia. But revenge-seeking settlers from the Paxton area of Lancaster County found and murdered twenty defenseless Indians in Conestoga.

Franklin, who had returned to the province in November 1762, wrote a *Narrative of the Late Massacres*, condemning the "Christian white savages" responsible for the massacre. Such expressions of outrage only confirmed the westerners' belief that in the Assembly where they were underrepresented, having but ten of the thirty-six representatives, they could not receive due support. But Governor John Penn, the nephew of Thomas and Richard who replaced Hamilton in October 1763—a surprising choice in view of the gravity of provincial problems and his mediocrity—was clearly not going to take strong steps to punish the offenders. Hence, the Paxton Boys again decided to act, this time marching toward Philadelphia to deal with both the Indians and the Assembly.

> The Paxton Boys are coming down
> to kill us all, and burn the Town.

Israel Pemberton and several other prominent Quakers

slipped away to New Jersey, a move that hardly aided the reputation of conscientious Friends who frequently served as scapegoats for frustration with the weakness of frontier fortifications. Governor Penn called on Dr. Franklin, who prepared a military reception for the Paxton Boys with more vigor than the Assembly had shown in response to earlier pleas for defensive aid against the Indians. And, accompanied by Galloway and a few others, Franklin went out to negotiate with the approaching marauders. The Paxton Boys lamely presented a *Remonstrance*, complaining of the Assembly's Indian policy and underrepresentation of the western counties, and agreed to return to their homes.

With Franklin established as a hero and Governor Penn illustrating the continuing unadaptability of his family by striking down two money bills for military appropriations and a militia bill in the wake of the crisis, the time was ripe for a full-scale attack on proprietary government, or so it seemed to Franklin and Galloway. Yet their strategy was ill-conceived for two reasons, one of which was almost overlooked at the moment despite its grim implications for the future, the other of which was strikingly obvious and immediately responsible for Franklin's and Galloway's defeat. The former was the imperial reorganization that began with the signing of the Treaty of Paris in 1763; the latter was provincial factionalism, latent and grudging, fostered by the devisiveness of the Paxton Boys affair and focused by the campaign against proprietary government.

The Treaty of Paris made England not only the most powerful nation in Europe but the largest landholder in North America. All of the area between the Appalachians and the Mississippi, plus Canada to the north and the Floridas in the south, were included in her newly gained domain. The war with France that led to these acquisitions had fastened attention on America, acquainting the home government with colonial behavior which may only have been parochial but was judged selfish and detrimental to the best interests of England: provincial legislatures laid claim to grand prerogatives while they were niggardly with military appropriations; Indians along the frontier were inflamed and the fur trade was interrupted by the constant westward movement of settlers; colonial merchants expected to reap commercial advantages in the empire while evading the rules. The tax burdens of an increased national debt inherited from the war together with the potential outlay for administering the enlarged empire, turbulence among the natives in the recently acquired territory, the cost of supporting an outmoded mercantile system—all of these problems had obvious causes in the colonial behavior London officialdom observed and resented during the war.

A fine line, easily crossed, existed between the attitude that colonials must bear their share of responsibility for empire and the belief that the Americans were in an inferior position, subject to control. Such theoretical questions as the nature of political decision-making or the limits of economic expectations were not considerations to policymakers in London. Rather, it was clear that new sources of revenue must be found to support English troops garrisoned on the North American frontier as well as royal officials stationed in the centers of colonial population.

The new king, George III, in casting about for cabinets had settled upon a ministry headed by George Grenville. As Chancellor of the Exchequer he directly faced the postwar budget with its increased administrative costs. In March 1764 he proposed levying specified taxes on the colonies. That news reached America on the heels of a proclamation, issued by the king the previous autumn, that all land west of the Appalachians would be under royal "sovereignty, protection, and dominion, for the use of the . . . Indians." White settlers were expected "forthwith to remove themselves," while traders needed official licenses to deal with the natives. Then, in April 1764, Parliament responded to Grenville's prodding with the American Revenue Act.

The Sugar Act, as it was popularly known due to the increased levy on that commodity, was designed to draw duties from imports into the colonies of sugar, molasses, wines, coffee, indigo, and textiles. It embodied a discriminatory policy against non-British ports of origin, a time-honored procedure, but it also contained a novel feature: the duties would be "for defraying the expences of defending, protecting and securing the said colonies." Earlier measures, such as the Plantation Duty Act of 1673 and the Molasses Act of 1733, were intended to regulate trade rather than raise money. A major motive for innovation was the fact that their yields were so low; the customs commissioners estimated an average annual revenue of less than £1,900 over the past thirty years, compared to an administrative cost of £7,600. Stricter enforcement was also expected to augment collections. A treasury investigation resulted in the charge that "neglect, connivance, and fraud" was detrimental to both revenue and regulation, the result being that several steps were taken to ensure enforcement. Warnings were issued to royal officials and colonial governors, seizure and search privileges were granted to naval officers, and enlarged jurisdiction was assigned to vice-admiralty courts before the Sugar Act was passed.

In face of this new imperial vigor, Franklin's plan for replacing proprietary with royal authority might have seemed foolhardy to Pennsylvanians had they not shared his provincial astigmatism. But while Franklin spoke of the "Care and Protection" of the king, a young lawyer of Quaker ancestry who had entered the Assembly in 1762 took a different tack. John Dickinson was born in 1732 in Maryland, the son of a planter-lawyer. He moved to Delaware where he was tutored until he traveled to London to study at Middle Temple for four years during his early twenties. Plagued by ill health and properly wary of "the vicious pleasures of London," young Dickinson was extremely sensitive to political degeneration in the capital, where he judged it "a vice here to be virtuous" and worried that England was in a condition which led to "the destruction of all empires." Once returned to America, he regarded the triumph of 1763 with alarm: commercial prosperity would breed luxury, corruption and "our ruin certain." He distrusted proprietary as well as royal authority, which led the Franklin forces to think that he would accept the report of an Assembly committee on grievances which concluded: "The Powers of Government ought, in all good Policy, to be separated from the Power attending that immense Property, and lodged, where only it can be properly and safely lodged, in the Hands of the Crown."

Instead, Dickinson opposed a petition asking the king to assume control over the colony. On May 24, 1764, he arose in the

Assembly chamber to warn: "If the change of government now meditated, can take place, with all our privileges preserved, let it instantly take place: but if *they* must be consumed in the blaze of royal authority, we shall pay too great a price." Dickinson directed much of his speech to the bad timing of the move: the home government was "designing, as we are told, the *strictest reformations*" in all the American colonies, while the Pennsylvania Assembly was notably out of favor and the Penns in with the authorities. But he also made clear his fear of power lodged in the English ministry and emphasized the significance and importance of the rights Pennsylvanians enjoyed under the Charter of Privileges of 1701. "Let any impartial person reflect how contradictory some of these privileges are to the most ancient principles of the English Constitution, and how directly opposite other of them are to the settled prerogatives of the crown, and then consider what probability we have of retaining them on a *requested* change." He did, however, express his distaste for the recent conduct of the proprietors.

Joseph Galloway's response showed how very different was the perspective of the antiproprietary forces. On the provincial level he was suspicious: the power of the Penns and their wealthy supporters must be arrested now, before it grew even greater; and, somewhat contradictorily, the inadequacy of the proprietary to promote law and order was intolerable. But on the imperial plane, he was trusting: colonials must rely on the British "Disposition to mild and equitable Measures" and a "just Sovereign." Galloway's attitude expressed the Assembly's outlook. Isaac Norris, later to become Dickinson's father-in-law, was one of the small band opposing the petition which called for a royal take-over. Consequently, Norris resigned the speakership and Franklin, elected his successor, endorsed the document and sent it off to Pennsylvania's agent, Richard Jackson, in May.

By autumn, however, popular opposition to royal government was developing, though not along the lines of principle enunciated by Dickinson. Rather, the campaign against proprietary government brought into clear focus divisions in Pennsylvania, regional and religious, ethnic and economic. There was, of course, already a nucleus of opposition to the Assembly party's program which other groups might cluster around: the proprietary faction which was attached to the Penns through patronage. Thomas Penn appointed not only the lieutenant governor but all members of the Council.

These men were multiple officeholders. Lawrence Growden, for example, formerly an assemblyman and the father-in-law of Joseph Galloway, was a justice of the peace, prothonotary of the Court of Common Pleas, clerk of the Orphans Court, recorder of deeds for Bucks County, and second justice of the Supreme Court. He was also chief stockholder in the Durham iron works, the enterprise James Logan had created in the Forks of Delaware region. His estate at his death was above £110,000. Benjamin Chew, a Quaker turned Anglican, was attorney general of the province from 1754 to 1774, when he succeeded William Allen as chief justice of the Supreme Court. He was also register general of wills and recorder of the City Corporation of Philadelphia, a proprietary stronghold.

Another apostate Friend was Edward Shippen, whose father had also been a councilor and the first mayor of Philadelphia. He himself was councilman, alderman, and mayor, as well as judge of the Court of Common Pleas in Philadelphia County before he moved business operations to Lancaster County. His son, Edward II, became a councilor in 1770, already having served as prothonotary of the Supreme Court and judge of the vice-admiralty court in Delaware Bay. Another son, Joseph, succeeded Richard Peters as provincial secretary in 1762 and later became a councilor, while Edward's nephew, Thomas Willing, was alderman, councilman, and mayor of Philadelphia, third justice of the Supreme Court, and financial chieftain of the proprietary faction by virtue of building the family shipping business, with the help of Robert Morris, into a fortune. Not only in shipping but in the fur trade and real estate speculation, these men were crowding the formerly preeminent Quakers. Although they usually remained aloof from the constant battles between the executive and the legislature, the threat to proprietary rule in 1764 was too crucial to be resisted. They organized, they published, and they ran for office.

Though Thomas Penn wanted the sternest punishments meted

out to the frontiersmen who had murdered defenseless Indians, the proprietary faction found it advantageous to seek support in the west. There the record of Quaker pacifism and underrepresentation in the Assembly could be used as appeals to the German and Scotch-Irish settlers against Franklin and his cohorts, who retained the allegiance of tradesmen in Philadelphia. The city, with 8 percent of the province's population of 250,000, furnished almost 50 percent of the 3,500 signatures on circulated petitions favoring royal government, with Quakers accounting for the majority of the signatories.

Religious rivalries intruded on regional hostilities, in the case of the Scotch-Irish Presbyterians intensifying them, but among some of the Germans abating such feelings. These rivalries could be traced to the Great Awakening which, through the heightening of spiritual awareness, led to lay participation in church affairs and denominational awareness—as each congregation defined itself, it also recognized its theological enemies. The quarreling within and among groups in the 1740s gradually gave way to a time of reconciliation, grudging tolerance of one another, and, in varying degrees, the emergence of an American identity.

In 1758 the two contending factions in the Presbyterian Church, both of which had vigorously vied for adherents, merged to form the largest denomination in the province. "The Quakers . . . are esteemed more wealthy," William Allen wrote in 1761, "but are not equal in numbers to the Presbyterians." The German Reformed (Calvinist) Church, second in size, flourished under the direction of Michael Schlatter until his energy carried him into the forefront of the Charity School movement, sponsored by Franklin and William Smith as a means of assimilating Germans by Anglicizing them. This movement was ridiculed by the sectarian newspaper editor Christopher Sauer, who constantly wrote to raise the political consciousness of Germans. Sauer charged that the school sponsors "care very little for religion or for the cultivation of Germans, they rather want the Germans to stick out their necks by serving in the Militia in order to protect the property of these gentlemen."

European brethren tried to repair the division in the Reformed

Church which Schlatter created. The growth of the Swedish Lutheran Church, on the other hand, was impeded by its transatlantic connection, while the German Lutherans sustained little supervision from abroad and grew in harmony under the leadership of Henry Muhlenberg, whose cautious participation in the Charity School movement illustrated his political dexterity. The Anglicans were in the least enviable position among the church groups, dependent on two English agencies, the Bishop of London and the Society for the Propagation of the Gospel, and committed to the establishment of an American bishopric. Rivals feared that a bishopric would lead to an established church. Presbyterian William Allen was at times almost hysterical on this point, but Thomas Penn refused to regard it as a threat.

While the churches organized and gained members, the sects struggled with internal problems. The Quakers underwent a reformation directed by conscientious Friends, while the Schwenkfelders proposed a program of education for children which similarly stressed group identity. The Moravians abandoned their far-flung missionary efforts and disbanded the General Economy at Bethlehem, ending an experiment in simultaneous proselytizing and insularity. Nevertheless the Moravians, like other sects, remained concerned with their peculiarity, unlike the church groups which were finding a way into the broader society.

Lutheran and Reformed Germans in the west resented the alliance of Moravians, Mennonites, and Schwenkfelders with Quaker pacifists and became dissatisfied with the sectarian mentality that blocked the organization and education of Germans. They now were inclined to vote for the proprietary group with their Scotch-Irish neighbors, though the tradition of supporting the Quakers was not easily broken. The Quakers themselves were anything but united, however, with English Friends and longtime leaders like Isaac Norris and Israel Pemberton actually opposing the party once labeled Quaker. But many Friends who feared royal government perceived an even greater threat in the unified and growing Presbyterian interest, which William Allen was welding to the proprietary faction. Anglicans were also divided, some seeing in the transition to

royal government visions of an American bishopric and the arrest
of Presbyterianism, others opposing royalization because of their
attachment to the proprietary group by family or friendship.

Perhaps Dickinson could be spokesman for the proprietary
cause because he stood apart from special interest groups,
isolated with his high principles in a campaign conducted at the
low level of name-calling, ridicule, and even slander. Galloway's
alleged aspiration to Allen's seat as chief justice was depicted in
verse:

> Thro' Rocks and Shelves our Bark they'll paddle,
> And fasten G_____ in Will's old Saddle;
> Just as they please they'll make him fit it,
> Unscrub'd, tho' Will, they say, be-sh-t it.

But scatalogical sloganeering was not limited to one side. A
Franklin partisan characterized the proprietary group as "Piss-
Brute-tarians." Whether it was this sort of electioneering, a
concern for the principles of government, or anxiety over
threatened interests, 1764 witnessed an unparalleled turnout at
the polls. When the votes were in, though the Assembly party (or
Old Ticket) won as expected, both Franklin and Galloway were
narrowly defeated in Philadelphia County. Six of its eight seats,
plus the two city seats, went to the proprietary group. "Mr.
Franklin died like a philosopher," noted one observer. "But Mr.
Galloway agonized in death, like a mortal deist who has no
hopes of a future existence."

Neither man gave up the ghost. Rather, both hovered about
the Assembly, admonishing their adherents to stand firm on the
petition to the king. On October 26, 1764, the legislature voted to
send Franklin back to England to lobby for royal government, an
appointment that prompted strong demurs from the pens of
Dickinson and others. But Franklin optimistically anticipated
the time "when the direct and immediate Rays of Majesty
benignly and mildly shine on all around us," instead of being
"transmitted and thrown upon us thro' the Burning Glass of
Proprietary Government." Thus far he personally had mini-
mized the potentially adverse effect of parliamentary action.

In June Franklin had noted that the Sugar Act caused "a

great stir among our Merchants. . . . My opinion is, that more is apprehended than will happen." He correctly assumed that Parliament would soon pass a Currency Act, prohibiting the issue of paper money, but he did not "apprehend much Inconvenience from that Currency's being no legal Tender" and sent Richard Jackson his plan, rejected by the Assembly, for issuing interest-bearing notes rather than bills of credit. Finally, Franklin commented on Grenville's projection of a Stamp Act, giving his opinion that no colony would agree to it but predicting that he "could propose a better mode by far." In September the Assembly objected to all three pieces of legislation, which may have prompted Franklin to think more seriously about an alternative plan. And Dickinson's injection of the imperial issue into the debate on royal government no doubt gave him pause; as agent his instructions, drawn up under his own and Galloway's direction, included an admonition to try for concessions to ease trade and paper money regulations.

Commercial conditions in Pennsylvania, or the merchants' pessimistic perception of them, might also have prompted a reaction to British policy, though not a strong one. Wartime prosperity had given way to a slump in trade by late 1760. Merchants owed large debts in England, paid high prices for imported goods, found money scarce and the price of sterling steep, while sales were slow and payments from country store-keepers only creeping in because farmers had no cash.

The situation of Quaker merchant John Reynell illustrated the problem. Although the market for British goods was depressed, Reynell ordered from London as usual in the late summer of 1762, incorrectly anticipating that the end of hostilities would bring better times. Like other merchants, he was having trouble settling his balances with England. In late 1763, he ordered his metalware directly from the factory, bypassing the supplier to save money. But with a continuing high rate of exchange and low volume of sales, he cut back his orders in the autumn of 1764 and was delinquent in his remittances. Like others in the dry goods trade, he was hit hard by the Currency Act, being used to a stable system of paper money capably managed by the provincial government and respected by English merchants, though never by the imperial authorities. Still, there was not as much resentment to the Sugar and Currency acts among Philadelphia merchants as there was elsewhere in the colonies. Indeed, some merchants such as Thomas Clifford hardly noticed that the British government's policy was changing. Clifford attributed stagnation in trade to bad practices of local and London merchants, but also to politics, the "Commotions we have been in amongst ourselves."

Probably the tightening up of the imperial system did not have a great effect on Pennsylvania's oceangoing commerce. Stricter enforcement of the existing rules was intended to prevent illicit trade, which was not a major problem in Philadelphia. Quakers prided themselves on abiding by regulations; John Reynell warned one of his captains to "bring no goods on frt or otherwise, but what can be legally shipt & is enter'd & clear'd according to law." Violation of the Molasses Act—the most widespread instance of smuggling in the colonies—was far less tempting to Pennsylvanians than to New Englanders. Customs officers, by their own admission, could not prevent illegal trade on the Delaware anyway, and they received little help from the British Navy. The Sugar Act did largely foreclose illicit commerce in sugar, and the Currency Act accentuated the scarcity of money which made it difficult both to collect and pay debts. But merchants, who had a reputation as perennial grumblers and who saw the economy through the lens of a constricted dry goods trade, were not blaming the new policies for their problems before 1765, though the government's measures were unpopular.

Indeed, from a long range perspective the merchants hardly had cause for complaint. The trend in Philadelphia as in other American cities was toward a greater concentration of wealth in the upper layers of society. Merchants, as well as lawyers, land speculators, and even some shopkeepers and master artisans in the City of Brotherly Love, fared better at accumulating estates in the course of the eighteenth century than did their counterparts in Boston. The gains registered by these entrepreneurs were not, however, universally beneficial. The real assets of the lower two-thirds of Philadelphians were declining, while by the early 1760s poverty was becoming a critical social problem.

Outside the city, however, the economic picture was much cheerier. Drought and crop failures in 1761 and 1762 and Indian depredations in 1763 were followed by large crop yields and high prices for agricultural products in 1764, the beginning of a trend which prevailed to 1775. Taxes on rural real estate during the same period were relatively light, while land values rose. With the end of the war had come a cessation in privateering and a decline in freight and insurance rates, while simultaneously there was an expansion in demand for agricultural produce from abroad. For the first time, export tonnage to southern Europe exceeded that to the West Indies. And a series of poor crops beginning in 1764 converted England from a grain exporting to a grain importing country.

From 1764 to 1768 the price of Pennsylvania wheat rose spectacularly, with flour, corn, pork, and beef also rising and remaining high. Grist mills, which usually produced only whole wheat flour, were in steady operation. Saw mills were busy, too, as Philadelphia developed an important lumber export trade as well as secondary manufacturing enterprises, such as coopering and furniture-making. The iron industry was also associated with agriculture; furnaces were located in the countryside where deposits of iron ore, forests for charcoal, limestone for flux, and water for power were found in one place. Most iron plantations were remotely situated, self-sufficient operations, often occupying thousands of wooded acres and employing a hundred or even more people in various enterprises. The pig iron produced at plantation furnaces was converted to bar iron at forges, some of which were located in Philadelphia, and further refined in slitting mills, plating forges, and steel furnaces, all of which were prohibited by the Iron Act of 1750 but operated nonetheless. The enumeration of iron and lumber in 1764 was relaxed a year later.

There was, however, a potential economic problem in Pennsylvania which the new imperial policy fostered: the tendency of urban merchants to favor oceangoing commerce over inland trade and development. Fundamental to Philadelphia's rapid ascent to preeminence in the eighteenth century was its commercial control of the productive surrounding countryside. In addition to all of southeastern Pennsylvania and the Three

Lower Counties, or Delaware, several regions of New Jersey and two or three counties in eastern Maryland were tributary to Philadelphia, a total trading area which embraced some 375,000 people. Within a twenty-mile westward radius of the city lay the most densely populated and productive part of the area, but the potential for economic growth was further toward the periphery. And competition loomed large for Philadelphia where an alternate port was available—not Wilmington, overshadowed and also controlled by Philadelphians, but New York and Baltimore.

In the 1760s the farmers and millers of southern New Jersey and Delaware were shipping goods upstream and inland by shallops, which carried as much as thirty-five tons yet drew no more than four or five feet of water. In the same vessels lumber producers from southernmost New Jersey could risk the Atlantic, also to reach Philadelphia. In central Jersey a competition with New York was evident in Monmouth, Middlesex, and Somerset counties. Hunterdon and Sussex counties generally shipped down the Delaware River, as did the residents of Northampton and Bucks, of course. But farther west the Susquehanna River was navigable only in its northern portion, which meant goods had to be transshipped, usually at Harrisburg or Middletown, to wagons going on to Philadelphia. In York County especially, but also in Cumberland, Lancaster, and southern Chester, the influence of a growing Baltimore was being felt. But in the 1760s Philadelphia was powerful enough to draw to it some of the produce from the decentralized commerce of the upper Chesapeake area of Maryland. Christiana Bridge in southern Delaware, which provided frequent boats to Philadelphia and resident merchants to handle business, was but ten miles from Head of Elk, Maryland, on the most heavily traveled road in North America.

The rise of Baltimore threatened not only this trade but, more important, that of the province's southern counties, a development viewed with alarm by some Pennsylvanians. Inhabitants of Berks and Northampton counties were generally sympathetic to their southern neighbors, but others, notably the settlers of overrepresented Bucks, Philadelphia, and northern Chester counties, did not want to improve western roads at provincial expense. Philadelphia merchants recognized the importance of lowering ferry rates across the major rivers and improving transportation between the city and the upper Susquehanna. Yet they did nothing about the lower reaches of the river. Ferry rates were scrutinized although ultimately not tampered with, the merchants seemingly willing to countenance a monopoly on river crossings where later they would not countenance a corner on the sale of tea. Road reform became a major political issue, most attention focusing on the King's Highway between Lancaster and Philadelphia, the major westward artery of trade. While the Assembly finally agreed on a grant for the road and another for improving passage over the falls on the upper Delaware, the stipulation being private matching funds for both projects, the merchants raised money only for better navigation, thereby contributing to the continued ascent of Baltimore and the decline of Philadelphia.

But this legislative action was almost a decade in the future as Franklin left for England in 1764, certain that the provincial economy was functioning well. He was under little pressure to protest the new imperial policy, and he would have been reluctant to do so in any case. The main tenet of his optimistic view of the future of the British Empire was its dependence on unhindered American growth; he thought the ministry recognized and would act upon the same principle. Furthermore, Grenville's program was almost in place, and Franklin's mode of operation was to accept what existed and, if necessary, work around it. Finally, since his major objective was to bring royal government to Pennsylvania, he did not want to offend London officialdom.

But when Grenville asked the colonial agents for an alternative plan to the impending Stamp Act, as Franklin later told Galloway:

This encourag'd me, to present him with a Plan for a General Loan-Office in America, nearly like ours, but with some Improvements effectually to prevent Depreciation; to be established by Act of Parliament, appropriating the Interest to the American Service, & c. This I then thought would be a lighter and more bearable Tax than the Stamps, because those that pay it have an Equivalent in the Use of the

Money; and that it would at the same time furnish us with a Currency which we much wanted, and could not obtain under the Restrictions lately laid on us [by the Currency Act]. Mr. Grenville paid little Attention to it, being besotted with his Stamp-Scheme, which he rather chose to carry through.

In fact, the success of Franklin's scheme depended on prosperity. Grenville's plan for direct taxation would be a more dependable way of raising revenue. Nor could Franklin's implicit acceptance of Parliament's right to tax the colonies have appealed to those Americans who, faced with the question, denied the right. Fortunately for Franklin, his counterproposal remained a secret.

He did, however, openly recommend assent to the Stamp Act which, despite the objections of six provincial assemblies and because of the protests of heavily taxed Englishmen, emerged from Parliament in March 1765. It called for the use of stamps or stamped paper, costing from a halfpenny to £10 and payable only in specie, on all sorts of items from mortgages to newspapers, college diplomas to playing cards. A few documents, such as religious publications and marriage certificates, schoolbooks, and assembly records, were exempt. Non-English articles were doubly taxed. The heaviest burdens were laid on the most articulate members of society: editors, lawyers, merchants, land speculators, and students. Franklin claimed helplessness and counseled acceptance: "We might as well have hinder'd the Suns setting. That we could not do. But since 'tis down, . . . Let us make as good a Night of it as we can. We may still light candles. . . . Idleness and Pride Tax with a heavier Hand than Kings and Parliaments."

Franklin's fellow Americans were far less philosophical. Charles Thomson, the recipient of Franklin's letter, wondered who would "labour or save who has not security in his property?" Rumblings about rights and representation thundered into charges that Parliament had exceeded its bounds, commerce would collapse, currency drain away, coercion be applied. Patrick Henry declaimed on freedom in the Virginia House of Burgesses, while Sons of Liberty emerged in towns and rural areas alike, protesting, threatening, and, finally, acting defiantly by marching and planting liberty trees, burning buildings, and attacking stamp collectors. From October 7 to 24, 1765, representatives from nine colonial assemblies, including Pennsylvania's, met in New York at a Stamp Act Congress; the remaining four colonies gave their blessings to the gathering. Although pledging loyalty to the king and subordination to Parliament, they asserted that the sole right of taxation lay in the local legislatures and requested repeal of the Stamp Act and other measures adversely affecting the commerce and political rights of the colonies. Nonimportation agreements in many ports lent substance to the barrage of words. London merchants soon joined colonial agents in the clamor for repeal.

If Franklin seemed strangely out of step with American sentiment, other agents had also not anticipated the upheaval which would take place, otherwise they would not have accepted Grenville's suggestion that they nominate stamp distributors. Franklin's nominee, his Assembly ally John Hughes, accepted the post with alacrity, though he soon had to be reassured by Franklin that he was making the right move in the long run, despite growing resentment against the act. Under increasing attack, he stood firm with Galloway on Parliament's right to tax, tried to keep Pennsylvania from participating in the Stamp Act Congress and her merchants from joining the nonimportation movement, though even the apolitical Thomas Clifford was saying at the time: "America is doing all they can to avert this heavy blow at Liberty."

Members of the Assembly party were still thinking in terms of the political issues of 1764, trying to prove to the British ministry that the province was worthy of royal government. When mob violence threatened, they called out their allies among the laboring men of Philadelphia to quell the disturbances. Thus, no Sons of Liberty emerged, no violence upset the City of Brotherly Love. Ironically, Governor John Penn got the credit for this unusual tranquillity, while the proprietary party was able to brand its opponents as allies of Grenville and his plan to subvert the liberties of the people. Imperial policy was still being viewed in Pennsylvania through the lens of provincial rivalries, a perspective easily as shortsighted as the home government's failure to recognize American maturity and probably more so; at least members of the Privy Council recognized that an attack on proprietary authority was an attack on royal prerogative as well.

Franklin, too, remained a victim of the provincial mentality. In early November 1765, aware now of colonial reaction to the Stamp Act as well as the temper of the home government, he took the petition for royal government before the Privy Council, only to have it dismissed three weeks later. But if his political judgment was poor regarding this issue which obsessed him for several more years, Franklin showed his characteristic adaptability regarding the Stamp Act, becoming a leader among the colonial agents and English merchants for repeal, constantly lobbying members of Parliament, issuing news to the press, and inadvertently benefiting when the uncommitted Rockingham cabinet replaced Grenville's coterie.

He was also rethinking his attitude toward the British Empire, arriving at the position that the colonies were dominions of the crown, not subject to parliamentary legislation, a viewpoint which did not gain widespread acceptance for another decade. Now he began his ascent to the unofficially recognized status of spokesman not for Pennsylvania, but for America. He appeared before the House of Commons in this capacity, testifying to his countrymen's "greatly lessened" respect for Parliament, their unwillingness to submit to a modified stamp tax or to force, and the possibility that in the future they would find external taxation as objectionable as internal. Shortly afterward, on March 18, 1766, the Stamp Act was repealed.

Franklin's activities and writings in England were used to retrieve his reputation in Pennsylvania, where the political landscape was changing as in no other colony. In the wake of news concerning the looming Stamp Act, the Assembly assumed the unfamiliar role of defending prerogative, while the proprietary amalgamation espoused popular rights, a position most of its older members found uncomfortable. The newer members, Presbyterians and Germans, dropped away from the organization as the threat of royal government receded. Furthermore, the massive American resistance to the Stamp Act could not go unnoticed by Pennsylvanians, especially with the formation of an association for nonimportation put together by Philadelphia importers and shopkeepers and in existence from January to May 1766. At this point imperial issues began to emerge from the shackles of old provincial politics.

Hastening this change was a local issue which meshed with the transatlantic conflict: the rivalry between Anglicans and Presbyterians. It was not a situation unique to Pennsylvania. The attempt to establish bishops in the colonies was always an object of the Society for the Propagation of the Gospel. Renewed impetus came from the appointment in 1758 as Archbishop of Canterbury of Thomas Secker, an enthusiastic proponent of an American episcopate who established an Anglican mission in Massachusetts. Strong resistance to a more vigorous and imperialistic Church of England existed among New England Congregationalists and Presbyterians in the Middle Colonies. Many believed that the Grenville legislation and an American bishopric were parts of the same plot against New World liberty.

In Philadelphia the drama was played out in the college and academy, where the Anglicans dominated the board of trustees and the Presbyterians controlled the faculty. The latter were led by Reverend Francis Alison, a Scotch-Irish Latin scholar who had been chosen, ironically, by Franklin because he favored development of the English School. Quakers, fearing such conflict, never participated. The provost, Reverend William Smith, reveled in it, openly and secretly intriguing to bring the institution under Anglican control from the day of his appointment. "I am ready to resign my place," a weary Alison wrote in 1766, while simultaneously informing a gathering of Presbyterians in New York that he favored "an Union among all anti-Episcopal Churches."

Several months earlier Galloway, a nominal Anglican, had written to Franklin: "A certain sect . . . seem to look on this [the Stamp Act] as a favorable opportunity of establishing their republican principles and of throwing off all connection with the mother country. . . . Besides, I have reason to think they are not only forming a private union among themselves . . . but endeavoring also to bring into their union the Quakers and all

Benjamin Franklin at age fifty-four, painted by Benjamin Wilson; mezzotint by James McArdell. *Benjamin Franklin Collection, Sterling Memorial Library, Yale University.*

Deborah Franklin, painted by Benjamin Wilson. *American Philosophical Society.*

other Dissenters." Up to this time Smith, who clearly wanted to
be a bishop, was a mainstay of the proprietary group along with
other prominent Philadelphians, most of whom were anxious to
return to a policy of currying favor with the British ministry.
Given the proroyal position of the Assembly party—Joseph
Galloway had referred to the strongest opponents of the Stamp
Act as "Madmen"—Pennsylvania was left without an enduring
patriot organization!

The exodus of Presbyterians from the proprietary conglomer-
ate filled this void. A new party was being formed which
opponents labeled with a religious tag but its partisans called
whig. Some church Germans moved into this orbit, while other
sect Germans resumed alliance with the Quakers who remained
in the Assembly party. Still other Germans returned to their
traditional aloofness from politics during the prerevolutionary
crisis. The acknowledged leader of the Presbyterian-whig organization was John Dickinson, who had led the Assembly protest
against the Stamp Act and drafted instructions for Pennsylvania
delegates, of which he was one, to the Stamp Act Congress.

Assisting at the helm of the new party was Charles Thomson,
more pragmatic and less aristocratic than Dickinson. An orphan
and a former pupil of Francis Alison at the academy, secretary at
the Easton conferences with the Indians, bright and ambitious
like Franklin and in constant touch with him after his departure
in 1764, Thomson's contacts with mechanics, artisans, and small
shopkeepers served the Presbyterian party well and gave him an
authoritative voice in its councils. Despite differences in background, Thomson and Dickinson were in fundamental agreement. When Thomson, now a Presbyterian elder and merchant,
advocated nonimportation, Dickinson concurred, arguing that
the home government could do no more than regulate trade.
Dickinson then contemplated the possibility of separation,
though with distaste, and soared into a discussion of colonial
rights based not on contract but the "immutable maxims of
justice and reason."

With virtue thus ranged on the side of the Presbyterian party,
the imperial conflict could only invigorate the new political
organization. A Quartering Act, passed only two months after

the Stamp Act, called for the housing, feeding, and transporting of British troops in the colonies under certain circumstances. The potential for coercion, creation of a standing army, invasion of privacy, and indirect taxation were charges leveled against this measure. Yet the Assembly party in its continuing quest for royal government approved the Quartering Act, leading to General Gage's observation that "Pennsylvania, I think, is now the only Province in which Troops have been stationed, that has not since passing the Act openly refused to provide for them."

Even more helpful to the emergent Presbyterian party was the ascendancy of Chancellor of the Exchequer Charles Townshend, a member of the new Pitt-Grafton ministry who pushed through Parliament legislation suspending the New York Assembly until it complied with the Quartering Act; establishing a board of customs commissioners in America for stiffer enforcement of rules; and assigning duties to glass, lead, paint, paper, and tea, the revenue from which would pay the salaries of royal officials, thus permanently settling a civil list in America. Franklin called it a "Grenvillianized Ministry."

Franklin had already been rethinking his attitude on the British Empire. The Townshend Acts finally demonstrated to him that royal government would be a grave mistake for Pennsylvania. He argued against the Townshend proposals while they were under debate in Parliament but, once passed, he anticipated the reaction of his constituents and continued to oppose the acts, unwilling to "change my political Opinions every time his Majesty thought fit to change his Ministers." English politics, which Franklin characterized as "party contentions about places of power and profit, . . . court intrigues and cabals, . . . [men] abusing one another," was leaving a bad taste. And his partnership with Galloway was withering as their viewpoints diverged, a development Franklin did little to arrest. Galloway remained so bound to the old politics that he not only accepted the Townshend legislation, informing Franklin that "I don't well see how the Publick Weal of the Province can be affected by it," but he viewed it positively as a prelude to royal government in Pennsylvania. Meanwhile the proprietary group abandoned its aggressive tactics of two years earlier and approached the acts cautiously. It remained for John Dickinson, spearheading the Presbyterian party, to seize the initiative through the publication of the *Letters from a Pennsylvania Farmer.*

Liberty was the watchword of Dickinson's lexicon. He attacked the act restraining the New York Assembly: "A dreadful stroke is aimed at the liberty of these colonies . . . for the cause of *one* is the cause of *all.*" He assailed the Townshend duties: "The single question is, whether the parliament can legally impose duties . . . FOR THE SOLE PURPOSE OF RAISING A REVENUE, *on commodities she obliges us to take from her alone.* . . . If they can, our boasted liberty is but A sound and nothing else." And he prescribed a course of action: "If at length it becomes undoubted that an inveterate resolution is formed to annihilate the liberties of the governed, the *English* history affords frequent examples of resistance by force." Constantly Dickinson hammered at the point that the Townshend Acts were no different in principle from the hated Stamp Act, returning again and again to the theme of taxation without consent as a clear denial of freedom.

Who was to blame for this travesty? "We cannot suppose, that any injury was intended us by his Majesty, or the Lords. . . . attribute it to the inattention of the members of the house of commons, and to the malevolence or ambition of some factions great man. . . . Mr. *Greenville,* and his party . . . not one half of the members of the house of commons . . . did perceive how destructive it was to *American* freedom." Dickinson reconciled his belief that the "love of liberty is natural to the human heart" with his patriotic attachment to England by latching onto an interpretation of politics which was rife in eighteenth-century Anglo-America: the belief in the existence of conspiracy, the real source of party, which meant to overthrow either constituted authority or constitutional rights.

The maintenance of constitutional rights was a source of constant concern and anxiety for the whig opposition to the government in England, and it worried colonists as well. Even so trusting a person as Franklin viewed the Townshend Acts in terms of "intrigues and cabals." The idea of conspiracy particularly fit Dickinson's unhappy recollection of the alien world of London when he knew it as a student. The *Letters,* not surprisingly, received tremendous acclaim in America, where "To The Farmer" became a favorite toast. It hardly mattered that Dickinson was no farmer at all, as his first letter showed: "My servants are few, but good; I have a little money at interest. . . . I spend a good deal of [my time] in a library." His audience expected aristocratic leadership. Praise poured in to the *Pennsylvania Chronicle*, where the letters first appeared. New England town meetings responded likewise. The *Letters* were republished at home and abroad. Franklin, who privately expressed his more radical stance that Parliament had the "power to make *no laws* for us," observed in his preface to the English edition that the *Letters* represented "the general sentiments of the inhabitants" of America.

And, indeed, there was a striking resemblance between the *Letters* and the Massachusetts House of Representatives' "circular letter" of February 1768 issued before Dickinson's writings were published in Boston. Lord Hillsborough, the first occupant of the secretaryship of state for the colonies created in January 1768, saw in the Massachusetts letter "a most dangerous and factious tendency, calculated to inflame" and referred to Dickinson's *Letters* as "extremely wild."

And in Pennsylvania Joseph Galloway, speaker of the Assembly and heretofore Franklin's ally, sputtered as the *Letters from a Pennsylvania Farmer* appeared: "Mere fluff! fustian! altogether stupid and inconsistent." He referred to his countrymen as "mad," a term he used recurrently and, judging by his last years, significantly. He added that "they knew not what they wanted . . . [and were] incapable of judging on such matters." Under his leadership, the Assembly hardly considered the Townshend Acts. The legislators were more worried about the "trespassing spirit of encroaching hogs," snapped Dickinson in a rare moment of humor, than the "most dangerous and daring outrages against the liberty of themselves." Thomson and Dickinson again pushed the merchants to send petitions to London and follow the lead of Boston in adopting nonimportation, but few of the traders were willing to curtail their activities.

However, Lord Hillsborough's demand that the Massachusetts House of Representatives rescind its circular letter, which it refused to do, and his order that the lower houses of other colonies not take similar action or even respond to Massachusetts on penalty of dissolution, provoked a response from the Assembly. The Pennsylvania legislature asserted that it could not be controlled from without; it would not be hindered from corresponding "with the Representatives of the Freemen in any of his Majesty's Colonies in *America*, relative to Grievances which may affect the General Welfare," in order to achieve redress; and it wanted an end to the Townshend duties, which were "unconstitutional taxes."

If Galloway and his followers were forced with some embarassment to defend the constitutional position of the Assembly by Hillsborough, they were dazed by their next news of him. A letter from Franklin which arrived in late October 1768 informed Galloway that Hillsborough was so hostile to the petition for royal government in Pennsylvania that the agent was dropping the matter. "I stay however a little longer here, till I see what Turn American Affairs are like to take." Franklin's perspective had so broadened that he was more interested in the affairs of all the colonies than in the plight of Pennsylvania alone; significantly, he became agent for Georgia in 1768, for New Jersey in 1769, for Massachusetts in 1770. And with the failure of his lobbying for royal government from 1764 to 1768, he turned to encourage American resistance to imperial power, an option he did not have in his own province.

Galloway's outlook, on the other hand, remained parochial. Having predicated his political behavior on the advent of royal government, he suddenly found his credibility at stake and his alliance with Franklin shaken. His weekly letters to his colleague ceased abruptly for almost a year, then became short and formal. He fell ill and gave up the speaker's chair from May to October 1769. Later he absented himself from the Assembly debates over nonimportation, and he had to retreat from Philadelphia to Bucks County to hold his seat in the legislature. His followers were also shaken by Franklin's news, but they could discover no broader program than abandoning their support for the Townshend Acts. Yet the fact that Galloway held the speakership until 1774 while most of his followers retained their Assembly seats meant that protest against imperial policies in Pennsylvania, when it occurred, was likely to be extragovernmental. The colony remained officially impervious.

Franklin's letter in October had not shaken Galloway's confidence that the "hotheaded indiscreet men" advocating nonimportation would fail. William Allen, however, viewed the situation as one of watchful waiting; if the ministry did not accept the petition against the Townshend Acts, "then, shall we begin our Constitutional war with our mother country . . . we will set up Manufactures and provide for ourselves." John Dickinson, Charles Thomson, and Thomas Mifflin, a socially prominent young merchant of Quaker descent, took direct action, wooing and winning the mechanics while putting pressure on the merchants until most of them agreed not to import commodities included in the Townshend Acts.

In March 1769 a committee was formed to supervise the nonimportation agreement, with subcommittees reaching even into the rural and frontier areas. John Reynell, the dry goods merchant who worried about the "great commotion among us" during the Stamp Act crisis, was again aware of the popular demand for nonimportation, largely the work of Charles Thomson. Reynell's decision to head a committee of merchants who would request their opposite numbers in England to work for repeal was based, at least partly, on a fear of otherwise losing control of the situation.

But when no word came back from English merchants and manufacturers, Reynell agreed to nonimportation until the Townshend Acts were voided. He now discovered the legislation to be unconstitutional and argued that without parliamentary representation his countrymen were "no longer Englishmen but Slaves." In July he presided over a meeting to determine whether a merchant had violated the general nonimportation agreement. His behavior confounded many Quakers, especially his old friend Israel Pemberton, who urged the Society to condemn Reynell's conduct as "a dangerous incitement to all the anarchical and revolutionary elements in the Province."

Soon Reynell had reason to respect Pemberton's caution, as Thomson and his cohorts, following the lead of Boston radicals, pushed the Philadelphia merchants to maintain nonimportation until Parliament repealed all laws imposing duties on American commerce. Reynell and most other dry goods traders resigned from the merchant committee, feeling it was being used for radical purposes and believing that repeal of the Townshend Acts was imminent. Furthermore, imports from England in 1769 were less than half the 1768 tonnage, giving Reynell further cause to reverse his position.

The ministry of Lord North, which would exist for a dozen years under the close control of the king, was formed in early 1770 and, by April, all the Townshend duties save for the one on tea were repealed. Franklin depicted partial repeal as "bad policy; . . . as it is bad surgery to leave splinters in a wound, which must prevent its healing, or in time occasion it to open afresh." He encouraged British merchants to lobby for removal of the tea duty, and he urged American merchants to continue nonimportation. Mechanics and merchants whose major business was not with England agreed as, of course, did Dickinson and Thomson. The dry goods merchants wanted to import all products but tea, especially after the boycott ended in New York.

In the ensuing power struggle between Reynell and Thomson the former won in September 1770 when trade was resumed, a development denounced by tradesmen as a sacrifice of the "credit and liberties of the province of Pennsylvania to the interests of a few merchants in Philadelphia." But Reynell and Thomas Clifford were satisfied that the imperial problem was solved. Clifford's emphasis on obedience, expressed in his anxiety regarding "the angry Countenance the Mother Country looks on her Children here with," stood in striking contrast to Dickinson's concern with liberty. And for the next three years most merchants went about their business as usual, or so it seemed.

In fact, there was an important change in mercantile relations with England and a major alteration in the landscape of provincial politics in the wake of the crisis in the empire. In the late 1760s the constitutional questions aroused by the Townshend Acts had assumed greater importance for merchants than their economic worries, despite the fact that 1767 witnessed colonial Pennsylvania's most colossal business failure: Baynton,

Wharton, and Morgan defaulted for £100,000. After 1770, though inventory had been cleared during nonimportation, merchants were again complaining of a depression.

The truth of the matter was that the traders had over-ordered, and supply was far in excess of demand; imports in 1771 were almost double the value of those in 1768. Much resentment was misdirected at the public auctions, or vendues, where large quantities of English goods were sold. And there was anger that the Assembly refused to regulate or end the practice which led people into the habit of buying the cheapest goods. By 1773 importers were curtailing their business. There was also a problem of scarce money, since the Currency Act of 1764 had been left untouched by colonial protest against home government policy. On the other hand, prices of agricultural exports remained high until after the war. The building of new wharves and rising rents of market stalls, not to mention the many public projects usually associated with Franklin, were testimony to prewar prosperity.

But in one important sense the economic scene changed in response to the agitation over imperial controls in the late 1760s: there was a dramatic increase in illegal trade. John Swift, deputy customs collector at the port of Philadelphia, wrote in 1771 that "smuggling was never carried to such a height as it has been lately. . . . The Officers of the Customs are but few & they have to contend with the whole body of Merchts many of whom think it no crime to cheat the King of his Duties." Two years later Swift added the lament that attempted enforcement cast the official in the role of "an enemy to the community."

Harassment of royal officers, which was indulged in by such eminent but politically diverse merchant-politicians as John Dickinson, Joseph Galloway, and proprietary placeman Benjamin Chew, and illicit commerce had an analogue in extralegal political activities of less eminent men. Philadelphia mobs carried away confiscated goods, damaged the property of port collectors, and physically assaulted informants and officials. In a society where deference had traditionally been paid to an economic and political elite, neither merchants nor politicians could expect such overt behavior to go unnoticed or unheeded.

If, indeed, the deportment of the time-honored leaders was not an index to their superiority, if the middling or lower sorts could be called upon to exert pressure on certain of the aristocrats, was not a more permanent alteration in political participation a logical next step? Four days preceeding the 1770 Assembly election there appeared in the *Pennsylvania Gazette* an anonymous letter questioning both the ability of the current party chieftains and the way candidates were agreed upon: "A certain Company of leading Men nominate Persons, and settle the Ticket, . . . without ever permitting the affirmative or negative voice of a Mechanic to interfere. . . . Have we not an equal Right of electing, or being elected? . . . I think it absolutely necessary that one or two Mechanics be elected to represent so large a Body of the Inhabitants." Both David Lloyd and Sir William Keith had politicized hitherto inactive elements of the body politic, far back in the province's past. But never before had it been suggested that mechanics share the leadership.

This political development was, however, a logical outgrowth of the social milieu of Philadelphia and the recent activities of the artisans. The city was not residentially segregated along class lines. Civic associations and family connections brought men of different occupations together. And there were no legal or institutional barriers in the way of movement from mechanic to merchant. Tradesmen were beginning to be elected to city posts such as commissioner, warden, and tax assessor in the late 1760s and early 1770s. But if social integration and the possibilities of occupational and political mobility encouraged the mechanics' aspirations, the redistribution of the community's assets could only have led to resentment.

Although affluence was ever more visible, it was becoming more and more concentrated in the apex of society. Among Philadelphians the median wealth of the top tenth had soared from £959 in the early years of settlement to £3,404 in the decade preceding the Revolution. In the bottom third of the population, however, the average amount of property held declined from £39 in the seventeenth century to £21 in the mid-eighteenth before it began slowly rising again. The graph of median wealth in the middle third of the city's people also showed a drop (from an initial £213 to £146 slightly before mid-century), slow growth, and leveling off at about £208 in the prerevolutionary years.

Mechanics, torn between a vision of success and the reality of immobility, might well have found a scapegoat in the "ruinous" competition of foreign goods. Nonimportation choked off these wares and sharpened the mechanics' instinct for power. They found, however, that when their interests collided with those of the merchants, the latter still wielded ultimate political control. The Assembly, for example, refused to regulate the price and quality of raw materials imported by merchants but used by artisans. Mechanics grew more active and were better organized in response to the Townshend Acts than ever before, putting pressure on the reluctant dry goods merchants and attempting to keep them in line on nonimportation through a "Mechanicks Committee." Unsuccessful on that front, the letter printed in the *Pennsylvania Gazette* was a prediction of their defection, but also a sign that they were working within the political system. Galloway knew what was about to happen. "As to our election, we are all in Confusion," he informed Franklin. "The White Oaks and Mechanics or many of them have left the Old Ticket and tis feared will go over to the Presbyterians."

But Franklin himself, though still friendly with Galloway, had in the course of nonimportation aligned himself with Thomson and his newly radicalized party, which had also added the urban tradesmen to its Presbyterian and church German supporters. As a result, Dickinson was elected to the Assembly from Philadelphia for the first time in six years, though he soon tired of politics and returned to his principles and his law practice from 1771 to 1774. Galloway, having retreated to Bucks County, nevertheless held on to the speakership until 1774. Though characterized as a tool of the British ministry, he and the Assembly party, kept afloat by rich merchants and content farmers, simply wanted to preserve the status quo from the anarchy to which the imperial crisis had momentarily exposed the province.

In this aspiration the Assembly party resembled nothing so much as its old rival, the proprietary group, with which it now found a community of interest, a basis of cooperation, and a common local enemy: the Presbyterians. While in other colonies during the early 1770s the lower houses battled the governors, in Pennsylvania there was needed only an Edward Hicks to depict the peaceable relations between legislature and executive. Charles Thomson tried to reawaken his provincial peers to the conflict with England, while the "respectable Tradesmen, Mechanics, &c." formed the Patriotic Society to promote their goals. But the Pennsylvania Assembly pursued its own pacific path, oblivious of the transatlantic gales of change.

10

BLOSSOMING:
THE REVOLUTIONARY MOVEMENT

The revolutionary storm blew up from a tempest in a tea port. The early 1770s were years of comparative calm, with dedicated partisans like Charles Thomson in Philadelphia and Sam Adams in Boston fighting singular and not notably successful battles to keep the spirit of the turbulent 1760s alive. Occasional incidents between customs agents and merchants did remind colonists of the recent past, while Adams' revival of committees of correspondence had its effect beyond the towns of Massachusetts. But as London was still the heart of empire, Parliament remained the center of controversy, at this point creating a situation whose ramifications led to war and American independence.

The British East India Company, once a private venture, had been transformed into a semipublic investment through large government loans. In an attempt to rescue the company from bankruptcy, Parliament passed a Regulating Act, giving itself greater control over the company, and a Tea Act, which allowed the company to sell its product directly to colonial buyers, thereby eliminating the payment of an English tax and the commission of the English middleman. The act also passed over the colonial importer and, in dropping the cost of East India tea, gave the company a monopoly of the market; the price would be competitive even with smuggled Dutch tea. This was not only bad practice but dangerous principle. Once the precedent was established, monopolies could be granted to other companies. "Beware of the East India Company," wrote John Dickinson,

whose sensitivity to precedent and principle summoned hyper-
bolic prose: "The Revenues of Mighty Kingdoms have centered
in their Coffers. And these not being sufficient to glut their
Avarice, they have, by the most unparalleled Barbarities,
Extortions, and Monopolies, stripped the miserable Inhabitants of their Property and reduced whole Provinces to Indigence
and Ruin."

Dickinson of late had been a moderate voice. His unbending
hostility now gave warning that the Tea Act had produced a new
situation. Charles Thomson and his radical followers were busily
organizing committees and associations in every county of
Pennsylvania, as well as in Philadelphia, on the basis of a lesson
learned in protesting the Townshend Acts. Thomson's plan was
to organize those "who were firmly persuaded that the dispute
would terminate in blood, . . . and thereby put it out of the
power of the merchants as they had done before to drop the
opposition when interest dictated the measure." Thus a mechanic writing to the *Pennsylvania Gazette* in defense of "the sacred
Liberties of the *Americas*" compared the "Industry, Oeconomy,
Prudence and Fortitude" of the tradesmen to the "Corruption,
Extravagence and Luxury" of English politicians. He reiterated
Dickinson's strong charges against the East India Company and
warned his readers that not only merchants would be affected
but "YOU, ME and every member of the whole Community."
Obviously, consensus was requisite for effective action.

The merchants to whom the tea was consigned were put under
the heaviest pressure. Abel James, Henry Drinker, Thomas and
Isaac Wharton (two other consignees were absent from the city),
all Quakers, had had little to do with the tea trade previously
and, like the stamp agents, became involved through the
intercession of friends in London. When a mass meeting held in
mid-October adopted resolutions depicting the tea scheme as a
plot to implement the Townshend duty and labeled anyone
involved in it as "an Enemy to his Country," these merchants
were persuaded to resign their tea commissions. Not even the
conservative Quaker meeting would say a word in support of
them. But that situation changed as John Reynell, recognizing
radical control of the committees and associations, refused to

participate in them. Instead, he used his influence in the Society of Friends to direct a campaign against the Thomson group through official statements. The first of these emerged from the Meeting for Sufferings in January 1774, warning Quakers to stay clear of public demonstrations or meetings directed by radicals.

Thomson, Mifflin, and their followers demonstrated their control of the situation through the formation of a Committee for Tarring and Feathering. Political activists were more radical and more unified than ever before. In response to rumors that a tea ship, the *Polly*, was on its way from England, Delaware River pilots were warned not to guide it up the river, while the vessel's captain was promised "a halter around your neck . . . ten gallons of liquid Tar decanted on your pate . . . with the feathers of a dozen live geese laid over that to enliven your appearance." Philadelphia had moved faster than any other American city in taking a public stand against the Tea Act. But the first tea ship arrived in Boston on November 28, 1773, almost a month before the *Polly* docked.

It was fitting that the Bostonians who dumped the tea into the harbor on the night of December 16 started a train of events which eventually led back to an intercolonial meeting in Philadelphia. But in fact, the radical residents of Pennsylvania's port were unprepared to take such astounding steps as had the Massachusetts Sons of Liberty. News of the Boston Tea Party was welcomed and the heady rhetoric was maintained. Thomson reported to Sam Adams and John Hancock that his handbills depicted the East India Company "as ravagers of Asia, the corrupters of their country, the supporters of arbitrary power, and the patrons of monopoly." The sentiments were no doubt sincere but also consciously manipulative, for Thomson admitted that he did "not think it unworthy the cause sometimes to borrow aid from the passions." Yet no tea was destroyed nor, as happened in Charleston, confiscated and stored. Rather, the intimidated captain of the *Polly* was sent back to England with his cargo.

The *Gazette*, retracing the events which led to the quiet disposal of Philadelphia's tea, concluded that "the Foundations of American Liberty [are] more deeply laid than ever." That opinion about the future of freedom could so quickly oscillate from deepest gloom to lofty optimism was an index of the instability and uncertainty of the times, an atmosphere of social stress that also explained the seemingly exaggerated statements of the participants. Hyperbole also signified the increasing importance of ideology in the resistance efforts. Yet one of the most extravagant judgments of the movement proved accurate. John Adams exclaimed: "This Destruction of the Tea is so bold, so daring, so firm, so intrepid, so inflexible, and it must have so important Consequences, and so lasting that I cannot but consider it an Epocha in History."

That it was. The dominant reaction in England was quite the opposite of American sentiment. Even Franklin, though a step ahead of many of his fellow colonists in believing that they were tied to England only through the crown and not Parliament, though he considered the Tea Act a mistake and wrote two magnificent satires in 1773 to ridicule imperial policy, could not see "any Necessity for carrying Matters to such Extremity, as, in a Dispute about Publick Rights, to destroy private Property"; and he recommended full compensation. The news of the Boston Tea Party arrived only days before Franklin was subjected to a humiliating scolding before the Privy Council for his part in supplying private letters, calculated to embarrass Massachusetts royal officials, to the Boston radicals during the Stamp Act crisis. The colonial agent for four colonies was ridiculed: "Dr. Franklin's mind may have been so possessed with the idea of a Great American Republic that he may easily slide into the language of a foreign independent state." But sarcasm was only partially indicative of the home government's furious reaction to the American situation. "The colonies must either submit or triumph," wrote the king, and the North ministry hastened to design the terms of submission.

Between March 31 and June 2, 1774, Parliament passed four bills, labeled the Coercive or Intolerable Acts by Americans. These legislative acts were calculated to close the port of Boston until the destroyed tea was paid for; regulate the government of Massachusetts through royal appointment of Council members and judges while severely restricting the function of town meetings; allow the governor of the Bay Colony to remove trials concerning acts of Parliament or suppression of riot from local jurisdiction to other provinces or England; and provide for quartering of English troops in the vicinity of popular disturbances, four more regiments having been sent to New England in the late spring of 1774. Almost simultaneously Parliament passed the Quebec Act, which Americans related to the previous punitive legislation because it extended the boundaries of that province southward, providing another barrier to settlement in the Ohio country. It also recognized French civil law and granted "the free exercize of Religion of the Church of Rome." Moderate and radical Americans alike were confirmed in the oft-expressed opinion that the English ministry was in the hands of diabolical men. And Parliament's display of power seemed a blatant assertion that colonial rights were subordinate in the empire. The consequence was American unity.

Yet, as immediately and generally provoking as the Coercive Acts were, a concerted reaction was achieved only by calculated political maneuvering. On May 18, 1774, news of the Boston Port Act reached Philadelphia. A day later Paul Revere arrived, seeking support for Boston's nonimportation proposal. The following day Thomson and Mifflin were joined by Joseph Reed, a moderate-minded, thirty-three-year-old lawyer of New Jersey Presbyterian background, who had studied at Middle Temple and arrived in Philadelphia only in 1770 but enjoyed both economic and professional success. This trio journeyed to the estate of John Dickinson. Here it was agreed that the first three men would present a plan for immediate nonimportation to a general meeting being held that evening at the City Tavern, after which Dickinson would present a counterproposal: the governor, John Penn, should be requested to call a special meeting of the Assembly and a committee of correspondence should be appointed to send a reply to Boston.

The strategy worked. Reed later recalled that Dickinson's reputation, and the contrast between Thomson's and his speech, described as "being so gentle in its appearance was a great relief against the violence of the first," led to the acceptance of both propositions. A nineteen-member committee of correspondence was chosen, mostly merchants and including Dickinson, which for a month directed extralegal activity. Indeed, from this point until independence was declared, committees were at the very heart of the revolutionary movement in Pennsylvania. They dated back, of course, to the mid-1760s. With the passage of time they had become more radical, despite the continuing consciousness of a need for community consensus, less wealthy, and less dominated by merchants, more under the control of Presbyterians who had initially had only a third the representation of either Quakers or Anglicans.

The emergent dissatisfaction with the committee movement was evident enough. Quaker merchants such as John Reynell were conspicuously absent from the May 20 meeting. And the Society of Friends refused to support the one-day suspension of business on June 1 in recognition of Boston's plight, though the organizers of this "solemn pause" tried to have full denominational representation in planning it. Indeed, Quakers continued to oppose any economic coercion of England. And twelve hundred mechanics who wanted more decisive action met independently in early June to consider measures promoting unity and strengthening "the hands of our patriotic merchants." Governor Penn rejected the request that the Assembly be convened. And yet there was harmony on one subject. "All ranks, with us," Mifflin wrote to Sam Adams, "agree to the Proposal of a general Congress previous to the fixing on any Plan of Reconciliation or Opposition." To the radicals it meant a gathering with such notables as Sam Adams. More moderate men viewed it as a respectable forum for enunciating their principles and advertising unity. Conservatives saw in it a means of delaying outright resistance to England which otherwise appeared imminent.

There was some difficulty agreeing on how delegates to the congress would be chosen. The mechanics, desirous of immediate action, pressured the committee of correspondence to request a special session of the Assembly where delegates would be selected. Reed, though he realized the improbability of an early meeting of the legislature, favored this method since it would reveal the true sentiment of anachronistic assemblymen and lead to victories for his men at the polls in October. Dickinson, once the governor had refused to call the legislature, wanted a special convention summoned to choose delegates. By way of compromise, the committee of correspondence agreed to pursue this plan but did not discard its appeal for an Assembly.

Furthermore, on June 18 at a general meeting of some eight thousand people in the State House Yard, a new and larger committee of correspondence was formed, with more weight given to the radical point of view; apparently the mechanics forced seven of their number onto the slate. Dickinson, Thomson, and Mifflin then toured the back counties, advising on local committees of correspondence and preparing for the provincial convention which was to meet on July 15. Meanwhile Governor Penn called the Assembly into special session on July 18, on the pretext of dealing with frontier troubles.

The provincial convention lived up to the high hopes of its creators and, acting generally under the guidance of Dickinson's *Essay of Instructions* and his *Argument*, the latter being subsequently published as *An Essay on the Constitutional Power of Great Britain*, represented nothing so much as a whig point of view. Reasoning from the simple principle that "the happiness of the people is the end . . . of the Constitution," Dickinson attacked any power of government which was not limited or was exercised without popular consent, even if, in the past, that power had been used without protest. Consequently, Parliament could not legislate the internal affairs of the colonies or even regulate trade if such control were not beneficial.

In accepting this doctrine, the provincial convention called on Parliament to renounce its authority within the colonies, including the levying of internal or external taxes, and its power to adopt new acts of trade. By way of compromise, the Americans would agree to the old Navigation Acts. They could not, of course, accede to the Declaratory Act and the Coercive Acts, which were specifically condemned. But they would compensate the East India Company for its losses and settle a permanent revenue on the king. Although it was hoped that an attempt at redress of colonial grievances would be made to the crown, the convention endorsed nonimportation and nonexportation in any case, should the congress agree on it.

Three members of the convention were selected to lay that body's work before the Assembly: Dickinson; the merchant Thomas Willing, who had recently played a leading and moderate role in the committee of correspondence; and James Wilson, a Scotch Presbyterian who, tiring of teaching classics at the college after his arrival in Philadelphia in 1765, studied law under Dickinson and practiced in Carlisle. None of them were members of the legislature. Speaker Galloway supported the convening of an intercolonial congress; his plan of reconciliation and unity between England and America had the added attraction, he thought, of restoring his political credit in Pennsylvania.

He would not, in his official position, underwrite the work of the provincial convention, and he prevailed on the Assembly to send as delegates to the forthcoming congress not Dickinson, Willing, and Wilson, but himself and four colleagues. Thomas Mifflin was the legislature's only delegate associated with previous whig activities. Dickinson, Thomson, and their followers, if they expected to have a hearing at the congress, would have to work around the Assembly, as they had done several times previously. In fact, in 1774 Pennsylvania was the only colony that held a provincial convention after it was apparent that the legislature would meet and could appoint delegates. But in any case the whigs might profit from the advantage of laboring in familiar territory, for the Pennsylvanians were to host the intercolonial gathering.

On June 17 the Massachusetts House of Representatives had called for "a meeting of Committees, from the several colonies on this Continent," suggested September 1 in Philadelphia as the time and place, and appointed five delegates. The Rhode Island and Connecticut legislatures had already appointed delegates, while in New Hampshire, as well as in New Jersey, Delaware, Maryland, and North Carolina, provincial congresses chose the representatives. In South Carolina a general meeting of voters elected the delegates, the lower house ratifying the act. Virginia's deputies were selected by the "convention," a body convened by a group of Burgesses. In New York the delegates elected in the city were approved by all but three counties, which chose their own. Only Georgia was not represented.

All converged on Philadelphia, the largest city in North America and one of the greatest in the British Empire. "The regularity and Elegance of this City are very striking," noted John Adams on arrival, though a few weeks later he seemed compelled to add: "The Uniformity of this City is dissagreable to some.—I like it." Finally, having been wined and dined in grand fashion, visiting museums and sampling churches, politicking and being subjected to the "Deliberations of the Congress . . . spun out to an immeasurable Length," Adams concluded: "Phyladelphia with all its Trade, and Wealth, and Regularity is not Boston. The morals of our People are much better, their Manners are more polite, and agreable—they are purer English. Our language is better, our Persons are handsomer, our Spirit is greater, our Laws are wiser, our Religion is superiour, our Education is better. We exceed them in every Thing, but in a Markett, and in charitable public foundations."

To concede Philadelphia material advantage while reserving spiritual superiority to his native land was typical of the flinty Puritan side of Adams' personality, if it did not convey as well a persisting intercolonial rivalry to be discovered in the provincialism of many of the delegates. Yet Adams was also a man curious about his surroundings. During his two-month sojourn in Philadelphia, he visited Anglican, Quaker, Presbyterian, Moravian, Baptist, and Roman Catholic services, an odyssey his Massachusetts ancestors would have considered unholy.

He could not have failed to recognize Philadelphia's achievements. While Boston's population had remained stationary at sixteen thousand, Philadelphia's had tripled to forty thousand over the past three decades. (New York, now twenty-five thousand, Charles Town, and Newport had each seen their populations roughly double during the same period.) Surely Philadelphia did have superior markets: the many stalls along High (now Market) Street, some 1,300 feet of covered accommodations, were supplemented by others on south Second Street

and in the Northern Liberties. As to charitable public foundations, the burden on the Alms House, overcrowded when the
French and Indian War and Pontiac's rebellion sent settlers
scurrying into the city, was shared by the Bettering House, built
in 1767 and run on principles Adams approved: the aged and
disabled were given free care but the able-bodied poor were
required to work for their sustenance. In addition, private
citizens such as Anthony Benezet and benevolent societies,
usually organized along national lines, provided charity for the
needy.

But Adams could not avoid seeing that Philadelphia was
surpassing Boston in other areas, traditionally the safe preserve of
the Yankee city. He dined with John Morgan, "an ingenious
Physician and an honest Patriot," but also a symbol of Philadelphia's superiority in the field of medicine. Only New York shared
with it the honor of having a medical school, while the
Pennsylvania Hospital, which Adams visited, was a colonial
achievement without precedent or equal. True, in the realm of
law, Pennsylvania's criminal code was the harshest of any among
the colonies. Nor did Philadelphia's extensive elementary and
secondary school system, largely controlled by religious denominations but including the nonsectarian academy, match Boston's
tax-supported education.

Yet the literary output of Philadelphia greatly outweighed
Boston's; Adams admired the "excellent Library" at Carpenter's
Hall and the "grand" one at John Dickinson's country seat. The
City of Brotherly Love was more friendly to music, which Adams
heard at a Moravian service, and had recently taken the lead
from Boston in painting. The revitalized American Philosophical
Society, which supported such luminaries as the astronomer
David Rittenhouse, was probably the clearest evidence of
Philadelphia's cultural eminence. Charles Thomson, who was
most responsible for infusing the society with new life, noted the
geographical and intellectual relationships which Adams overlooked: "As Philadelphia is the Centre of the Colonies, as her
Inhabitants are remarkable for encouraging laudable and useful
undertakings, why should we hesitate to enlarge the plan of our
Society, called to our Assistance Men of Learning and Ingenuity

Plan of Boston, 1722. Map Division, New York Public Library, Astor, Lenox and Tilden Foundations.

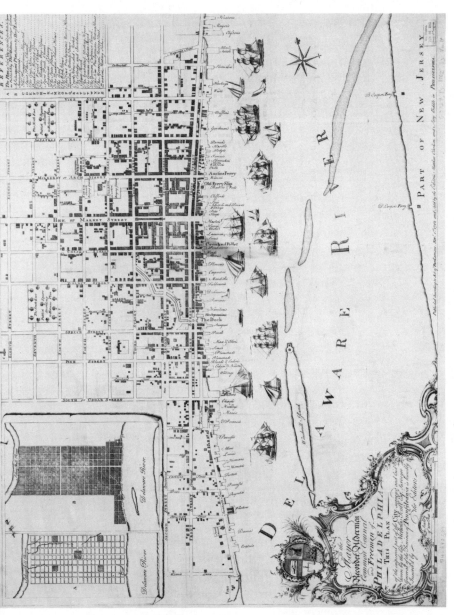

Plan of Philadelphia, 1762. *Library of Congress.*

from every Quarter and unite in one generous, notable attempt not only to promote the Interest of our Country, but to raise her to some eminence in the rank of polite and learned nations."

Perhaps Adams' astigmatism resulted, in part, from the tiring pressures of politics, which Thomson played no small part in applying. Before the Massachusetts delegation reached the city limits of Philadelphia it was greeted by several local gentlemen, including Thomas Mifflin and Benjamin Rush, who cautioned against "bold measures" and rendered the whig portrait of local politics. The following day John Adams met Charles Thomson, bestowing on him the accolade "the Sam. Adams of Phyladel-phia—the Life of the Cause of Liberty, they say." A day later he was visited by John Dickinson: "He is a Shadow—tall, but slender as a Reed—pale as ashes. One would think at first Sight that he could not live a Month. Yet upon more attentive Inspection, he looks as if the Springs of Life were strong enough to last many Years." The next day Adams encountered Joseph Galloway: "He looks like Ben. Davis the Sandamanian . . . Dr. [William] Smith, Mr. Galloway . . . and others in this Town, are now just where the Huchinsonian Faction were . . . when We were endeavoring to obtain a Repeal of the Stamp Act." And two days after that, Joseph Reed, Adams' frequent companion in the ensuing weeks, was described as "a very sensible and accomplished Lawyer of an amiable Disposition . . . He is a friend to his Country and to Liberty."

It was important that Adams and the other delegates be rightly disposed, for the politics of Pennsylvania immediately intruded on this first Continental Congress. On September 5 at ten in the morning, the representatives assembled in the City Tavern and walked two blocks to Carpenter's Hall, the newly completed meeting place of America's oldest builder's associa-tion, which housed the Library Company on its second floor. "The General Cry was, that this was a good Room," Adams recorded, and shortly afterward Thomas Lynch of South Caro-lina, whom Adams had met in the City Tavern the night of his arrival, proposed Charles Thomson as secretary for the Congress, "which was accordingly done without opposition."

Supporting the outward unanimity of action, however, was a

well-laid groundwork. Galloway had offered the State House, the Assembly's regular quarters a few blocks farther up Chestnut Street which, thought one delegate, was a better place but had been rejected to spite Galloway. Proponents argued that Carpenter's Hall would be "highly agreeable to the mechanics and citizens in general," hardly the speaker's political allies. The choice of Thomson "to my surprise," Galloway wrote William Franklin, was personally and ideologically offensive to him. "Both of these measures," sniffed Galloway, "it seems were privately settled by an Interest made out of Doors."

Yet the speaker, though he recognized the strength and strategic agility of the whig opponents, did not give up the battle. The Congress had convened, after all, to seek redress of grievances from and restore harmony with the mother country: the instructions to the Massachusetts delegates were hardly more radical than those to the Pennsylvanians. But after two committees had been formed, one to state colonial rights and the means to restore them, the other to report on legislation affecting trade and manufacturing in the colonies, the placidity of the Congress was disrupted by Resolves that arrived from Boston's Suffolk County. Denouncing the recent acts of Parliament and declaring that "no obedience is due from this province to either or any part of the acts," the Suffolk Resolves proposed breaking commerical relations with England, promised to resist enforcement of the acts with force and, yet, paid "all due respect and submission" to Congress' recommendations. The assembled delegates responded with a unanimous vote of sympathy; "one of the happiest days of my life," exulted John Adams. They agreed to nonimportation, nonconsumption, and, unless their grievances were recognized within a year, nonexportation.

Into this radical celebration Galloway burst with a plea for moderation and a plan of union. Earlier, the delegates had debated whether their rights as colonists were natural or political. This argument was resolved in the Declaration of Rights, which found the basis in "the immutable laws of nature, the principles of the English constitution, and the several charters or compacts." Galloway then put forward a third explanation: "We might reduce our Rights to one. An Exemp-

John Dickinson.
*Historical Society
of Pennsylvania.*

Charles Thomson.
*Historical Society
of Pennsylvania.*

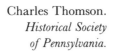

Joseph Reed.
*Historical Society
of Pennsylvania.*

Thomas Mifflin.
*The Metropolitan
Museum of Art, gift of
Mr. J. William Middendorf II,
1968.*

Benjamin Rush.
*Courtesy, the Henry Francis
du Pont Winterthur Museum.
Gift of Mrs. T. Charton Henry.*

tion from all Laws made by British Parliament, made since the Emigration of our Ancestors." This viewpoint, logically inconsistent, historically fallacious, and altogether novel, spotlighted Galloway as a sturdy defender of the Americans, thus preparing the way for his plan of union. Taking some inspiration from Franklin's Albany Plan, Galloway provided for a president general, appointed by the king and with veto power over the "British and American legislature," or Grand Council. This body was composed of representatives elected by the provincial legislatures and endowed with the rights, liberties, and privileges of the House of Commons. It shared with Parliament the responsibility for general regulation of the colonies but lacked the power to interfere in their internal affairs.

The idea gained immediate support from conservatives in the Congress, but radicals led by the Massachusetts and Virginia delegates feared in its acceptance the death of nonexportation and, perhaps, corruption by close association with Parliament. They moved to postpone consideration, and within a month they had obliterated the plan of union from the minutes of the Congress. To add to Galloway's dismay, the Pennsylvania election on October 1 had brought Thomson and Dickinson into the Assembly. When that body met two weeks later, Galloway lost the speaker's chair which he had occupied since 1766 and Dickinson was named a delegate to the Congress, where he immediately distinguished himself by drafting a petition to the king which denounced and demanded repeal of the legislation passed since 1763. Surely this would serve as an antidote to Galloway's pleas for reconciliation. In addition to the petition and the Declaration of Rights, one part of which served as a criticism of Galloway's plan, Congress concluded its work with a design for implementing the ban on trade with England: the Association.

This agreement—for the Congress could not give its most important act the force of law—was more than a means of putting into effect nonintercourse with England and nonconsumption of British products. It was a way of promoting American self-sufficiency, both material and spiritual. The associators pledged that they would "encourage frugality, and

industry, and promote agriculture, arts and the manufactures of
this country, especially that of wool." To leave no doubt that
they had in mind an invidious comparison between colonial
virtue and ministerial vice, the associators promised to "discoun-
tenance and discourage every species of extravagence and
dissapation." As important as self-regulation was to self-sufficiency, the delegates to Congress were also aware of human
frailty and self-interest. Consequently they added to the Association the machinery for extralegal enforcement: "That a committee be chosen in every county, city, and town . . . whose business
it shall be attentively to observe the conduct of all persons
touching this association; and when it shall be made to appear
. . . that any person . . . has violated this association, that [they]
cause the truth of the case to be published in the gazette."

If mutual surveillance seemed at odds with self-control, the
delegates could reconcile the contradictions by reference to John
Locke, whose familiar ideas were fundamental to the debates on
the state of nature and colonial rights. Those who thought in
terms of the mother country and the father king were reminded
by Locke that parenthood did not abridge "that *equal Right* that
every Man hath, *to his Natural Freedom*. . . . [although] *Children*
. . . are not born in this full state of equality, . . . they are born
to it." Self-sufficiency was a sign of maturation, but colonials
were still adolescents, finding their way, not adults. And Locke,
in his writings on child rearing, though he emphasized the
development of internal restraints, made it clear that careful
supervision would be necessary to foster self-control. He provided
the intellectual paternity which approved, or rationalized,
American experience.

The work of the Congress completed, the delegates agreed to
convene again in May 1775 if their grievances had not been set
right. But, as he left for Massachusetts, John Adams doubted
"that I shall ever see this part of the world again," a wistful
expression, perhaps, of a hope for the return of provincial
normality, now lost like the innocence of childhood. The
Association had no sudden effect on Pennsylvania's economy
because a surplus of wheat and West India staples allowed the
colony to respond slowly to inflationary pressures. But the impact

of the congressional action on Pennsylvania politics was as immediate as the reverse situation a few months earlier. The Assembly in Philadelphia was the first of the lower houses in the colonies to meet after Congress adjourned. On December 8 a report on the continental gathering was signed by Dickinson and Mifflin but not Galloway, and two days later it was approved, with Dickinson spurring the whig forces and Galloway absent at his country estate.

Galloway's leadership was now in almost full eclipse. His place in the speaker's chair had been taken by Edward Biddle of Berks County, who in a meeting in Reading on July 2, 1774, spoke strongly of the danger to the colonies from unconstitutional British measures. Furthermore, the delegates visiting in Philadelphia during September and October had left a favorable impression. Yet there remained an undercurrent of caution, if not outright opposition, to the program of Congress. The Society of Friends instructed members not to join "any of the city, country, provincial or general committees," and testimony was rendered against "every usurpation of power and authority in opposition to the Laws and Government, and against all Combination, Insurrections, Conspiracies, and Illegal Assemblages."

Dickinson himself, pleased with the Assembly's endorsement of Congress, and sensitive to the timidity of moderate political opinion, opposed convening a second provincial council. "The great Point, *at Present,* is to keep up the appearances of an unbroken Harmony in public Measures, for fear of encouraging Great Britain to Hostilities, which, otherwise, she would avoid." But the situation was already too politicized for a middle or conciliatory position to prevail. "A spirit of domination in the mother country has produced a spirit of libertinism rather than liberty here," wrote the moderate whig Joseph Reed in December 1774.

A Committee of Observation and Inspection, younger and more radical than the previous committees which were dominated by major merchants, had been elected a month earlier in Philadelphia. And similar local committees were springing up throughout the province, while nonparticipating Quakers and partisans of England were beginning to be branded as tories. The radical whigs called a provincial convention for late January 1775. Although Galloway enjoyed a momentary renaissance in the Assembly, by mid-March he was defeated, and he retired from politics. The time for thoughts of reconciliation and tempered argument was quickly passing, in England as well as America.

For in the mother country opinion had been hardening as much in one direction as it had in the other in the colonies. Two major bridges across the Atlantic had been the merchant community and the colonial agents. But English traders were becoming less responsive to the American cause in the 1770s as the emergence of prosperity and new markets diminished dependence on traditional channels of commerce. The colonists were placing more faith in economic boycotts, less in the colonial agents. The agents contributed to their own demise by betraying their disenchantment with English politics and thus fostering the reluctance of provincials to pursue conventional political routes rather than resist extralegally. And as the transatlantic conflict heightened, British-born agents lost sympathy with their American constituents while sympathetic agents lost credibility with the English government. Not only did colonial behavior during 1773 and 1774 lose Americans many of their best friends, but by the end of the latter year five colonies were without agents and four were represented by Franklin, whose effectiveness had been largely dissipated in 1773.

The Philadelphian had recommended united economic resistance to the Continental Congress, and in early 1775 he assured both Thomson and Galloway that adherence to that plan would bring the ministry around within a year. Meanwhile, he worked for reconciliation, and he found others, even in high places, who were similarly optimistic. Through Quaker intermediaries Franklin negotiated with members of the North ministry. The Earl of Chatham, accompanied by Franklin, went before the House of Lords. Edmund Burke waxed eloquent on conciliation. It was all to no avail. Only Lord North's plan, which neither renounced the right of taxation nor recalled the troops, was acceptable to a Parliament which declared Massachusetts in a

William Franklin.
Rutgers University Library.

Joseph Galloway.
Benjamin Franklin Collection,
Sterling Memorial Library,
Yale University.

state of rebellion, laid trade restrictions on New England, and extended these prohibitions to most of the other colonies. Franklin saw it was useless and perhaps dangerous to remain in England. On the first day of spring he sailed for America.

While he was at sea, the news reached Pennsylvania that Parliament had declared Massachusetts in rebellion. Then came word of the fighting at Lexington and Concord, followed by a letter from Franklin that more troops were coming to America. When Governor Penn came before the Assembly on May 2 with Lord North's proposal, he spoke in the outmoded language of empire, urging the representatives "to weigh and consider this Plan of Reconciliation, held forth and offered by the Parent to her children." The Pennsylvania legislature, first in America to be presented with the ministerial scheme, did not desert the familial metaphor: to agree unilaterally to North's plan would be "a dishonorable desertion of sister colonies . . . engaged with us by solemn ties in the same common cause." Four days later Franklin arrived, his landing "announced by ringing bells, to the great joy of the city." The Assembly unanimously elected him a delegate to the Continental Congress, about to convene in the State House that he knew so well.

Though Franklin appeared to adapt with his usual aplomb, the territory was not altogether familiar nor even congenial to him. His wife had died the previous winter. His son, William, was a tory. His legislative lieutenant was an anachronism. Galloway had resigned as a delegate to the Congress and retired to his home in Bucks County, where Franklin journeyed to find him ravaged by ill health as well as by the political situation. For two or three months he tried to convert his old partner to the revolutionary cause, not giving up until a midsummer meeting which included William Franklin proved the futility and, no doubt, the personal strain, of continued encounters.

Over a decade before, Franklin had left Pennsylvania for the purpose of overthrowing the proprietary government and replacing it with royal control. He departed from England just as Thomas Penn, his longtime enemy, died. The proprietary cause was in decline. Richard Peters, Penn's former secretary, was an invalid but a year from the grave. William Allen had resigned the previous spring as chief justice and now, along with his old political ally in the proprietary cause, William Smith, stood in the difficult position of a moderate, favoring conciliation rather than independence. John Dickinson favored both, but he believed one last attempt at the former should precede the latter, and he was preparing a program of reconciliation to present to Congress.

The contrast between Franklin's and Dickinson's political behavior was striking. The dilemma that all but the most radical and conservative American politicians now faced was centered on the awkward and perhaps contradictory activities of waging war, considering conciliation, and moving toward independence. The second Continental Congress convened on May 10, 1775, with many of its former members and two notable new ones, Franklin and Jefferson. All delegates carried less definite instructions than previously. On the matter of conducting the war there was little problem: Washington was appointed general of the continental forces, other officers were named, commissioners of Indian affairs were designated, and naval business was dealt with. The issues of conciliation and independence were far more difficult to handle.

John Dickinson came with a program for which he found support among other delegates from the middle colonies. His emphasis was on reconciliation, which the firmness communicated by military strength would bolster. In turn, political gestures would delay the main force of England's power, giving Americans opportunity for further preparation. And, if negotiations failed, the colonists would feel justified at having explored all avenues to peace before an all-out war effort. American agents to Parliament should seek repeal of recent legislation, adoption of a "permanent" system of commercial relations, and judicial reform, in return for which they would offer colonial recognition of royal prerogative and a guaranteed revenue to the king. Congress found the general thrust of Dickinson's proposals acceptable and appointed committees to draft a petition to the crown and a justification of Congress' establishment of a continental army.

The first committee, which included Dickinson and Franklin,

as well as Adams, Jefferson, and others, drew up a Second Petition, referred to as "humble and dutiful" and later labeled the olive branch petition. It focused on British tyranny rather than colonial rights and asked the repeal of offensive statutes, the end of military offensives, and reconciliation on rather vague terms. Congress accepted this document as well as the "Declaration of the Causes and Necessity of Taking up Arms," a collaborative effort of Dickinson and Jefferson predicated on the belief that Britain had consistently driven the colonies to act in ways which she then condemned: "Our cause is just. Our nation is perfect. Our preparations are nearly completed. Our internal Resources are great; and our Assurance of foreign Assistance is certain."

Thus stood Dickinson in early July, his work approved by Congress, his attitude both defiant and conciliatory, the latter stance dictated in part by provincial politics—or so argued Charles Thomson in his defense of his colleague a few years later. Thomson observed that the olive branch petition did not meet Dickinson's full approval, "yet on account of the people of Pennsylvania it was both prudent and politic to adopt it." But if Dickinson thought the people of Pennsylvania had to be gently persuaded that the British ministry was adamantly anti-American, he soon found that his approach was less than appealing to some of his Congressional colleagues, to whom the unobtrusive but firm behavior of Franklin was more attractive.

Remarking on Franklin's faithful attendance and reserved manner in Congress, John Adams observed in late July: "He has not assumed any Thing, nor affected to take the lead; but has seemed to choose that Congress should pursue their own Principles and sentiments and adopt their own Plans: Yet he has not been backward. . . . He does not hesitate at our boldest Measures, but rather seems to think us, too resolute and backward. . . . I wish his Colleagues from this City were All like him, particularly one, whose Abilities and Virtues, formerly trumpeted so much in America, have been found wanting." Adams had chafed under Dickinson's moderate leadership, especially after the news of Bunker Hill, and his impatience in Congress was unfortunately coupled with his characteristically intemperate language in an intercepted and widely published letter. He referred to Dickinson as "a certain great Fortune and Piddling Genius," a remark which led to an open break between the two men.

Franklin, on the other hand, now came forward with two startling propositions: that the colonies open their ports to world trade and that Congress adopt a plan of union which he had drafted. Both were premature in a body that was willing to take only the most hesitant steps toward independence. But these schemes established the fact that Franklin was looking toward the future; his plan of union aided in establishing a basis for the Articles of Confederation. Dickinson, despite the tactical meaning of his attempt at reconciliation, seemed to be yearning for the past. Even when the olive branch petition was spurned and the king, on August 23, 1775, declared the colonies to be in a state of rebellion, Dickinson clung to the idea that reconciliation was a real possibility.

His attitude, hardly unique, was unrealistic not only regarding the home government but provincial politics as well. However reluctant many Pennsylvanians, and particularly Quakers, were to take up arms or consider independence, there was a small but powerful motive force always pushing in the direction of radical political behavior that ultimately became revolutionary activity. Charles Thomson, an authority on the subject, when he commented on David Ramsay's manuscript narrative of the Revolution a decade after independence was declared, recalled that in the reaction to the Townshend Acts lay the origins of an extralegal network covering the colonies, "so that when any intelligence of importance which it was necessary the people at large should be informed of reached the Capital, it was immediately dispatched to the county Committees and by them forwarded to the Committees of the districts, who disseminated it to the whole body of the people." Maintained by private subscription and zealous individuals, by 1774 the Committees of Correspondence had been "revised, extended and reduced to a system."

The first Continental Congress had called for an expansion of activities to include surveillance during the economic boycott, thus giving birth to the Committees of Observation and Inspection. The city of Philadelphia, holding its election in mid-November 1774, created a committee of sixty-six members, only seventeen of whom (Dickinson, Thomson, Mifflin, and Reed among them) had served on the old Committee of Correspondence. The new members included a dozen mechanics and such outspoken radicals as William Bradford, editor of the *Pennsylvania Journal.* Philadelphia County acted soon afterward, followed by Berks and Bucks. "A Committee has been appointed for this County," wrote Galloway, "by a few warm People of neither Property or significance among us." Then in order came York, Chester, Northampton, Cumberland, and Lancaster, while in Bedford County the Committee of Correspondence simply took on the surveillance function. No action was taken in the frontier counties of Northumberland or Westmoreland. When the second provincial convention met in January 1775, its summons largely due to committee pressures, it resolved that any county committee facing opposition to enforcement of the Association could call on other county committees for aid. The Philadelphia Committee was empowered to call another provincial convention whenever necessary, a clear challenge to the Assembly but one not actuated until May 1776. While some men charged that the committees "aimed at general revolution" and were "drunk with the power they had usurped," Dickinson and others did serve as moderating influences in their councils.

News of Lexington and Concord provoked activity of a different sort, the formation of military associations. Not surprisingly, the frontier areas were quickest to respond to the stimulus of armed conflict, but the reaction was widespread. John Adams, when he reached Philadelphia for the convening of the second Continental Congress, wrote home in surprise: "The Martial Spirit throughout this Province is astonishing, it arose all of a Sudden . . . Quakers and all are carried away with it." The exaggeration was pardonable, for the wave of patriotism produced an unexpected conformity. "It's admirable to see the alteration of the Tory class in this place," noted one local diarist in early May.

It was not only the press of conformity but the fear of anarchy that accounted for some enlistments. William Allen's son James, a lawyer watching his business decline as indebtedness rose and prophesying ruin for America if there were to be a long struggle with England (itself "running fast to slavery"), finally joined up in October 1775: "I have no opinion that this association, will be very useful in defending the City: as they have refused to be bound by any Articles & have no subordination. My inducement to join them is; that a man is suspect who does not; & I chuse to have a Musket on my shoulders, to be on a par with them; and I believe discreet people mixing with them, may keep them in Order."

A concern for system was also manifest by Philadelphia's Committee of Observation and Inspection, which in 1775 boasted some thirty mechanics among its ranks. It was nevertheless orthodox enough to petition the Assembly for a military association and a Committee of Safety, both of which were approved. The military organization was funded in case of British attack; by autumn legislative action had virtually converted the "Associators" into a regular militia. The Committee of Safety, presided over by Franklin, was empowered to call the soldiers into service. The committee, composed equally of assemblymen and leaders from the towns of Philadelphia and Chester, was zealous yet respectable, a composite of the community with connections to every social and economic group.

Radical political activity was not co-opted by such association with establishment institutions but, rather, emerged elsewhere. The most notable instance was the Committee of Privates, organized in September 1775 for delegates from the city's neighborhood military associations to discuss their articles of association. Once convened, local radicals urged the committee to communicate its concerns to enlisted men elsewhere, thus creating a propaganda network of obvious utility in the coming months. The committee was also pressed to voice concern for extramilitary matters. In February 1776 the committee petitioned the Assembly concerning the avoidance of martial duty, a complaint aimed at the Quakers, and demanded the right to vote on the grounds that to put one's life in jeopardy should ensure the rights of citizenship. This ultimatum was an index of the

Thomas Paine by John Wesley Jarvis. *National Gallery of Art, Washington. Gift of Marian B. Maurice.*

inferior economic status of the petitioners, although by early 1776 radicalism was no longer the preserve of struggling artisans.

Long after the event John Adams observed in his *Autobiography* that "in the course of this Winter appeared a Phenomenon in Philadelphia *a Star of Disaster* . . . , I mean Thomas Paine." Adams could accept the familiar arguments favoring independence found in *Common Sense*, most of which, along with the title, came from Benjamin Rush. But he thought (or recalled thinking) that the section on the illegality of monarchy was based on either ignorance and superstition or sophistry and hypocrisy, while the "third part relative to a form of Government I considered as flowing from simple Ignorance, and a mere desire to please the democratic Party in Philadelphia, at whose head were Mr. Matlock, Mr. Cannon and Dr. Young." Among this new cast of characters, none of them mechanics, all of them novices in public affairs, lay the future of radical politics in Pennsylvania.

Thomas Young, a physician and recent arrival in Philadelphia, had worked with Sam Adams in Boston and participated in the Tea Party. James Cannon had lived quietly in the city as a school teacher for over a decade before he was drawn into politics through military activity, specifically as creator of the Committee of Privates. Timothy Matlack, disowned from the Society of Friends for his financial failures but back on his feet as a beer bottler, now served as clerk to Charles Thomson in the Congress. Benjamin Rush, youngest of these middle-aged men, of an old but undistinguished Pennsylvania family, had studied at the College of New Jersey and the University of Edinburgh, visiting London and borrowing money from Franklin on the way home in 1769. Medical practice absorbed his attention until 1773, when he issued an antislavery pamphlet and, in tandem with Mifflin, began writing for newspapers in response to the Tea Act. By 1774 he was deep into politics, welcomed the Adams cousins to the city in August, and remained a friend of John's until his death, a testimonial to the attractiveness of Rush's passionate temperament.

Early in 1775 Rush had met Thomas Paine, eight years his senior and recently arrived in Philadelphia from London with a letter of introduction from Franklin. Bright, restless, polemical, inclined to drink, Paine had left behind him a broken marriage and a dead-ended career as an excise collector. He brought with him, as Joel Barlow later observed, "a surprising memory and brilliant fancy; his mind was a storehouse of facts and useful observations; he was full of lively anecdote, and ingenious original pertinent remark, upon almost every subject." In America he discovered, according to John Adams, "the great Question was concerning Independence" and proceeded to write on it with Rush's encouragement.

Unlike the learned and reasoned treatises that had preceded it in the prerevolutionary period, *Common Sense* was racy, epigrammatic, and iconoclastic. It ridiculed government in general: "like dress, . . . the badge of lost innocence"; the British Constitution: "to say that the Constitution of England is an *union* of three powers, reciprocally *checking* each other, is farcical"; the British Empire: "there is something very absurd, in supposing a Continent to be perpetually governed by an island"; and the British king: George III was a "Royal Brute."

However much John Adams may later have resented *Common Sense*, it carried forward an imagery familiar to all Americans, including himself. As Paine was laboring on his tract, Adams entered in his *Diary* a thought on Lord North: "He rocks the cradle, and sings Lullaby, and the innocent Children go to Sleep, while he prepares the Birch to whip the poor Babes." John's wife, Abigail, earlier had expressed her belief that there was to be "no reconcilliation between our, no longer parent State, but tyrant State, and these Colonies." Paine attacked George III as a "wretch . . . with the pretended title of FATHER OF HIS PEOPLE." Only among a few pro-Americans in England was a similar theme heard. Thus, Dr. Richard Price wrote: " 'But we are the PARENT STATE.' These are the magic words which have fascinated and misled us . . . at the very time when our authority should have been most relaxed, we have carried it to the greatest extent . . . they have turned upon us; and obliged us to remember that they are not children." Still, the father-king was not slandered.

Though Paine was writing in a way directly relevant to his own childhood, he managed also to strike resonant chords in the consciousness of Americans. Patriarchal authority was notably on the decline in the colonies. Parents realized they could not withstand the pressures of population growth and disappearing land, economic expansion and urban growth, increasing class division. All these forces militated against family cohesion and filial subordination. Americans had begun to realize in the public arena what they experienced in private when the Great Awakening demonstrated that survival was possible in the face of declining authority. Then, in the late 1760s and early 1770s, it was seen that British superiority could be challenged, that England did not respond to rivalry as a loving parent, that colonials could endure despite this denial of affection. *Common Sense* crushed the remains of respect by revealing the betrayal of the father.

The tract had astounding impact. Benjamin Franklin, whose life was an outstanding example of familial disintegration, received the first copy off the press. George Washington, quite unaware that he would have to assume the paternal role of George III, noted that "by private letters, which I have lately received from Virginia, I find 'Common Sense' is working a powerful change there in the minds of many men." Abigail Adams thanked John for her volume, commenting, "'Tis highly prized here and carries conviction wherever it is read." Not recognizing the continuing need for a personalized father, she had stated: "Our country is as it were a Secondary God, and the first and greatest parent." There were more flamboyant claims for Paine's immediate influence, and there was resistance to his message as well.

John Dickinson, still in the moderate whig camp, was embarrassed that a tract refuting *Common Sense*, entitled *Plain Truth*, was dedicated to him. The dedication was hardly illogical, since Dickinson, though he had recognized by late autumn 1775 the virtual impossibility of reconciliation and, probably, the inevitability of independence, remained hesitant about an explicit declaration. He therefore stood in the way of any such instructions to delegates coming from the Pennsylvania Assembly while in the Congress. When Sam Adams attempted to resurrect

Franklin's proposed articles of confederation, Dickinson and his former law student James Wilson opposed the move.

Dickinson's active role as colonel in the Philadelphia Associators on an expedition to New York in late February moved him toward independence. But he returned to defend the Assembly, with the aid of Thomson and Reed, against the attacks of the radical whigs, who were proposing a convention to replace government under the charter of 1701. The radical efforts were undermined in mid-March, when the Assembly faced the charge of unequal representation by granting seventeen new seats to the frontier counties and the city of Philadelphia in an election to be held May 1. Dickinson then turned to deal with *Common Sense*, whose arguments he claimed largely to agree with. Yet he could not make the final commitment, though his metaphor was fitting: "Independency . . . ought to be the child of Necessity."

For conservatives who had thus far stood in opposition to British policy, Paine's tract was as much a turning as for American patriots. The close-knit Shippen family was supportive of colonial protests until early 1776. "A most extraordinary *Pamphlet*, entitled *Common Sense* . . . was published here last Week," wrote Joseph Shippen III, and "to the great Surprise & Alarm of many People . . . it openly avows an absolute Independency on Great Britain." Edward Shippen III echoed his sentiments: "I dread the Consequences of a State of Independency." Their fear was for the social consequences of the act, which were becoming increasingly evident already. When "a few Gentlemen" on the Philadelphia Committee of Observation and Inspection failed to block the election in mid-February of Timothy Matlack and "a number of other violent wrongheaded people of the inferior Class," Joseph looked forward to "the greatest Confusion Anarchy & discension." The Shippens' recourse was to remain silent and inactive, ultimately leaving the city for their country estates.

The Allen family had been even more active in the American cause, though none of them favored independence. William's eldest son John was one of the gentlemen on Philadelphia's Committee of Observation and Inspection, Andrew was on the

Committee of Safety and a delegate to the second Continental Congress, William a lieutenant colonel of a Pennsylvania regiment in Canada. All went over to the British by December 1776 including James, who made a last attempt at establishing the order congenial to his class.

"The plot thickens," he noted in March, "peace is scarcely thought of—Independency predominant. Thinking people uneasy, irresolute & inactive. The Mobility triumphant. . . . The madness of the multitude is but one degree better than submission to the Tea-Act." James Allen decided to run for the Assembly in the special election on May 1, and he won in Northampton County without opposition. But his worries were not allayed. "I think the Assembly of this province, will not consent to change their constitution; and then heigh for a convention! A Convention chosen by the people, will consist of the most firey Independents; they will have the whole Executive & legislative authority in their hands."

Allen understood the opposition. The Independents, a coalition of the Philadelphia Committee of Observation and Inspection, now under radical control, the Committee of Privates, and the Patriotic Society, a mechanic's organization, had narrowly lost the May 1 special Assembly election in Philadelphia, gaining only one of four seats; Andrew Allen was one of the three moderates elected. And they had been crushed in the back counties, where they had misjudged frontier resentment at underrepresentation and forgotten, or would not admit to themselves, that backcountry politics was in the hands of a few men who owed their allegiance to an elite established in Philadelphia. Members and minions of the Shippen and Allen families lived in Berks and Lancaster and Northampton counties; James Wilson came to the Assembly from Carlisle.

But this situation did not reconcile the radicals to defeat; it only caused them to revise their strategy. They were aided by allies in the Congress. John and Sam Adams were determined to get a declaration of independence, and however much John may have been dismayed with Paine's "democratical notions," he was willing to cooperate with the Pennsylvania Independents to attain his objective. The Middle Colonies were blocking the way.

On May 10 John moved and Congress resolved to recommend establishing new governments in states "where no government sufficient to the exigencies of their affairs have been hitherto established," a motion supported by Dickinson, who thought it showed colonial firmness without affecting Pennsylvania. He confidently departed for Delaware while the drafting committee added a preamble to the motion: "It is necessary that every kind of authority under the said crown should be totally suppressed." Despite James Wilson's pleas that this statement endangered government in Pennsylvania, since the political institutions rested on a royal charter granted to the Penns, Congress passed the whole motion (barely) on May 15. When the measure was read to a Philadelphia crowd, James Allen recorded, "My feelings of indignation were strong, but it was necessary to be mute." For the Independents, Adams' motion was the legal justification needed to overthrow the Assembly which they could not dominate.

In a well planned public meeting in the State House Yard on May 20, 1776, some four thousand people approved radical resolves condemning the Assembly's instructions to its congressional delegates to oppose independence; stating the legislature's lack of popular authority and competency and warning it not to meet again; and calling for a provincial conference of county committees to plan for a constitutional convention. Proprietary backers such as William Smith and whigs like Joseph Reed responded to this activity with a Remonstrance, which was carried even into the backcountry, but the Philadelphia Independents were prepared and, working through county Committees of Observation and Inspection as well as the military associations, did an effective job of undermining the efforts of the moderates and discrediting the Assembly. All counties chose delegations for the provincial conference.

Meanwhile, in early June, Dickinson was working to save the authority of the legislature by drafting new instructions for Pennsylvania's delegates while blocking Richard Henry Lee's motions in Congress for independence and confederation until Pennsylvania could get in step. In Jefferson's view "the people of the middle colonies were not yet ripe for bidding adieu to British connection; but . . . they were fast ripening, and in a short time would join in the general voice of America." Congress put off a decision on independence for three weeks, at the same time appointing a committee of Jefferson, Franklin, John Adams, Roger Sherman, and Robert R. Livingston to draft a declaration. Two other committees were also designated, one to deal with the matter of confederation, the other concerned with foreign treaties. Both committees included Dickinson, an attempt to win him to independence.

Courted in Congress, Dickinson was pummeled in the province. Although Pennsylvania's delegates were released from their earlier instructions and authorized, though not directed, to vote for independence, the radicals continued to attack, undermining the operation of the Assembly by absenting themselves and preventing a quorum. Moderates such as Dickinson, prizing an atmosphere in which reasoned debate could take place, were confronted with intolerance for divergent views. "Reconciliation is thought of now by none but knaves, fools and madmen," shouted a voice from the *Pennsylvania Evening Post.* For some, the change was unbearable; they left, while others mourned. "This day the amiable family of Shippens set of[f] for the Jerseys," wrote the radical editor William Bradford in his diary on June 20. "Mournful was the hour of parting. I pursued the Coach with my eyes & then retired to the office disconsolate and forlorn. Every beauty had left the place: the usual scene that I had so often seen with pleasure charmed no more. A heavy heart finds comfort no where. . . . I have hastened home & will retire to bed rather than to rest: Yet why this uneasiness: what concern have I with their going—None."

But there was a very different mood among those who anticipated success instead of reflecting on the past. Benjamin Rush exulted to his wife that "our cause continues to prosper. . . . The Remonstrance was burnt as a treasonable libel upon the liberties of America in Reading in Berks county. . . . Dr. Franklin's arrival gives great spirit to the independents. . . . I will never desert the cause I am [embar]ked in, till I see the monster tyranny gnash [his] impotent teeth in the dust in the Province of Pennsylvania. This I think will be the case of the

18th of next June, the day appointed for the provincial Convention." The Assembly adjourned on June 14, its members unaware that the body would never meet again, and four days later the delegates to the provincial convention met in Carpenter's Hall. Nearly all of Philadelphia's twenty-five representatives were drawn from its Committee of Observation and Inspection, and this was true of the various county delegations as well. Only two of the 108 members had previous parliamentary experience: Benjamin Franklin, now seventy and confined to his bed with gout during the seven-day meeting of the convention; and Thomas McKean, a lawyer in politics for half of his forty-two years, who was elected president.

The task of the provincial convention was simply to determine the rules and timing for the forthcoming constitutional convention. Unsurprisingly, in view of agitation from the Committee of Privates during the past year, the franchise was broadened to include any adult male in the military who had been resident in the province for a year and paid taxes, thus flouting the £50 property qualification. Nor was it amazing that voters would have to affirm their independence of the king and their belief that government should be established "on the authority of the people only." However, having to declare faith in the Trinity and the divine inspiration of the Scriptures in order to cast a ballot raised considerable opposition before it passed. As to the number of delegates, eight were to be sent from every county and the city of Philadelphia, which marked the culmination of a trend of increasing western representation in Pennsylvania politics. At the constitutional convention the eight western counties would have two-thirds of the delegates; even at the present provincial convention, Philadelphia and the three eastern counties sent more than half the deputies. The election was to be held on July 8, and the convention to meet a week later.

The contrast between these activities and the colony's foot-dragging role in Congress illustrated again the lack of synchronization between provincial and intercolonial politics; Pennsylvania was at once more radical and more conservative than its siblings. The eccentricity of the once-holy experiment continued. On July 1, when Lee's postponed motion for independence was put before the Congress, John Dickinson spoke against it, again arguing that delay would benefit the American cause. He took this position despite the change in instructions to the Pennsylvania delegates and the activities in the province, despite Franklin's place on the committee to draft the declaration and his own on the committees to consider confederation and foreign treaties.

Pennsylvania and South Carolina cast the only negative votes on independence; Delaware split its ballots and New York abstained. On July 2, South Carolina having changed its position, Pennsylvania reluctantly joined the others. Benjamin Franklin, James Wilson, and John Morton outweighed Charles Humphreys and Thomas Willing in the delegation, with Robert Morris and Dickinson abstaining. The question of independence thus carried without dissent. On the evening of July 4, Jefferson's amended declaration was accepted, again without dissent.

On July 8 the Declaration of Independence was proclaimed for the first time, to a great crowd in Philadelphia. "The battalions paraded on the Common, and gave us the *feu de joie,* notwithstanding the scarcity of powder. The bells rang all day and almost all night. Even the chimers chimed away," exclaimed John Adams. Despite his agitated impatience with delay over the past year, Adams had written to his wife a few days earlier: "Time has been given for the whole people maturely to consider the great question of independence, and to ripen their judgment, dissapate their fears, and all their hopes, so that the whole people, in every colony of the thirteen, have now adopted it as their own act. This will cement the union, and avoid those heats, and perhaps convulsions, which might have been occasioned by such a Declaration six months ago." As a description of and prediction for Pennsylvania, where the election of delegates to the constitutional convention was held the day the declaration was proclaimed, Adams' message was wrongheaded, as he soon would admit.

On July 15 delegates to the constitutional convention gathered in Philadelphia. Voters had been advised through the propaganda network of the Committee of Privates "to chuse no rich men, and few learned men as possible to represent them," and the gathering generally reflected obedience to this counsel. One

Congress voting independence, July 4, 1776. *Historical Society of Pennsylvania.*

of the few who had a legal education, Thomas Smith, admitted that "not a sixth part of us ever read a word on the subject" of government but he pinned the blame for "being ridiculous in the eyes of the world" on a few overly enthusiastic members who "would go to the devil for popularity, and in order to acquire it, they have embraced leveling principles."

Neither the voters nor the delegates bore full responsibility for the situation. When John Dickinson spoke of "cheerfully & deliberately sacrificing my popularity . . . to Principles" only to be shabbily treated, Charles Thomson delicately replied: "I know the rectitude of your heart & the honesty & uprightness of your intentions; but still I cannot help regretting, that by a perseverance which you were fully convinced was fruitless, you have thrown the affairs of this state in the hands of men totally unequal to them." Even Franklin, elected president of the convention, was so occupied with national affairs that he turned his duties over to the vice-president and, in the exaggerated view of one contemporary, "even declined the trouble of thinking. As to the constitution, whose provisions it was sometimes necessary to consider, it did not appear to him [the vice-president], that he had ever read it; or if he had, that he deemed it worthy of remembering." If 1776 marked the beginning of America's heroic age, the great men of Pennsylvania were preoccupied when it came to local affairs.

Yet the document produced by the state's minor figures, who probably were no less intelligent than assemblymen, reflected not only the very recent course of events but the political experience of the province over past decades. Neither the Preamble nor the Declaration of Rights contained any surprising or radical statements. In the latter section the time-honored principles of religious liberty and freedom of speech were respected. The reappearance of the stipulation of a belief in the divine inspiration of the Scriptures, required only of members elected to the Assembly, caught the supposedly somnolent Franklin's attention, but his opposition did not prevail.

The frame of government established the most democratic structure among the American states. The unicameral legislature was perpetuated; John Adams rightly attributed the "single

Assembly" to "the force of habit," but he was surprised at Franklin's zealous advocacy of it. The executive, vested in a president and council, had no veto power but was confined to executing laws. Geographical representation, six representatives from each county and from Philadelphia, was to prevail for two years, while the Assembly compiled complete lists of taxable inhabitants to be used in applying the principle of proportional representation.

The most striking feature of the new constitution was the elimination of property or financial qualifications for the franchise. Suffrage reform during the revolutionary era took place in only six states—New Hampshire, Vermont, New Jersey, Maryland, and Georgia were the others—and Pennsylvania provided the beacon that was followed. Any white male over twenty-one, resident in the state for a year and a taxpayer, could vote. Elections were to be held annually and, to further amplify the voice of the people in the legislature, all bills were to be printed and circulated before final debate and amendment, a provision that never worked.

A letter writer to the *Pennsylvania Evening Post* in late July had observed: "The rich, having been used to govern, seem to think it their right; and the poorer commonality, having hitherto had little or no hand in government, seem to think it does not belong to them to have any." The convention delegates believed, and they said so in the constitution, that honest work established the independence of the freeman whereas "offices of profit" led not only to "dependence and servility" but "faction, contention, corruption, and disorder among the people." This was the colonial perspective on English politics. Yet to encourage the common people to engage in public affairs, to keep politics from being the preserve of the rich, there must be "reasonable compensation." But when an office became too profitable the legislature was to reduce that compensation. And the power of impeachment was lodged in the Assembly.

An attempt was made to establish an independent judiciary by having the executive appoint, rather than the people elect, judges who served seven years on fixed salaries with the possibility of reappointment. The most unusual feature of the constitution was the creation of a Council of Censors, elected every seven years, to review the operation of government from the viewpoint of constitutionality and judge whether the legislature and executive had "performed their duties as guardians of the people." The feature was no more successful than the public printing of bills before the Assembly.

For all the talk of popular approval of political action, the constitutional convention simply assumed the powers of government in Pennsylvania. This situation could be explained if not excused by the collapse of the Assembly, the precedent set by the provincial convention, the blessings received from Congress, the military predicament and, of course, the delegates' belief in their own grass-roots support. Furthermore, the convention failed even to submit the constitution to a popular vote, nor did any other state but Massachusetts in 1780. Working from mid-July into September, the delegates dallied in anticipation of the return of the associators, who would surely support the constitution. Then, as signs of opposition grew, a few hundred copies of the document were hurried into print and the vote was taken on September 28. Paine, who with Matlack, Cannon, and Young led the radical forces, observed that "as the general opinion of the people in approbation of it was then known, the constitution was signed, sealed, and proclaimed on the authority of the people." Even within the convention, a quarter of the delegates, mostly from the eastern part of the state, cast dissenting votes. It was not a good omen for public tranquillity.

"Good God!" exclaimed John Adams as he read the document, "the people of Pennsylvania in two years will be glad to petition the crown of Britain for reconciliation in order to be delivered from the tyranny of their Constitution." Adams took no responsibility for creating an environment congenial to a radical triumph, nor did he acknowledge that conditions of war and continuing social friction, which the constitution symbolized rather than created, could produce the political misery which he accurately predicted. An eminent physician, named by the convention to the reformed Pennsylvania delegation to Congress in August, a sympathizer with the new government, was writing less than a year later: "I need not point out to *you* [General

Anthony Wayne] the danger and folly of the Constitution. It has substituted a mob government to one of the happiest govern- ments in the world. Nothing more was necessary to have made us a free and happy people than to abolish the royal and proprietary power of the state." It had appeared otherwise in the rush of revolution. Or, perhaps more accurately, war was catering to nostalgia, that pleasantly distorted view of the past from a troubled present.

11

HARVEST: THE WAR YEARS

Independence appeared to transform Pennsylvania from a placid province into an emotional state. But the forces responsible for the turbulence were not novel, nor was open dispute untypical of politics in Philadelphia. The new development in the revolutionary period was the inability of the Assembly to confine controversy to certified channels. Legislators clung to the anachronism of antiproprietary, which was to say proroyal, politics, thereby blunting their response to imperial issues. Furthermore, these established leaders were unable to respond to economic and social realities in Pennsylvania. In this situation, extralegal activity was virtually inevitable. The committee movement whose actions ultimately superseded the Assembly's function was increasingly radical in behavior yet constantly aware of the importance of consensus. Indeed, it was recognition of the whole society, Presbyterians as well as Quakers, mechanics as well as merchants, which yielded the ever growing resistance to England's provocative measures. By the time moderates began to absent themselves from the committees, the movement was too well established to be compromised. This, the dual heritage of a proprietary form of government which exacerbated ordinary provincial quarrels and a policy of toleration which made Pennsylvania the most heterogeneous of all the colonies, contributed directly to the coming of the Revolution. Furthermore, the economic growth fostered in Philadelphia had not led to harmony through mutual affluence but had accentuated class differences through maldistribution of wealth.

By the spring of 1776 the old leaders of the province were being openly referred to as "a minority of rich men," rulers who were always intent on making "the common and middle class of people their *beasts of burden.*" As the repressed portion of the population took hold of power, the hidden issues were articulated. Among the catalytic forces that produced revolutionary behavior in Pennsylvania, the press played a major role in heightening the awareness of the province's inhabitants. The very vitality of the printing business was a testimony not only to widespread literacy but also general interest, especially in Philadelphia where the ability to read was notably higher than in the surrounding rural areas. The forty-two printers who worked in the city in the quarter century preceding the Revolution, by the nature of their work, were both laborers and intellectuals, often trained abroad and frequently in contact with local aristocrats as well as other colonial printers. They were artisans whose outlook encompassed a breadth of interests. Though their working environment was urban, they knew that their products circulated to a rural constituency as well.

The eleven thousand issues from Philadelphia printing shops between 1740 and 1776, about 15 percent of which were in German, included business and legal forms, catalogues and almanacs, but also more controversial items. Sermons were best sellers, especially after the Great Awakening, but pamphlets on political issues were almost as popular. Seven newspapers, both English and German, were available in the city in 1776, five of them dailies, with circulation not only in the backcountry but in other seaboard colonies and the West Indies. Reprints of English authors abounded, though school textbooks were the greatest single source of business, thus preparing the way for an even greater expansion of printing in the future. Neither sex nor class was an insurmountable barrier to literacy or, observed one resident in 1772, to opinion: "Such is the prevailing taste for books of every kind, that almost every man is a reader; and by pronouncing sentence, right or wrong, upon the various publications that come in his way, puts himself upon a level, in point of knowledge, with their several authors." The climate was ripe for controversy in revolutionary Pennsylvania.

In 1776 dispute centered on the state constitution, attacked and defended because of its democratic features. Among the men most sensitive to this new challenge to authority and, therefore, most anxious to combat it were the religious leaders who had weathered the Great Awakening and knew the consequences of lay participation in affairs theretofore the domain of professionals. With a few exceptions, they had been conspicuous by their absence from the prerevolutionary protest movement. They did not want to forfeit control again. On September 16, 1776, the Reverend William Smith, Anglican provost of the College of Philadelphia, unexpectedly called on the Reverend Henry Muhlenberg, senior minister of the united German Lutheran Congregations, and warned him "that the condition of the Christian religion seemed in danger after independence had been declared and a new form of government was in process of formation; that no care at all had been taken to acquire even the outer ramparts." Despite the religious professions required of electors and officeholders, as well as a section of the constitution supporting laws for "the encouragement of virtue and prevention of vice and immorality," Muhlenberg agreed. He met with a few other ministers in order to point out that "it now seems as if a Christian people were ruled by Jews, Turks, Spinozists, Deists, perverted naturalists," hyperbole deflated by the Presbyterian vice-provost of the college, the Reverend Dr. Francis Alison, whose unalarmed assessment was that these worries were "of no consequence."

Nevertheless Alison, along with Smith, Muhlenberg, the Reverend L. Weyberg of the Reformed Church, and other ministers, approached Franklin, who had not favored any religious tests in politics, and petitioned the convention to have included in the constitution a guarantee to all religious and charitable societies that the "Privileges, Immunities and Estates" enjoyed under the old government would continue under the new. Still there was consternation, expressed in the popular press as well as by the clergy, that the required oath was too latitudinarian. Possibly there was also the fear, though it was never mentioned, that Roman Catholics, earlier excluded from government by a law of 1705, might be elected to the state legislature. Muhlenberg again sounded the siren of suspicion: "The good, honest men who sit in conventions and the like may indeed be good fathers, citizens, mechanics, and even Christians but there are always among them cunning heads and perverse hearts, who, by false speech and art of disputing, outwit and entrap the simple-headed ones." The freedom of conscience guaranteed in the constitution was, he believed, an invitation to overthrow the Christian religion.

Opposition to the new constitution was only too apparent. But the expression of dissent was hardly encouraged. Each official of government and every elector was called on to swear or affirm that he would not "directly or Indirectly do any Act or Thing prejudicial or Injurious to the Constitution or Government thereof as established by the Convention." This oath did not deter protest, however, but became another rallying point for it. On October 21 in the State House Yard, John Dickinson and Thomas McKean attacked the document and, despite a spirited defense of it by James Cannon, Timothy Matlack, and James Young, resolutions denouncing both the convention and the constitution were passed and sent on to county committees to stir further opposition.

These efforts came too late to revive the Assembly on the traditional election day, October 1, but plans were laid to subvert the new government on November 5, the new election day, by sending opponents of the constitution to the legislature and by refusing to take the oath. Yet only in the city and county of Philadelphia did the anticonstitutionalist candidates score a complete victory and the electors refuse the oath. Although the constitutionalists held the majority in the legislature, the Philadelphians, including Dickinson and Robert Morris, entered with instructions to block execution of the constitution and seek its revision. When they were unable to achieve this plan, they withdrew, leaving the Assembly often without a quorum and the government paralyzed. The Supreme Executive Council remained unorganized, leaving executive duties to the Council of Safety.

Getting a new government started would have been difficult under the best of circumstances, but in Pennsylvania the burden of opposition was made heavier by the weight of inexperience. None of the executive or judicial officers of the old regime appeared in the new, while less than a quarter of the men elected to the Assembly between 1750 and 1776 gained a place in the new legislature. In the colonial period the continuity from one Assembly to the next had always been higher than 70 percent whereas now it was lower than 25 percent. However, if experience on the local level was counted, half the assemblymen and councilors were the beneficiaries of previous governmental employment. The moderate increase in the number of state offices and the shift in representation to the West made the entrance of these new men inevitable and probably laid claims on their loyalties, as well. But the problems of governing remained.

A more striking if less paralyzing change, though not surprising in view of Pennsylvania's immigrant past, the composition of the revolutionary committees, and the recent consternation of the clergy, was the alteration in religious and ethnic background of the newly elected state officers. Up to 1776, Quakers or their descendants dominated the Assembly. The exodus of 1756 had been reversed in 1765, when James Pemberton and others returned; while Friends such as Isaac Norris never left the legislature. They composed 40 percent of the membership of the last provincial Assembly, followed by Anglicans and Presbyterians with about 20 percent each; the Baptists and the Reformed comprised approximately 6 percent each. Ethnic division paralleled the religious: almost half the assemblymen were English and Welsh, over a quarter were Scotch-Irish or Scottish, while less than a fifth were German. As a result of the election for the Assembly and Council held in November 1776 Quakers held only 14 percent of the offices and Anglicans but 9 percent, while the Reformed and Lutheran groups together reached 20 percent. Expressed ethnically, the combined English and Welsh officeholders dropped to a quarter the total, the Germans rose to a quarter, while Scottish and Scotch-Irish composed the remaining half.

This dramatic alteration was the consequence not only of the urban committee movement but of a political awakening among groups in the newly represented west that had been preoccupied with the basic problems of settlement and earning a living and, additionally, were internally divided by religion. The Scotch-Irish were split into New Light and Old Light Presbyterianism; the Germans into Lutheran, Reformed, and sectarian groups. Germans faced an unfamiliar language and form of government and seemed content to be led by the Quakers, while the Scotch-Irish Presbyterians took their cues from a small group of men within the proprietary faction, especially William Allen. But the problems created by the Seven Years War and Pontiac's rebellion demonstrated that the governing elite in Philadelphia was far more ready to rule than respond. The Scotch-Irish Presbyterians, particularly, were politicized in the years immediately preceding the Revolution and could point to such eminent leaders as Charles Thomson, Joseph Reed, and Thomas McKean. The men who came to the Assembly in 1776, younger on the average than their predecessors, had become involved in politics through the revolutionary movement and brought with them to Philadelphia an American identity based on an anti-English bias as well as an ethnic and religious awareness.

These were not, however, qualifications for governing, and certainly not conditions for producing unity. The winter of 1776–77 was dark indeed. The British had invaded nearby New Jersey. Efforts to get the Pennsylvania militia into action failed. Brigadier General John Lacey of Bucks County attributed the rejection of officers' commissions by two Philadelphians to domestic politics: they "had leaged themselves with the party hostile to the New Constitution, determined to oppose all measures used to carry it into operation—Their enmity to it was so great, they entirely overlooked the fatal effects their opposition might produce in distroying the general Cause of Independence."

Congress retreated to Baltimore in alarm in mid-December, at which time the Assembly adjourned for a month. Washington's victories at Trenton and Princeton gave some sense of safety, but division in state politics persisted as the Assembly reconvened and dismissed its congressional delegation, except Franklin and Morris, ostensibly because of opposition to the constitution.

Though James Allen noted that the "reason for leaving out so many old members, it is said, is that the new light Presbyterian Party have the ascendant in Assembly." Special elections held in mid-February to fill the vacated Assembly seats for Philadelphia were won by the radicals, or Constitutionalists, as they were now labeled.

The change in appellation was paralleled by a change in political appeal. With the government in their hands, the Constitutionalists made patriotism rather than participation their attraction, promising political stability and demanding fidelity. Indeed, the loyalty oaths of 1777, which disfranchised nonjurors and deprived them of many legal rights, and the oaths of 1778, which subjected nonjurors to double taxation, made suffrage in Pennsylvania less democratic than it had been before the Revolution, even though property tests had been abandoned. And Congress again intervened to shore up the radical-Constitutionalist cause. The rhetoric of winning the war rather than reforming the government was institutionalized in the Whig Society of 1777, which espoused an economic nationalism meant to reach merchants and mechanics alike. Support for the Constitutionalists was not lodged in one class.

But the commercial situation in Pennsylvania demanded more than a patriotic platform. The favorable price trends of the prerevolutionary years involved upward movement for domestic produce, especially wheat (which led to acreage expansion), and stability of West Indian imports. These trends were reversed in the early years of the war. The economy was healthy enough to absorb the initial issues of Continental currency and changes in production without prices being affected, but the closing of the port eventually sent the cost of West Indian goods up and of domestic staples down, a fluctuation accentuated by the rising cost of mercantile insurance. Farmers, already the worst victims of the price situation and hardest hit by the scarcity of salt, suffered a bad wheat harvest in 1776. The prices of West Indian staples, especially sugar, rose considerably faster than prices on other goods into 1777. Consequently, mechanics pressed for wage increases to keep pace with prices. British naval patrols disrupted trade and slowed shipbuilding, causing unemployment in those areas, and merchants found themselves unable to penetrate enough new markets to compensate for the loss of trade with England.

Furthermore, the tremendous increase in government spending, once sources of borrowing were exhausted, led to the issue of more and more currency and its steady depreciation. In April 1777, John Adams observed: "There is so much injustice in carrying on a war with a depreciating currency that we can hardly pray with confidence for success." For merchants in 1776 and 1777, this began to mean that it was better to have nonperishable goods than liquid capital, which led to vigorous trade in West Indian goods, less likely to spoil than wheat or flour, and—another characteristic of an inflationary period— speculation, which brought on appeals for government controls. The reversal of the price situation in 1778 and 1779, with the cost of grain, grain products, and bar iron rising sharply, did not quiet protests against the economic situation. Rather, once fears of military conquest were subsiding, anger was better organized and directed, as civilian committees arose in every town and county in the state. Monopolists were denounced, lower price schedules were set, and trade in essential goods stagnated, creating more unrest than high prices. The ratio of wheat to flour prices only complicated the situation, which was not fully overcome until 1781.

There was not sufficient economic sophistication to realize that it was not only the war but structural changes in the economy that created price fluctuations and attendant problems: the agricultural situation reflected the past, urban industrialization anticipated the future, and a new equilibrium had to be reached. The Pennsylvania government had no experience with price controls. The extralegal Association of 1774 had been the first attempt to deal with prices publicly rather than privately. Politicians were inadequate to the economic situation. And, of course, they could not control the war.

In late July 1777 General William Howe left New York City with a plan to seize Philadelphia from the south, sailing up the Chesapeake and landing at Head of Elk with fifteen thousand troops. Washington threw his ten thousand troops against the

British at Brandywine Creek in late August but without success. Wayne was covertly attacked and defeated at Paoli. On September 26 Howe marched into Philadelphia in triumph, Congress hastening off to Lancaster and later to York, Washington hovering outside the city and engaging the British unvictoriously at Germantown before settling into a terrible winter at Valley Forge. Although only three hundred loyalists responded to Howe's request for volunteers, he and his officers were wined and dined by wealthy tories. If further proof was needed of British decadence, it was provided by the poet:

> Sir William he, snug as a flea
> Lay all this time a snoring;
> Nor dream'd of harm as he lay warm
> In bed with Mrs. Loring.

The contrast between the situations of the British and American troops that winter was the source of much bitterness. When Sir Henry Clinton replaced Howe in May 1778 with orders to evacuate Philadelphia, at least three thousand loyalists left with him, fearing to remain in the city.

Someone had to bear the brunt of the patriot anger, and the Quakers were a convenient target. They had consistently opposed the war and refused to support the revolutionary government. In the midst of their own reformation, they viewed as imperative a testimony against war, disowned those Friends who would not honor pacifism, and declared their intention to resist "with Christian firmness" any efforts to conscript them into the fighting or to impose "tests not warranted by the precepts of Christ or the laws of the happy constitution under which we and others long enjoyed tranquility and peace," a resolution referring to the affirmation of support for the new constitution. Quakers remained aloof from a second loyalty oath, originating in 1777 and evolving through 1779, which was intended to divide loyalists from patriots. The Quakers attempted to maintain neutrality, assisting neither army, attending only to their private and religious duties. When John Adams returned to Philadelphia in the spring of 1778, he observed that the city was "a dull place, in comparison to what it was. More than one half of the inhabitants have removed into the country . . . The remainder are chiefly Quakers, as dull as beetles. From these neither good is to be expected nor evil to be apprehended. They are a kind of neutral tribe, or the race of the insipids."

In fact, neutrality was out of the question. When Howe approached Philadelphia, Congress advised the Pennsylvania government of Quaker disaffection, which led to arrest, imprisonment, and deportation to Virginia of some Quakers, including Israel Pemberton who died shortly afterward. When the patriots returned to Philadelphia after the British and the loyalists exited, two Friends were hanged, most were subject to public ridicule, and the property of any of them was easily seized. Stories were spread of Quaker avarice; the Lutheran leader Muhlenberg claimed that Friends "laughed at the Associators, and meanwhile raised the price of all necessities and amassed money for their tender consciences." Jail was sometimes the sentence for failure to take oaths of allegiance, not only for Quakers but for members of similar groups, Moravians, Schwenkfelders, United Brethren, Mennonites, and even some Baptists and Lutherans. It was the penalty as well for Anglicans, whose refusal to swear fidelity was due to different reasons.

The reformation in the Society which led to the adamant attitude on war as an expression of self-purity also raised the question of the Friends' relationship to the surrounding civil community. Previous to and even during the revolution, the British government generally accepted the Quaker desire to stand apart. But idealistic revolutionaries, in other states as well as in Pennsylvania, were suspicious of passivity and virtually forced Friends to take a role in society. In response, Quakers made a contribution of their virtue. They conducted a large-scale program of war relief in the form of money, clothing, and provisions for noncombatants. And they publicly proclaimed their morality, most notably their views on slavery. The captive in the clutches of a tyrannical master was a metaphor used liberally by American propagandists after 1763, but to Friends it was more than imagery. It fit a judgment they had already made on the institution of black slavery. As other Americans drew back from the implications of total equality, Friends moved forward.

And there could be found a final irony in the Society's new social role. As the Revolution began, Quakers looked to their origins, when they were similarly at odds with the state. Thus, they conceived of their role as apocalyptic, quoting in 1777 Penn's *To the Children of Light*: "We are the people, above all others, that must stand in the gap, and pray for the putting away of wrath, so that this Land may be not made an utter desolation." As Quakers pressed their principles on the larger society, Penn's idea of a final purifying upheaval sent from on high was less relevant to their lives than active reforming carried on below, though abolitionism would later create an earthly cataclysm.

While the Quakers underwent their own peculiar revolution in response to the war for independence, politics in Pennsylvania continued to manifest the ebullient spirits of '76. The anti-Constitutionalists took up the cause of those groups which refused to sign loyalty oaths, a fusion which gained them almost a third of the Assembly seats in the November 1778 election. As a result their opponents agreed both to hold a referendum the following spring on whether there should be a new constitutional convention and to the test acts which created hardships for Quakers and other sectarians as well as Anglicans. The receding military threat may also have prompted this conciliatory attitude, but it was only temporary. By spring 1779 the majority in the Assembly had reneged on the convention and voted against an amendment to liberalize the test acts, approving an even harsher act in the fall.

Although radical propagandists talked of a union of artisan and agricultural interests, voting in the Assembly followed the lines neither of class nor section but, more clearly than before, of religious background. The Calvinists—Scotch-Irish Presbyterians and, less prominently, Reformed Germans—in the 1778 Assembly supported the constitution and the harsh test acts, and they voted together on other issues, most notably the action which purged the College of Philadelphia of its Anglican influences and put Presbyterians such as Joseph Reed, David Rittenhouse, and George Bryan in charge. The same alignment was evident outside the legislature. The anti-Constitutionalist

Republican Club was distinctly non-Calvinist in composition, while voting patterns in some counties gave testimony to a relationship between religious affiliation and political position.

The elections of 1779 gave even clearer evidence of this ethnic and religious pattern. America's first demographer, himself a study in mobility, observed in 1784: "It is a fact that the Irish emigrants and their children are now in possession of the government of Pennsylvania by their majority in the Assembly, as well as of a great part of the territory." It appeared that Penn's "holy experiment," insofar as it was a venture in republicanism, was vindicated by the constitution of 1776, only to be undermined by the loyalty oaths which not only restricted the suffrage but did violence to the founder's belief in toleration. From another and more positive viewpoint, however, these new developments could be viewed as the consequence of strangers to politics handling power for the first time, the very presence of these newcomers being a result of Penn's policy of toleration.

The problems of governing were not peculiar to Pennsylvania but existed everywhere in the immature republic. Experimentation was rife; both the United States and Pennsylvania had changed constitutions by 1790. Yet this turbulence could not obscure the most salient of all political facts: a new nation had emerged and was functioning. One Pennsylvanian, Benjamin Franklin, had served as major midwife to this birth. His work in welding an alliance with France in 1778, the turning point of the revolutionary war, and negotiating a peace treaty with England was further evidence of his prominence. Concurrently he was writing his *Autobiography*, which to many observers seemed to be the embodiment of American values.

Yet for all these changes, the imprint of William Penn had not been erased. The principles of his "holy experiment" became tenets of the American faith, if not always of national practice. And when profession did not square with reality, it was the Quakers, more than any other single religious group, who would serve as the conscience of the nation.

BIBLIOGRAPHY

PRIMARY SOURCES

The *Pennsylvania Magazine of History and Biography* contains not only a wealth of useful articles on colonial Pennsylvania but also primary source material in printed form. The first 75 volumes are indexed (Philadelphia, 1954). Manuscript collections in Pennsylvania can be traced through Philip M. Hamer, ed., *A Guide to Archives and Manuscripts in the United States* (New Haven, 1961). The richest source of documents can be surveyed through the *Guide to the Manuscript Collections of the Historical Society of Pennsylvania*, 2nd ed. (Philadelphia, 1949); a brief description here could not do justice to the wealth of materials to be found at 1300 Locust Street in Philadelphia. Primary sources in print are cited under relevant topical headings below.

SECONDARY SOURCES

Norman B. Wilkinson, *et al., Bibliography of Pennsylvania History* (Harrisburg, 1957) is a useful compendium of other bibliographical aids as well as of secondary works.

THE QUAKERS

The Journal of George Fox, rev. ed. (Cambridge, Eng., 1952), which one nineteenth-century historian called "gibberish" and another characterized as "one of the most extraordinary and instructive narratives in the world," should at least be sampled by students of Quakerism. Many other journals followed it. The first attempt at a history was William Penn's *Brief Account of the Rise and Progress of the People called Quakers, in which their Fundamental Principles, Doctrines, Worship, Ministry, and Discipline are plainly declared* (London, 1694), which depicts the emergence of the Society of Friends as the revival of primitive Christianity. An earlier and more comprehensive examination of Quaker beliefs can be found in Robert Barclay's *An Apology for the True Christian Divinity: being an Explanation and Vindication of the Principles and Doctrines of the People Called Quakers* (London, 1675) which, though criticized by some of Barclay's contemporaries as being too Calvinistic, has stood as the classic systemization of seventeenth-century Quakerism.

Joseph Besse, also a Quaker, carefully gathered and indexed *An Abstract of the Sufferings Of the People call'd Quakers For the Testimony of a* Good Conscience . . . *Taken from* Original Records, *and other* Authentick Accounts (3 vols.; London, 1733–1738), covering the years 1650 to 1666, which was later expanded into *A Collection of the Sufferings of Quakers, 1650–1689* (2 vols.; London, 1753).

Besse's work was preceded by two histories. Gerald Croese's *Historia Quakeriana* (Amsterdam, 1696) was the work of a Dutch reformed clergyman which was translated into English in the year of its publication by George Keith, who had probably aided Barclay and later left the Society. Croese's work was poorly regarded by Quakers, especially William Sewell, who had lent Croese materials, and thus prepared an *errata* of *Historia Quakeriana*, and later published *The History of the Rise, Increase, and Progress of the Christian People called Quakers, Intermixed with several Remarkable Occurances* (London, 1722), doing the English translation himself. It is an accurate narrative of the Society in England down to 1717.

Other notable accounts by Quaker historians in the eighteenth and nineteenth centuries include John Gough's *A History of the People called Quakers. From their first Rise to the present Time* (4 vols.; Dublin, 1970), most of which concerns the seventeenth century, with some attention paid to Pennsylvania; Charles Evans' *Friends in the Seventeenth Century* (Philadelphia, 1875); Samuel M. Janney's *History of the Religious Society of Friends from its rise to the year 1828* (4 vols.; Philadelphia, 1860–1867), which includes the American side of the story; and James Bowden's *The History of the Society of Friends in America* (2 vols.; London, 1850–1854), which begins with the persecutions in early New England and narrates the events of two hundred years.

In the late nineteenth century Joseph Smith, a Quaker who operated a bookstore in London, compiled *A Descriptive Catalogue of Friends' Books . . . from their first rise to the present time, interspersed with critical remarks . . .* (2 vols.; London, 1867; supplement, London, 1893); *Bibliotheca Anti-Quakeriana; or, A Catalogue of Books Adverse to the Society of Friends . . . with biographical notices of the Authors . . .* (London, 1873); and *Bibliotheca Quakeristica, A Bibliography of Miscellaneous Literature relating to the Friends (Quakers), Chiefly written by Persons not Members of the Society* (London, 1883).

In the early twentieth century Rufus M. Jones, a tireless American Friend whose life was a combination of thought and action in the best Quaker tradition, undertook the editing and a large part of the writing of a "history of Quakerism, treating it as an experiment in spiritual religion." The concept was that of Jones' deceased companion, John W. Rowntree, after whom the series was named. Jones wrote the first two volumes, *Studies in Mystical Religion* (London, 1909) and *Spiritual Reformers in the 16th and 17th Centuries* (London, 1914), in which George Fox does not appear until the last chapter, the leader of a movement whose roots are deep in mysticism. This contention has been disputed by Hugh Barbour, himself a Friend, in *The Quakers in Puritan England* (New Haven, 1964). Focusing on the 1650s, Barbour establishes a close relationship between Puritanism, more radical in response to its new working-class constituency, and Quakerism.

Edward Grubb, in "The Early Quakers," *The Cambridge History of English Literature* (14 vols.; New York and London, 1907), VIII, 101–114, states that the Quaker conception of religion "was essentially the rediscovery, by men and women whose whole training and environment were puritan, of the metaphysical element which lies close to the heart of religion but which Puritanism, with all its strength, had strangely missed." Frederick B. Tolles maintains, in *Meeting House and Counting House. The Quaker Merchants of Colonial Philadelphia, 1682–1763* (Chapel Hill, 1948), that the presence of both Calvinism and Anabaptism (or mysticism) in Quakerism was responsible for the dichotomies which ran through the lives of Pennsylvania's early settlers. Melvin B. Endy, Jr., in *William Penn and Early Quakerism* (Princeton, 1973), returns to an emphasis on spiritualism in the movement's beginnings.

The third and fourth volumes in the Rowntree Series are William C. Braithwaite's *The Beginnings of Quakerism* (London, 1912; rev. ed., Cambridge, Eng., 1955), covering the same period as Barbour's book but more detailed and comprehensive while less interpretive, and *The Second Period of Quakerism* (London, 1919; rev. ed., Cambridge, Eng., 1961), which deals in the same exhaustive manner with the remainder of the seventeenth century, including a chapter on Quaker colonization. To complete the series, Jones wrote *The Quakers in the American Colonies* (London, 1911), with sections on Pennsylvania contributed by Isaac Sharpless, and on New Jersey by Amelia M. Gummere, a book which ends at the time of the American Revolution, and *The Later Periods of Quakerism* (2 vols.; London, 1921), which carries the story into the nineteenth century. Elbert Russell's *The History of Quakerism* (New York, 1942) concisely covers the same period as the Rowntree Series and profits greatly from Jones' labors. Frederick B. Tolles has considered some of the foregoing literature as well as non-Quaker work in "1652 in History. Changing Perspectives on the Founding of Quakerism," *Bulletin of the Friends Historical Society*, 41 (1952), 12–27.

Arnold Lloyd, in *Quaker Social History, 1669–1738* (London, 1950), discusses the achievement of internal discipline but deprecates the role of George Fox. Alan Cole, also a revisionist in his approach, argues the case for changes in Quaker belief as a reflection of political awareness in "The Quakers and the English Revolution," *Past and Present*, 10 (November 1956), 39–54. William Beck and T. Frederick Ball's *The London Friends' Meetings* (London, 1869) and Robert J. Leach's The First Century of London Yearly Meeting, 1660–1761 (typescript, Quaker Collection, Haverford College Library), both deal with the centralization of authority more in detailed description than concept. Luella M. Wright, in *The Literary Life of the Early Friends, 1650–1725* (New York, 1932), emphasizes the control George Fox exercised over Quaker writing and the subordination of individual experiences to a pattern of presentation which would promote group consciousness.

Richard T. Vann's *The Social Development of English Quakerism, 1655–1755*

(Cambridge, Mass., 1969) is a model of scholarship: wide-ranging but thorough in its use of sources; imaginative yet rigorous in its application of other academic tools to history; comprehensive in coverage, precise in presentation, and well written. Several previously held beliefs about Quakers are disputed in this study.

WILLIAM PENN, HIS FAMILY, AND EARLY SETTLEMENT

William I. Hull's *William Penn. A Topical Biography* (New York, 1937) is a reliable mine of facts. A more readable biography is Catherine O. Peare's *William Penn* (Philadelphia, 1957), while Mary Maples Dunn's *William Penn. Politics and Conscience* (Princeton, 1967) is a first-rate analysis of the Quaker leader's intellect. Joseph E. Illick's *William Penn the Politician. His Relations with the English Government* (Ithaca, 1965) is primarily political; it contains a bibliographic note on Penn biographies.

Considering the volume of literature on William Penn, there is a paucity of writing on his family. Sophie H. Drinker's *Hannah Penn and the Proprietorship of Pennsylvania* (Philadelphia, 1958) is a lifelike portrait, with much correspondence reprinted. Arthur Pound's *The Penns of Pennsylvania* (New York, 1932) has a few scraps of useful information but far less than Howard M. Jenkins, "The Family of William Penn," *Pennsylvania Magazine of History and Biography*, 20 (1896), 1–29, 158–175, 370–390, 435–455; *ibid.*, 21 (1897), 1–19, 137–160, 324–346, 421–444; 22 (1898), 71–97, 171–195, 326–349. Edward O. Smith's Thomas Penn, Chief Proprietor of Pennsylvania. A Study of his Public Governmental Activities from 1763 to 1775 (Ph.D. diss., Lehigh University, 1966) is a detailed study, though one lacking a personal dimension.

There have been many accounts of Penn's province published. For a review of this literature see Joseph E. Illick's "The Writing of Colonial Pennsylvania History," *Pennsylvania Magazine of History and Biography*, 94 (1970), 3–25. John E. Pomfret has written knowledgeably about Penn's role in *The Province of West New Jersey. 1609–1702* (Princeton, 1956). His "The First Purchasers of Pennsylvania, 1681–1700," *Pennsylvania Magazine of History and Biography*, 80 (1956), 137–163, is also solid and comprehensive. William R. Shepherd's *History of Proprietary Government in Pennsylvania* (New York, 1896) is an institutional approach to the questions of land and government in Pennsylvania, often technical but always illuminating. Edwin B. Bronner's *William Penn's "Holy Experiment." The Founding of Pennsylvania, 1681–1701* (New York, 1962), is of more value for American developments than the English background. Anthony N. B. Garvan's "Proprietary Philadelphia as Artifact," in Oscar Handlin and John Burchard, eds., *The Historian and the City* (Cambridge, Mass., 1963), 177–201, is an imaginative essay. Gary B. Nash's *Quakers and Politics. Pennsylvania, 1681–1726* (Princeton, 1968), characterized by abundant scholarship, fresh viewpoint, and sprightly style, has influenced my interpretation considerably.

Staughton George, *et al.*, eds., *Charter to William Penn, and Laws of the Province of Pennsylvania, Passed Between the Years 1682 and 1700* (Harrisburg, 1879), contains not only the royal patent but the Frame of Government of 1682 and the Forty Laws agreed upon in England, as well as court laws and useful historical notes in the appendices. Samuel Hazard's *Annals of Pennsylvania, from the Discovery of the Delaware, 1609–1682* (Philadelphia, 1850), in addition to a number of pertinent letters, includes Penn's "Conditions and Concessions" to purchasers, published July 11, 1681, his instructions to his "Commissioners for settling the present colony," September 30, 1681, a list of "First Purchasers" as of May 22, 1682, documents concerning the Free Society of Traders, Indian deeds, and a chronology of events.

Hope Frances Kane's "Notes on Early Pennsylvania Promotion Literature," *Pennsylvania Magazine of History and Biography*, 63 (1939), 144–168, thoroughly covers the years 1681 and 1682. The same material for the remainder of the century is more briefly treated in Justin Winsor, ed., *Narrative and Critical History of America* (7 vols., 1884–1889), III, 495–502. Several of these tracts are reproduced in A. C. Myers, ed., *Narratives of Early Pennsylvania, West New Jersey and Delaware, 1630–1707* (New York, 1912), as is Penn's letter of 1683 to the Free Society of Traders. The most practical advice, including itemized costs, can be found in Penn's "Information and Direction to Such Persons as are inclined to America," *Pennsylvania Magazine of History and Biography*, 4 (1880), 329–342.

Plantation Work the Work of this Generation (London, 1682), probably written by William Loddington, argues so strongly the case of "such as are weightily inclined to Transplant themselves and Families to any of the English Plantations in America" that the reader can sense the nature of the opposition in the Society of Friends. Marion Balderston's edition of *James Claypoole's Letter Book. London and Philadelphia, 1681–1684* (San Marino, Calif., 1967) provides an intimate view into the life and thoughts of a Quaker merchant who migrated. Marion D. Learned's *The Life of Francis Daniel Pastorius* (Philadelphia, 1908) is a mine of information, but it should be supplemented by Samuel W. Pennypacker's "The Settlement of Germantown, and the causes which led to it," *Pennsylvania Magazine of History and Biography*, 4 (1880), 1–41. Charles H. Browning's *Welsh Settlement of Pennsylvania* (Philadelphia, 1912) is extremely detailed.

Literature on earlier European settlements along the Delaware is rather limited. The standard works are Amandus Johnson, *The Swedish Settlements on the Delaware, 1638–1664* (2 vols., Philadelphia, 1911), and two books by C. A. Weslager, *Dutch Explorers, Traders, and Settlers in the Delaware Valley, 1609–1664* (Philadelphia, 1961) and *The English on the Delaware: 1610–1682* (New Brunswick, N. J., 1967).

Paul A. W. Wallace's *Indians in Pennsylvania* (Harrisburg, 1968) is the best starting point on the subject of the aborigines; the treatment is at once clear, concise, and comprehensive, with an emphasis on the Delawares. Frank G. Speck's "The Wapanachki Delawares and the English," *Pennsylvania Magazine of History and Biography*, 67 (1943), 319–344, ethnohistory of the highest order, contains penetrating insights on beliefs, relationships, and customs. Speck's

"The Delaware Indians as Women: Were the Original Pennsylvanians Politically Emasculated," *Pennsylvania Magazine of History and Biography*, 70 (1946), 377–389, also demonstrates well the technique of applying current knowledge of Indian lore to past events. Anthony F. C. Wallace, son of Paul Wallace and for years a colleague of Speck's in the Department of Anthropology at the University of Pennsylvania, writes along the same vein in "Women, Land, and Society: Three Aspects of Aboriginal Delaware Life," *Pennsylvania Archaeologist*, 17 (1947), 1–35, and "Some Psychological Characteristics of the Delaware Indians During the 17th and 18th Centuries," *ibid.*, 20 (1950), 33–39. The bibliography in the former article shows the wide range of primary materials in print. William W. Newcomb, Jr.'s *The Culture and Acculturation of the Delaware Indians* (Ann Arbor, 1956) is also a useful study.

Allen W. Trelease's *Indian Affairs in Colonial New York: The Seventeenth Century* (Ithaca, 1960), while focusing on the Five Nations of the Iroquois, discusses their relations with the tribes along the Susquehanna. For a one-volume collection of primary documents, see H. Frank Eshleman, *Lancaster County Indians. Annals of the Susquehannocks and other Indian Tribes of the Susquehanna Territory from about the Year 1500 to 1765, the date of their extinction* (Lancaster, 1908). Francis P. Jennings' "Glory, Death, and Transfiguration: The Susquehannock Indians in the Seventeenth Century," *Proceedings* of the American Philosophical Society, 112 (1968), 15–53; "The Indian Trade of the Susquehanna Valley," *ibid.*, 110 (1966), 406–424; "The Delaware Interregnum," *Pennsylvania Magazine of History and Biography*, 89 (1965), 174–198; and "Incident at Tulpehocken," *Pennsylvania History*, 35 (1968), 335–355, are penetrating and enlightening studies deriving from an excellent but unpublished doctoral dissertation, *Miquon's Passing. Indian-European Relations in Colonial Pennsylvania, 1674 to 1755* (University of Pennsylvania, 1965). Nancy Lurie's "Indian Cultural Adjustment to European Civilization," in James M. Smith, ed., *Seventeenth-Century America* (Chapel Hill, 1959), is mildly revisionist and very convincing in its argument for the similarity in European and Indian material cultures.

The beginnings of Philadelphia can be followed in Hannah B. Roach's "The Planting of Philadelphia: A Seventeenth-Century Real Estate Development," *Pennsylvania Magazine of History and Biography*, 92 (1968), 3–47, 143–194, and Gary B. Nash, "City Planning and Political Tension in the Seventeenth Century: The Case of Philadelphia," *Proceedings* of the American Philosophical Society, 112 (1968), 54–73, much of which appears in *Quakers and Politics*, as well as Garvin's "Proprietary Philadelphia as Artifact," already cited. John Reps' *The Making of Urban America* (Princeton, 1965), a comparative study of city plans, is most useful in understanding the origins of Penn's thinking on Philadelphia. A good synthesis of Philadelphia materials can be found in Mary M. and Richard S. Dunn's "1609–1701: The Founding of the City," an essay lent to me by the authors. Interesting details of early Philadelphia life can be found in John F. Watson, *Annals of Philadelphia and Pennsylvania in the Olden Time* (2 vols.; Philadelphia, 1857); J. Thomas Scharf and Thompson Westcott,

History of Philadelphia. 1609–1844 (3 vols.; Philadelphia, 1884), which also includes a number of useful maps; and Luther P. Eisenhart, ed., *Historic Philadelphia from the Founding until the Early Nineteenth Century* (Philadelphia, 1953), a volume replete with illustrations. Nicholas B. Wainwright's "Plan of Philadelphia," *Pennsylvania Magazine of History and Biography*, 80 (1956), 164–226, shows the lots recorded under original surveys in the oldest part of the city.

Richard R. Pillsbury's The Urban Street Patterns of Philadelphia before 1815 (Ph.D. diss., Pennsylvania State University, 1968) provides a unique way of looking at the cultural landscape. Judith Diamondstone's "Philadelphia's Municipal Corporation, 1701–1776," *Pennsylvania Magazine of History and Biography*, 90 (1966), 183–201, the distillation of a doctoral dissertation of the same title (University of Pennsylvania, 1969) contains material on attempts at incorporation before the eighteenth century. Carl Bridenbaugh's *Cities in the Wilderness. Urban Life in America, 1652–1742* (New York, 1938) and *Cities in Revolt. Urban Life in America, 1743–1776* (New York, 1955) are useful for comparative purposes.

THE BACKCOUNTRY

Stevenson W. Fletcher's *Pennsylvania Agriculture and Country Life. 1640–1840* (Harrisburg, 1950) is a readable if rather old-fashioned book on rural life. Russell Nelson's Backcountry Pennsylvania (1709–1744): The Ideals of William Penn in Practice (Ph.D. diss., University of Wisconsin, 1968) capably covers a wide range of topics from immigration to politics. Henry Glassie's "Eighteenth-Century Cultural Process in Delaware Valley Folk Building," *Winterthur Portfolio 7* (Charlottesville, 1972) shows the provocative use nonliterary materials can be put to. James T. Lemon's *The Best Poor Man's Country. A Geographical Study of Early Southeastern Pennsylvania* (Baltimore, 1972) demonstrates remarkable breadth in dealing with fundamental questions of land settlement. See also James T. Lemon and Gary B. Nash, "The Distribution of Wealth in Eighteenth-Century America. A Century of Change in Chester County, Pennsylvania, 1693–1802," *Journal of Social History*, 2 (1968–69), 1–24. Jerome H. Wood's Conestoga Crossroads: The Rise of Lancaster, Pennsylvania, 1730–1789 (Ph.D. diss., Brown University, 1969) is a thorough study. James A. Henretta's *The Evolution of American Society, 1700–1815. An Interdisciplinary Analysis* (Lexington, Mass., 1973) is most provocative and, despite its formidable title, is gracefully written.

Activities in mid-eighteenth century frontier Pennsylvania can be followed through Paul A. W. Wallace's *Conrad Weiser, Friend of Colonist and Mohawk* (New York, 1945), Nicholas B. Wainwright's *George Croghan, Wilderness Diplomat* (Chapel Hill, 1959), and Anthony F. C. Wallace's *King of the Delawares: Teedyuscung, 1700–1763* (Freeport, N.Y., 1949).

EARLY INSTITUTIONAL, POLITICAL, AND ECONOMIC LIFE

Institutional aspects of early Pennsylvania history are well treated in E. R. I. Gould, "Local Self-Government in Pennsylvania," *Pennsylvania Magazine of*

History and Biography, 6 (1882), 156–173; Lawrence Lewis, Jr., "The Courts of Pennsylvania in the Seventeenth Century," *ibid.*, 5 (1881), 141–190; William H. Loyd, *The Early Courts of Pennsylvania* (Boston, 1919); Sister Joan de Lourdes Leonard, "The Organization and Procedure of the Pennsylvania Assembly, 1682–1776," *Pennsylvania Magazine of History and Biography*, 72 (1948), 215–239, 376–412, and "Elections in Colonial Pennsylvania," *William and Mary Quarterly*, 3rd Ser., 11 (1954), 385–401; Thomas Wendel, "The Speaker of the House, Pennsylvania, 1701–1776," *Pennsylvania Magazine of History and Biography*, 97 (1973), 3–21. Clair W. Keller's Pennsylvania Government 1701–1740: A Study of the Operation of Colonial Government (Ph.D. diss., University of Washington, 1967) is a thorough, accurate, and constantly useful study which I have relied on considerably. A convincing interpretation of the role played by the Assembly in colonial life is given in Jack P. Greene's *The Quest for Power. The Lower Houses of Assembly in the Southern Royal Colonies, 1689–1776* (Chapel Hill, 1963), 3–18. A similar point of view, which emphasizes the stabilizing forces of local government, can be found in Clarence Ver Steeg's *The Formative Years, 1607–1763* (New York, 1964), 129–151.

Among the major personalities of early Pennsylvania, Thomas Lloyd suffers for lack of a biography. Roy N. Lokken's *David Lloyd, Colonial Lawmaker* (Seattle, 1959) contains a wealth of detail, mostly concerned with the legal side of Lloyd's life; the reader must draw his own conclusions about the personal aspects, such as motivation. Similarly, Michael G. Hall's *Edward Randolph and the American Colonies, 1676–1703* (Chapel Hill, 1960) focuses on the career of a civil servant in the context of imperial policy. Frederick B. Tolles, in *James Logan and the Culture of Provincial America* (Boston, 1957), takes a more personal tack and acknowledges a "high debt" to Joseph E. Johnson's A Statesman of Colonial Pennsylvania: A Study of the Private Life and Public Career of James Logan to the Year 1926 (Ph.D. diss., Harvard, 1943). My own interpretation of Logan's career, however, is not the roseate one depicted in these works but a harsher and more convincing portrait found in Jennings' Miquon's Passing. See also Nicholas B. Wainwright, "Governor John Blackwell," *Pennsylvania Magazine of History and Biography*, 74 (1950), 457–472, and Ethyn W. Kirby, *George Keith (1638–1716)* (New York, 1942).

The deputy governors have been largely neglected by biographers, probably for the obvious reason of their collective colorlessness, but one of the most interesting is the subject of Thomas Wendel's The Life and Writings of Sir William Keith, Lieutenant-Governor of Pennsylvania and the Three Lower Counties, 1717–1726 (Ph.D. diss., University of Washington, 1964), part of which appears in Wendel's "The Keith-Lloyd Alliance: Factional and Coalition Politics in Colonial Pennsylvania," *Pennsylvania Magazine of History and Biography*, 92 (1968), 289–305.

Two different interpretations of Quaker pacifism related to governing are Guy F. Hershberger's "The Pennsylvania Quaker Experiment in Politics, 1682–1756," *Mennonite Quarterly Review*, 10 (1936), 187–221, and Hermann Wellenreuther's "The Political Dilemma of the Quakers in Pennsylvania, 1681–1748," *Pennsylvania Magazine of History and Biography*, 94 (1970), 135–172.

Early economic development and policy in Pennsylvania can be traced through A. L. Jensen's *The Maritime Commerce of Colonial Philadelphia* (Madison, Wisc., 1963), a first-rate study which is also useful for the revolutionary period; Curtis Nettles, "The Economic Relations of Boston, Philadelphia and New York, 1680–1715," *Journal of Economic and Business History*, 3 (1930–31), 185–215; Harry D. Berg, "The Organization of Business in Colonial Philadelphia," *Pennsylvania History*, 10 (1943), 157–177; John W. Weidman, The Economic Development of Pennsylvania until 1723 (Ph.D. diss., University of Wisconsin, 1935); Raymond E. Haynes, "Business Regulation in Early Pennsylvania," *Temple Law Quarterly*, 10 (1936), 155–178; James G. Lydon, "Philadelphia's Commercial Expansion, 1720–1739," *Pennsylvania Magazine of History and Biography*, 91 (1967), 401–418.

NON-ENGLISH IMMIGRANTS

The background of Africans transported to America is discussed in Melville J. Herskovits, *The Myth of the Negro Past* (New York and London, 1941), where it is observed that "the greatest significance of the African heritage lies in the fact that most of it quickly and inevitably was lost," a point perhaps debatable but certainly truer in Pennsylvania than elsewhere since Negroes came to the Quaker province by way of other white societies, according to Darrold D. Wax, The Negro Slave Trade in Colonial Pennsylvania (Ph.D. diss., University of Washington, 1962). Portions of Wax's study appear in recent volumes of *Pennsylvania Magazine of History and Biography* and *Pennsylvania History*. The standard study of the subject is E. R. Turner, *The Negro in Pennsylvania* (Washington, 1911), but two recent works should also be read to broaden institutional and psychological perspectives on the topic: David B. Davis, *The Problem of Slavery in Western Culture* (Ithaca, 1966), and Winthrop D. Jordan, *White Over Black. American Attitudes Toward the Negro, 1550–1812* (Chapel Hill, 1968). Gary B. Nash's "Slaves and Slaveowners in Colonial Philadelphia," *William and Mary Quarterly*, 3rd Ser., 30 (1973), 223–256, shatters some long-held myths.

The story of the Scots who migrated to Ireland, then to Pennsylvania, is graphically rendered by James G. Leyburn in *The Scotch-Irish. A Social History* (Chapel Hill, 1962). The German situation is less easily found in English language books. John G. Gagliardo's *From Pariah to Patriot. The Changing Image of the German Peasant, 1770–1840* (Lexington, Ky., 1969) has some useful background material. John D. Brite's The Attitude of European States Toward Emigration to the American Colonies and the United States, 1607–1820 (Ph.D. diss., University of Chicago, 1937) is crammed with facts. Several older studies are pertinent: Walter A. Knittle, *Early Eighteenth Century Palatine Emigration* (Philadelphia, 1936); Oscar Kuhns, *The German and Swiss Settlements of Colonial Pennsylvania* (New York, 1901); Arthur B. Faust, *The German Element in the United States* (New York, 1927); Frederic Klees, *The Pennsylvania Dutch* (New York, 1951). Hallock F. Raup's The Pennsylvania Dutch at the Forks of the Delaware, Northampton County, Pennsylvania (Ph.D. diss., University of California, Berkeley, 1935) is a careful study of the environment and the people in it. Gottlieb Mittelberger's *Journey to Pennsylvania* (Cambridge, Mass., 1960) is a firsthand account by a discouraged immigrant.

The standard account of servitude is Abbot E. Smith's *Colonists in Bondage. White Servitude and Convict Labor in America, 1607–1776* (Chapel Hill, 1947), which contains useful appendices. Cheesman A. Herrick's *White Servitude in Pennsylvania. Indentured and Redemption Labor in Colony and Commonwealth* (Philadelphia, 1926) is a thorough study of the subject.

RELIGION

The problems posed for religion as a result of immigration to Pennsylvania are perceptively treated in Martin E. Lodge's "The Crisis of the Churches in the Middle Colonies, 1720–1750," *Pennsylvania Magazine of History and Biography*, 95 (1971), 195–210. A useful general study is C. H. Maxson's *The Great Awakening in the Middle Colonies* (Chicago, 1920). Richard Hofstadter's *America at 1750* (New York, 1971) contains several chapters on the Awakening. Dietmar Rothermund, in *The Layman's Progress. Religious and Political Experience in Colonial Pennsylvania, 1740–1770* (Philadelphia, 1961), considers the effects of the Awakening. Guy S. Klett's *Presbyterians in Colonial Pennsylvania* (Philadelphia, 1937) is a helpful survey. Unfortunately, I have not read Charles H. Gladfelter's The Colonial Pennsylvania German and Reformed Clergyman (Ph.D. diss., The Johns Hopkins University, 1952). *Moravians in Two Worlds* (New York and London, 1967) is Gillian L. Gollin's thoughtful and thorough study of one sect's attempt at creating a unique community.

Frederick B. Tolles' "Quietism Versus Enthusiasm: The Philadelphia Quakers and the Great Awakening," originally having appeared in *Pennsylvania Magazine of History and Biography*, 69 (1945), 26–49, is reprinted in a collection of Tolles' always thoughtful work, *Quakers and the Atlantic Culture* (New York, 1960). David R. Kobrin's The Saving Remnant: Intellectual Sources of Change and Decline in Colonial Quakerism, 1690–1810 (Ph.D. diss., University of Pennsylvania, 1968) is interesting, if somewhat one-dimensional in its focus on ideas alone. Jack D. Marietta's Ecclesiastical Discipline in the Society of Friends, 1682–1776 (Ph.D. diss., Stanford University, 1968) is a first-rate study of the relationship of changing behavior to ideology, and I have consulted him personally on some questions relating to Quakers and politics. See also Marietta's "Quaker Family Education in Historical Perspective," *Quaker History*, 63 (1974), 3–16, and "Wealth, War and Religion: The Perfecting of Quaker Asceticism, 1740–1783," *Church History*, 43 (1974), 230–241.

Sydney V. James' *A People Among Peoples. Quaker Benevolence in Eighteenth-Century America* (Cambridge, Mass., 1963) focuses on the Friends' extension of humanitarianism to those outside the Society. His thesis is partially summarized in an article, "The Impact of the American Revolution on Quakers' Ideas about Their Sect," *William and Mary Quarterly*, 3rd Ser., 19 (1962), 360–382. Richard Bauman's *For the Reputation of Truth. Politics, Religion and Conflict among the Pennsylvania Quakers, 1750–1800* (Baltimore, 1971) is a rather fresh approach to an often-treated subject. And I benefited very much from reading a study of ideology and social conditions among mid-eighteenth-century Friends by Gloria Stoft, a San Francisco State University graduate student. Marjorie Lasky, also of San Francisco State, and Patricia Cline Cohen, of the University of California, Berkeley, also provoked my thinking about Pennsylvania as a result of seminar papers they wrote.

Two other works on Friends are also valuable and interesting: J. William Frost's *The Quaker Family in Colonial America. A Portrait of the Society of Friends* (New York, 1973); and Robert V. Wells, A Demographic Analysis of Some Middle Colony Quaker Families of the Eighteenth Century (Ph.D. diss., Princeton University, 1969), parts of which appear as "Family Size and Fertility Control in Eighteenth-Century America: A Study of Quaker Families," *Population Studies* 25 (1971), 73–82, and "Quaker Marriage Patterns in Colonial Perspective," *William and Mary Quarterly*, 3rd Ser., 29 (1972), 415–442.

BENJAMIN FRANKLIN AND MID-CENTURY POLITICS

Individual Quakers in public affairs receive kind treatment in Isaac Sharpless' *Political Leaders of Provincial Pennsylvania* (New York, 1919). Edwin B. Bronner's "The Disgrace of John Kinsey, Quaker Politician, 1739–1750," *Pennsylvania Magazine of History and Biography*, 75 (1951), 400–415, supplies a necessary corrective portrait for one of these leaders. Theodore Thayer's *Israel Pemberton, King of the Quakers* (Philadelphia, 1943) has an economic and political rather than religious or personal emphasis, and the same should be said of William T. Parsons' Isaac Norris II, The Speaker (Ph.D. diss., University of Pennsylvania, 1955). Carl L. Romanek's John Reynell, Quaker Merchant of Colonial Philadelphia (Ph.D. diss., Pennsylvania State University, 1969) is also basically an economic study, with a little attention devoted to his religious upbringing; it includes a thorough coverage of his political activities before the Revolution. Grace H. Larsen's Profile of a Colonial Merchant: Thomas Clifford of Pre-Revolutionary Philadelphia (Ph.D. diss., Columbia University, 1955) concerns a successful Quaker trader who did not participate in politics.

As for political friends of the proprietors, Burton A. Konkle's *The Life of Andrew Hamilton, 1676–1741* (Philadelphia, 1941) is inadequate, but there is no other biography except Foster C. Nix's "Andrew Hamilton's Early Years in the American Colonies," *William and Mary Quarterly*, 3rd Ser., 21 (1964), 390–407. Norman S. Cohen's William Allen: Chief Justice of Pennsylvania, 1704–1780 (Ph.D. diss., University of California, Berkeley, 1966) is comprehensive and helpful; a small portion of it is published as "The Philadelphia Election Riot of 1742," *Pennsylvania Magazine of History and Biography*, 92 (1968), 306–319. Hubertis Cummings' *Richard Peters: Provincial Secretary and Cleric, 1704–1776* (Philadelphia,

1944) has been superseded by Joseph H. Fairbanks, Jr., Richard Peters (c. 1704–1776): Provincial Secretary of Pennsylvania (Ph.D. diss., University of Arizona, 1972). Also helpful is Don Roy Byrnes' The Pre-Revolutionary Career of Provost William Smith, 1751–1780 (Ph.D. diss., Tulane University, 1969). Two larger portraits of very different kinds are G. B. Warden's "The Proprietary Group in Pennsylvania, 1754–1764," *William and Mary Quarterly*, 3rd Ser., 21 (1964), 367–389, and Rudolph S. Klein's The Shippen Family: A Generational Study in Colonial and Revolutionary Pennsylvania (Ph.D. diss., Rutgers University, 1972). In "Local Politics in Pre-Revolutionary Lancaster County," *Pennsylvania Magazine of History and Biography*, 97 (1973), 45–74, Wayne L. Bockelman shows the influence of the proprietary group.

The obvious starting point for an understanding of Benjamin Franklin is his *Autobiography*, revealing not only for what it includes but what it omits. Leonard W. Labaree, ed., *The Papers of Benjamin Franklin* (18 vols. [1706–1771], New Haven, 1959–1974), is a useful and fascinating supplement to Franklin's interpretation of his life, and the *Pennsylvania Gazette* is available in 25 bound volumes covering the years 1728 to 1789 (Philadelphia, 1968). Among the many Franklin biographies, the best advice is probably to consult first the shortest: Carl Becker's fourteen-page essay in the *Dictionary of American Biography*; and the longest: Carl Van Doren's *Benjamin Franklin* (New York, 1938). Verner W. Crane, in *Benjamin Franklin and a Rising People* (Boston, 1954), depicts his protagonist as a popularizer of emerging middle-class values, while Carl and Jessica Bridenbaugh, in *Rebels and Gentlemen. Philadelphia in the Age of Franklin* (New York, 1942), portrays a city populated by many Franklins attempting to innovate in the face of entrenched conservatism. Sam B. Warner's *The Private City. Philadelphia in Three Periods of Its Growth* (Philadelphia, 1968) contains some relevant material.

I. Bernard Cohen's monumental *Franklin and Newton* (Philadelphia, 1956) is a comprehensive and convincing interpretation of Franklin as a Newtonian, but for a contrary point of view read the relevant section of Daniel J. Boorstin's *The Americans: The Colonial Experience* (New York, 1959). Brooke Hindle's *The Pursuit of Science in Revolutionary America, 1735–1789* (Chapel Hill, 1956) has considerable material on Pennsylvania.

Thomas Wendel's *Benjamin Franklin and the Politics of Liberty* (Woodbury, N. Y., 1974) is pleasantly written and reliable on the subject in its title. Gerald Stourzh's *Benjamin Franklin and American Foreign Policy* (Chicago, 1954) is also a dependable source. And there is a good deal of material on Franklin's public life in more general approaches to politics.

Each of the three most recent books on mid-eighteenth-century Pennsylvania politics has a point of view to which Franklin is central. Theodore Thayer's *The Growth of Democracy, 1740–1776* (Harrisburg, 1953) depicts political life in terms of principles, while William S. Hanna's *Benjamin Franklin and Pennsylvania Politics* (Stanford, 1964) portrays many of the same conflicts as matters of power. James H. Hutson's *Pennsylvania Politics, 1746–1770. The Movement for Royal Government and*

Its Consequences (Princeton, 1972) argues for the predominance of one issue. These volumes should be supplemented by a number of articles: John J. Zimmerman's "Benjamin Franklin and the Quaker Party, 1755–56," *William and Mary Quarterly*, 3rd Ser., 17 (1960), 291–313; Ralph L. Ketcham, "Conscience, War, and Politics in Pennsylvania, 1755—*1757*," *ibid.*, 20 (1963), 416–439; G. B. Warden, "The Proprietary Group in Pennsylvania, 1754–1764," *ibid.*, 21 (1964), 367–389; Francis Jennings, "Thomas Penn's Loyalty Oath," *American Journal of Legal History*, 8 (1964), 303–313; Ralph L. Ketcham, "Benjamin Franklin and William Smith: New Light on an Old Philadelphia Quarrel," *Pennsylvania Magazine of History and Biography*, 88 (1964), 142–163; James H. Hutson, "Benjamin Franklin and Pennsylvania Politics, 1751–1755: A Reappraisal," *ibid.*, 93 (1969), 303–371; Jack D. Marietta, "Conscience, the Quaker Community, and the French and Indian War," *ibid.*, 95 (1971), 3–27.

Mabel P. Wolff provides the background for Franklin's London sojourn in *The Colonial Agency of Pennsylvania, 1712–1757* (Philadelphia, 1933), while the story is continued in Michael Kammen's *A Rope of Sand. The Colonial Agents, British Politics, and the American Revolution* (Ithaca, 1968). A general review of the literature leading up to and including the imperial crisis can be found in Joseph E. Illick's "Recent Scholarship Concerning Anglo-America Relations, 1675–1775," *Anglo-American Political Relations, 1675–1775*, edited by Alison G. Olson and Richard M. Brown (New Brunswick, 1970). Consequently, most of that material will be omitted here.

REVOLUTIONARY POLITICS

Charles H. Lincoln's *The Revolutionary Movement in Pennsylvania*, 1760–1776 (Philadelphia, 1901) makes a strong case for internal divisions creating political strife, while David F. Hawke's *In the Midst of a Revolution* (Philadelphia, 1961) sees the crisis as the work of a few radicals. Arthur M. Schlesinger's *The Colonial Merchants and the American Revolution, 1763–1776* (New York, 1918) puts developments in Philadelphia into a larger context.

In Merchants and Politics: The Revolutionary Movement in Philadelphia, 1765–1776 (Ph.D. diss., University of Southern California, 1970), Robert F. Oaks disputes Schlesinger's thesis concerning the unity of the merchants, focusing on 520 Philadelphians, mostly merchants, who for reasons of age, religion, and wealth, sustained or lost interest in the revolutionary movement. A portion of this work appears as "Philadelphia Merchants and the First Continental Congress," *Pennsylvania History*, 40 (1973), 149–166. Charles Olton's Philadelphia Artisans and the American Revolution (Ph.D. diss., University of California, Berkeley, 1967), as well as his "Philadelphia's Mechanics in the First Decade of Revolution, 1765–1775," *Journal of American History*, 59 (1972–73), 311–326, should be read in conjunction with Schlesinger and Oaks not only because it focuses on another group but because it represents a different view of class division. In Leadership in Crisis. The Radical Committees of Philadelphia and the Coming of the Revolution in Pennsylvania,

1765–1776: A Study in the Revolutionary Process (Ph.D. diss., The Johns Hopkins University, 1973), Richard A. Ryerson, like Oaks, carefully analyzes the makeup of his subject and, additionally, finds the committee movement to be at the heart of revolutionary activity from 1774 to 1776.

Benjamin H. Newcomb's *Franklin and Galloway: A Political Partnership* (New Haven and London, 1972) is thorough, reliable, and contains the only modern portrait of Galloway; an older one is Ernest H. Baldwin's "Joseph Galloway, the Loyalist Politician," *Pennsylvania Magazine of History and Biography*, 26 (1902), 161–191, 289–321, 417–442. John E. Ferling's "Joseph Galloway: A Reassessment of the Motivations of a Pennsylvania Loyalist," *Pennsylvania History*, 39 (1972) is a sympathetic portrayal of Galloway's ideas. David L. Jacobson's *John Dickinson and the Revolution in Pennsylvania, 1764–1776* (Berkeley and Los Angeles, 1965) is useful not only for the depiction of its protagonist but for a general view of provincial politics. It may be supplemented with H. Trevor Colbourn's "A Pennsylvania Farmer at the Court of King George, John Dickinson's London Letters, 1754–1756," *Pennsylvania Magazine of History and Biography*, 86 (1962), 241–286, 417–453. A sympathetic rendering of "Charles Thomson, 'The Sam Adams of Philadelphia,' " *Mississippi Valley Historical Review*, 45 (1958–59), 464–480, is the work of John J. Zimmerman. "The Papers of Charles Thomson, Secretary of the Continental Congress" are in *Collections of the New York Historical Society for the Year 1878* (New York, 1879), 1–286.

Kenneth R. Rossman's *Thomas Mifflin and the Politics of the American Revolution* (Chapel Hill, 1952) is a rather thin treatment of a whig leader; John F. Roche's *Joseph Reed, A Moderate in the Revolution* (New York, 1957) is better. Charles Page Smith's *James Wilson, Founding Father. 1742–1798* (Chapel Hill, 1956) renders a complete portrait. Brooke Hindle's *David Rittenhouse* (Princeton, 1964) has the virtue of competently handling its subject within the realm of both science and politics. David F. Hawke has risen to the height of his interesting protagonist in *Benjamin Rush: Revolutionary Gadfly* (Indianapolis, 1971), though readers will probably want to consult, as well, George W. Corner, ed., *The Autobiography of Benjamin Rush* (Princeton, 1948), and Lyman H. Butterfield, ed., *Letters of Benjamin Rush* (2 vols.; Princeton, 1951).

John Adams' acerbic commentaries on the events around him are to be found in L. H. Butterfield, ed., *Diary and Autobiography of John Adams* (4 vols.; Cambridge, 1961). The "Diary of James Allen, 1770–1778," is in *Pennsylvania Magazine of History and Biography*, 9 (1885), 176–196, 278–296, 424–441. Also useful for contemporary views are J. S. Littell, ed., *Memoirs of His Own Time . . . By Alexander Graydon* (Philadelphia, 1846), and Joseph Doddridge, *Notes on the Settlement and Indian Wars of the Western Parts of Virginia and Pennsylvania from 1763 to 1783* . . . (Pittsburgh, 1912), the latter observing: "Every man, by a law of his own, pursuing that of nature, has appointed a time for the enfranchisement of youth; and America had perhaps completed her years of minority."

Alfred Owen Aldridge's *Man of Reason. The Life of Thomas Paine* (Philadelphia and New York, 1959) is probably the best of many biographies of Paine.

Winthrop D. Jordan's "Familial Politics: Thomas Paine and the Killing of the King, 1776," *Journal of American History*, 60 (1973-74), 294-308, demonstrates how creatively *Common Sense* can be used; a comparison might be made to another very thoughtful use of the same document in Felix Gilbert's *To the Farewell Address. Ideas of Early American Foreign Policy* (Princeton, 1961). Along the lines of Jordan's work, reference can be made to Edwin G. Burrows and Michael Wallace, "The American Revolution: The Ideology and Psychology of National Liberation," *Perspectives in American History*, 6 (1972), 167-308; the closing remarks in Philip J. Greven, Jr., *Four Generations. Population, Land, and Family in Colonial Andover, Massachusetts* (Ithaca and London, 1970); and the chapters by Joseph E. Illick and John F. Walzer in Lloyd deMause, ed., *The History of Childhood* (New York, 1974).

The intercolonial perspective on protest is excellently captured in Benjamin W. Labaree's *The Boston Tea Party* (New York, 1964). Edmund C. Burnett's *The Continental Congress* (New York, 1941) is comprehensive and useful; it can be supplemented by his edition of *Letters of Members of the Continental Congress* (8 vols., Washington, 1921-1938). Chilton Williamson's *American Suffrage from Property to Democracy, 1760-1860* (Princeton, 1960) also deals in the context of the Atlantic seaboard, while J. Paul Selsam, in *The Pennsylvania Constitution of 1776. A Study in Revolutionary Democracy* (Philadelphia, 1936), notes the connections between the Congress and local politics, though its focus is mainly on the latter. James E. Gibson has compiled useful data on "The Pennsylvania Provincial Conference of 1776," *Pennsylvania Magazine of History and Biography*, 58 (1934), 312-341. James M. Aldrich concludes that there was no correlation between section and political ideology in "A Quantitative Reassessment of the Effects of Sectionalism in Pennsylvania during the War for Independence," *Pennsylvania History*, 39 (1972), 334-361, an article derived from The Revolutionary Legislature in Pennsylvania: A Roll Call Analysis (Ph.D. diss., University of Maine, 1969).

Robert L. Brunhouse's *The Counter-Revolution in Pennsylvania, 1776-1790* (Harrisburg, 1942) is detailed and reliable from an informational standpoint, though its political interpretation has been recently challenged in two articles: Owen S. Ireland, "The Ethnic-Religious Dimension of Pennsylvania Politics, 1778-1779," *William and Mary Quarterly*, 3rd Ser., 30 (1973), 423-448; and Wayne L. Bockelman and Owen S. Ireland, "The Internal Revolution in Pennsylvania: An Ethnic-Religious Interpretation," *Pennsylvania History*, 41 (1974), .125-160. Bockelman's Continuity and Change in Revolutionary Pennsylvania: A Study of County Government and Officeholders (Ph.D. diss., Northwestern University, 1969) is an exhaustive study which also shatters some conventional wisdom about the nature of the Revolution. Gordon Wood's *The Creation of the American Republic, 1776-1787* (Chapel Hill, 1969) is a reliable general survey of the period.

John R. Alden's *A History of the American Revolution* (New York, 1969) contains full accounts of the military campaigns. Robert F. Oaks' "The City under Military Occupation: Philadelphia 1777-1778," in Oaks, *et al.*, *Essays on Urban*

America (Austin, 1975), and John K. Alexander's "The Fort Wilson Incident of 1779: A Case Study of the Revolutionary Crowd," *William and Mary Quarterly*, 3rd Ser., 31 (1974), 589–612, depict some of the problems faced during war. Henry J. Young's The Treatment of Loyalists in Pennsylvania (Ph.D. diss., The Johns Hopkins University, 1955) is comprehensive but not interpretive. See also Young's "Treason and its Punishment in Colonial Pennsylvania," *Pennsylvania Magazine of History and Biography*, 90 (1966), 287–313. Arthur S. Mekeel's The Society of Friends (Quakers) and the American Revolution (Ph.D. diss., Harvard University, 1940) is helpful for the period before as well as during the Revolution.

ECONOMIC AND SOCIAL DEVELOPMENTS

The economic scene in mid-eighteenth-century Pennsylvania can be studied through Arthur C. Bining, *Pennsylvania Iron Manufacture in the Eighteenth Century* (Harrisburg, 1938); William S. Sachs "Agricultural Conditions in the Northern Colonies Before the Revolution," *Journal of Economic History*, 13 (1953), 274–290; John F. Walzer, "Colonial Philadelphia and Its Backcountry," *Winterthur Portfolio* 7 (Charlottesville, 1972), and Transportation in the Philadelphia Trading Area, 1740–1775 (Ph.D. diss., University of Wisconsin, 1967); Anne Bezanson, "Inflation and Controls, Pennsylvania, 1774–1779," *Journal of Economic History*, Supplement 8 (1948), 1–20; Willard O. Mishoff, "Business in Philadelphia During the British Occupation, 1777–1778," *Pennsylvania Magazine of History and Biography*, 61 (1937), 165–181; Clarence L. Ver Steeg, *Robert Morris, Revolutionary Financier* (Philadelphia, 1954); and Jensen's already cited *Maritime Commerce*.

In addition to Gary B. Nash's "The Transformation of Urban Politics 1700–1765," *Journal of American History*, 60 (1973), 605–632, I was fortunate enough to see three unpublished essays by Nash, which added considerably to my understanding of the relationship between the changing economic picture in Philadelphia and the emergence of a socially revolutionary ideology espoused by the lower classes: "Urban Wealth and Poverty in Pre-Revolutionary America"; "Poverty and Poor Relief in Pre-Revolutionary Philadelphia"; "Social Change and the Origins of Revolution in the Cities." Ramon S. Powers, in Wealth and Poverty: Economic Base, Social Structure and Attitudes in Pre-Revolutionary Pennsylvania, New Jersey and Delaware" (Ph.D. diss., University of Kansas, 1971), deals with these topics in the countryside as well as the city.

In "The Press and the Book in Eighteenth Century Philadelphia," *Pennsylvania Magazine of History and Biography*, 65 (1941), 1–30, Carl Bridenbaugh shows that a wide range of reading materials were available. But in "Literacy Levels and Educational Development in Rural Pennsylvania, 1729–1775," *Pennsylvania History*, 39 (1972), 301–312, Alan Tully takes issue with the idea that there was a "liberating" literacy in eighteenth-century America, as argued by Lawrence Cremin in *American Education: the Colonial Experience, 1607–1783* (New York,

1970). Further information can be gained from John J. Stoudt's "The German Press in Pennsylvania and the American Revolution," *Pennsylvania Magazine of History and Biography*, 59 (1935), 74–90, and James O. Knauss' *Social Conditions among the Pennsylvania Germans in the Eighteenth Century, as Revealed in German Newspapers Published in America* (Lancaster, 1922). Robert A. Feer, in "Official Use of the German Language in Pennsylvania," *Pennsylvania Magazine of History and Biography*, 76 (1952), 394–405, demonstrates that German was not considered as an official language, but H. L. Mencken, in *The American Language* (4th ed., New York, 1937), 616–621, shows the durability of Pennsylvania Dutch nonetheless. William T. Parsons kindly lent me a copy of his unpublished paper, The Pennsylvania Dutch: Partners in the War for Independence.

INDEX

Page numbers in boldface refer to illustrations.

339